DEBTS OF HONOUR

Co\

DEBTS OF HONOUR

MICHAEL FOOT

faber and faber

This edition first published in 2010
by Faber and Faber Ltd
Bloomsbury House, 74–77 Great Russell Street
London WC1B 3DA

Printed by CPI Antony Rowe, Eastbourne

A CIP record for this book is available from the British Library

ISBN 978-0-571-27019-4

To Jill
the biggest creditor of the lot,
and to the people of Tredegar, Ebbw Vale,
Rhymney and Abertysswg.

Contents

Foreword

Half the pieces in this book have been written especially for it, and the other half were previously published, in a more abbreviated form than appears here, in *Tribune*, the *Evening Standard* or the *Observer*. One of them, the first, on my father, was commissioned for the *Sunday Telegraph* by an old friend of mine, Hugh Massingham, who devised a series in which various present-day politicians wrote about their fathers. It was my first attempt at a portrait of him which I hope at some stage to elaborate into a proper biography, but this sketch, I trust, has the merit of freshness, and certainly no such book as this could be devised by me except under my father's auspices and without his constant instructions and incitements jogging my memory. He loved books and taught me how to read and love them too; not, alas, on his own comprehensive, catholic scale but at least in such a manner that every other activity—politics especially—has become associated with books, and, in particular, with books about books.

It was my father who first introduced me to William Hazlitt; I like to pretend that I can recall the note of scheming resignation in his voice when I finally defended my decision to leave the family's Liberal faith and become a Socialist, and when he in turn recommended me to test my ideas by reading Hazlitt. He could never quite accept the Hazlittean assault on the apostasies of *his* heroes, William Wordsworth and Edmund Burke and a few others. Hazlitt was too much of a flaming radical to suit my father's temperament. But if a son of his was determined to stampede down radical or revolutionary paths, what better guide could there be than Hazlitt?

He also introduced me, for quite different reasons, to Jonathan

Swift. It was his idea to write a book in which the conflict between Swift and the Duke of Marlborough was described in day-by-day detail, and he told the story with so many marvellous dramatic touches that I became captivated. But he himself was always too busy reading to waste time writing; he was happy that I should take over the idea, which I did in *The Pen and the Sword*. However, my notions of Swift were transformed into something quite different from his. Mostly his markings in his books show that he still saw Swift as the great Whig historians and as Sarah, Duchess of Marlborough, had seen him—the furious, vicious, unconscionable enemy of the great Whig captains and statesmen and their theme of English freedom and English greatness. But there was another Swift altogether, the Drapier, the author of *Gulliver's Travels*, the precursor of William Hazlitt. I hope that together, placed at the different ends, they may hold this book together.

Hazlitt may also be invoked to excuse the fact that some sections of this book and some sentences in the other pieces have been printed before. Hazlitt was paid by the page or the word, and, like all good journalists, he therefore regarded the number of words he had to write as a question of some significance. He sometimes had to re-publish what he had written before, in an elaborated or abbreviated form, and good luck to him and good luck to all journalists with similar requirements! Moreover, I recall in this connection a piece of wise advice given me by John Strachey which was based—so he told me—on previous advice which he had received from Arthur Koestler. All writers, especially journalists, find it difficult to cut their own copy, even when style or clarity or the demands of publishers suggest that they should or must. So Koestler, according to Strachey, devised the idea of establishing a special file which he called 'useful bits'. He was able to ease the pain of making necessary cuts in words he had already written by transferring them to the file instead of destroying them altogether, and they—both Koestler and Strachey—did find that the bits could be most usefully revived at a more appropriate time and in a more appropriate context. I recommend the alleged Koestler method to all journalists who aspire to produce books.

One last word: I hope the selection of people to appear in the various chapters in this volume will not be cited to mean that others are excluded from my list of creditors. I think I could easily select at least another fifteen names to compile a new list and threaten to do so if this book meets with any success. I mention two. I wanted to include here Robert Blatchford: among his other claims to fame, he was just about the best writer of books about books there ever was—to be ranked with Montaigne or Disraeli's father or Arnold Bennett or Hazlitt himself. But the more I looked, the more I thought he cried out for separate treatment. And finally, there is Aneurin Bevan; to him I owe the biggest political debt of all, and it is not yet discharged. Since I concluded my biography of him in 1973, some new material has appeared—in particular the claims and accusations contained in Philip Williams's monumental life of Hugh Gaitskell. Then also the Cabinet papers of the 1945–51 period are now becoming available. Meantime, Jennie Lee has written a new volume of autobiography, to be published just at the time this book appears. So perhaps the best time for me to contemplate a fresh contribution to the counter-attack against Gaitskellite revisionism will come a little later.

As with the two volumes on Aneurin Bevan, I must also offer my special thanks to Una Cooze, my secretary, without whom the necessary work could never have been done, and to Elizabeth Thomas who helped so much with those previous volumes.

MICHAEL FOOT
Tredegar, June 1980

ONE

A Rupert for the Roundheads

> I recalled a favourite passage from Milton, that, next to the
> man who gives wise and intrepid counsels of government, he
> places the man who cares for the purity of his mother tongue.
>
> JOHN MORLEY

MY FATHER must have been just about the happiest man who
ever lived. Of course, he had his ailments, irritations, bouts of
testiness, and what might be considered an unfair share of
political disappointments and defeats. But all these and all else,
during his eighty years, were governed by his zest for living and
reading, a seemingly single, unquenchable quality. He was
Wordsworth's happy warrior, the servant of high causes, and yet
he also knew with Wordsworth, maybe learnt from him, that

> *The wise*
> *Have still the keeping of their*
>   *proper peace,*
> *Are guardians of their own*
>   *tranquillity.*

He was, almost from his cradle, a dedicated spirit, yet he could
indulge his vices, if such they were, with the abandon of a Turkish
sultan. He had the best of both worlds, fashioned for himself the
perfect synthesis, or so it seems when I recall him in his
Promethean moments; full days and weeks on end of complete
absorption and exultation, so recurrent and characteristic that
the darker intervals look quite insignificant.

He left school at fourteen, taught himself almost everything he
ever knew, sat for a Civil Service examination in London, but
soon preferred to train as a solicitor in his home town, Plymouth,

and earned every penny he ever acquired. In his early twenties he
went on a Wesley Guild excursion and set eyes on one whom only
Wordsworth could describe:

> *A perfect woman, nobly*
> * planned*
> *To warn, to comfort and*
> * command:*
> *And yet a Spirit still, and*
> * bright*
> *With something of angelic*
> * light.*

He proposed the day after he saw her, intensified the pursuit
week after week in her Cornish home of Callington, swept aside
her Scottish caution, brought her back in triumph to Plymouth,
reared seven children, and thenceforward bowed to her charm and
superior will on almost every question but one. For in those early
days, with all the odd sixpences he could spare, he also started to
build a library.

Or maybe the trouble had started even earlier, at the Band of
Hope of all places. He saw the effects, or the causes, of addiction
to alcohol in the crowded, violent back streets of Plymouth.
Once he saw a particular carpenter friend of his reeling into the
street, fighting drunk, and, when his mother came out to protest,
striking her a cruel blow across the face. So Isaac Foot, aged nine,
signed the pledge, but at the Band of Hope meetings temperance
was not all they preached. At one meeting he heard someone
recite the words:

> *Lars Porsena of Clusium*
> *By the Nine Gods he swore*
> *That the great house of*
> * Tarquin*
> *Should suffer wrong no*
> * more . . .*

'I walked home that night on air. A fire was kindled within me
which has never ceased to burn.' Lars Porsena's rhetoric was, for

my father, more potent than any wine; and certainly no one in his strict nonconformist home had ever sworn by the Nine Gods. Not that that home was oppressive; it was, like so many Puritan households, suffused with music and song, and my father's love for them merged with his new-found taste for declamation.

Macaulay was a chief companion again as he moved back and forth from his lodgings to his work, during his stay as a boy-clerk in London. Since every minute was precious, he acquired the trick of reading and declaiming as he walked. The great passages from Macaulay's essay on Hampden he could recite by heart. 'The nation looked round for a defender. Calmly and unostentatiously the plain Buckinghamshire Esquire placed himself at the head of his countrymen and right before the face and across the path of tyranny.' Soon the little yellow volumes of W. T. Stead's Penny Poets added to his repertoire Milton, Shelley, Keats, Coleridge and, most important of all, an abridged version of Carlyle's Letters and Speeches of Cromwell. He rolled secular words round his tongue as readily as the hymns he learnt at Sunday school, trained himself to wake ever earlier in the mornings to snatch more time for reading, lavished a prodigious proportion of his fourteen shillings a week salary on the second-hand book-shops in the Charing Cross Road. On his return to Plymouth and thereafter, new authors were his milestones. He remembered the 1906 election, not only for the thumping Liberal victory, but for the visiting speaker who mentioned a name he had never heard—Burke, Edmund Burke. Next day he bought the little Temple Classics edition of Burke's American speeches, price one shilling but 'worth a thousand pounds to me.'

Poetry and politics, literature and living, the heritage from the past and the onward march of Christian soldiers; for my father the interweaving never ended. He never talked about commitment, would have been puzzled by the argument. We must fight the good fight and keep the faith. Books were weapons, the most beloved and the sharpest. And there spread out before us were enemies enough for a lifetime: historical figures and their modern counterparts melted into one; brewers, Protectionists, Papists, apologists for Lord North and the Chamberlain family; Spanish tyrants and Stuart kings; Simonites and appeasers, men of

Munich and Suez; sons of Belial or Beelzebub, normally disguised as West Country Tories, an especially reprehensible branch of the species.

In 1910, thirty years old, he crossed the Tamar into Cornwall again on another notable expedition; he just failed to become Liberal M.P. for Bodmin by forty-one votes. In 1919 he fought Lady Astor in Plymouth when Waldorf Astor became a peer, lost his deposit, and the family, all seven of us, or at least all old enough to know what was what, sang in unison:

> *Who's that knocking at the door?*
> *Who's that knocking at the door?*
> *If it's Astor and his wife, we'll stab 'em*
>   *with a knife*
> *And they won't be Tories any more.*

Then in 1922 he returned to Bodmin and won a sensational by-election victory as a Liberal Wee Free Asquithian against the Lloyd George Coalition. Meantime the teetotal Astors became family friends. Lady Astor charmed my father, my mother and the rest, and only in the later Cliveden Set era could we raise a full chorus for our 1919 Marseillaise.

Normally my father fought with the gloves off. When he unmasked Sir Edgar Sanders, director of the Brewers Society, initiating a campaign to make 'the younger customer the mainstay of the public house' and proposing that sportsmen should be recruited to advertise their wares, his pamphlet in reply was called *Blood Money?*, and part of the text insisted:

> Footballers, cricketers, prize-fighters, and so on. Why did you stop there? Why not give us poster pictures of the chauffeur or bus driver at the wheel, saying 'I drive on beer', and 'I am the mainstay of the public house?' Would anyone of your brewers trust this gentleman with his lorry or his Rolls Royce?

Sir Edgar did not reply. Sometime later in the House of Commons a spokesman of the brewers or distillers was dilating on the virtues of strong drink. 'Who says it interferes with health? Who says "drink" does anyone any harm? In bygone days

W. G. Grace used to sit up all night drinking and go out next day and make a century.' To which, my father interrupted: 'Yes, that was because the bowlers were up all night.' But usually the rebuke for the brewers was less temperate. 'Your scheme', he told Sir Edgar, 'is concerned with *profit*. Here is a passage on profit: "But who shall cause one of these little ones . . . to stumble, it is profitable for him that a great millstone should be hanged about his neck, and that he should sink in the depth of the sea".'

Such was the tone of controversy down our way in the twenties and thirties, when my father was at his peak. When a fellow candidate in a neighbouring constituency inquired how to deal with some customary Tory trick, he replied: 'Tell them it is a lie. Tell them it is a damned lie. Tell them it is no less a lie because it is uttered by a Tory gentleman of title.' Into every town and village he carried his war, and the Tory agents lamented as he invaded their territories: 'There's Isaac Foot holding another of his bloody little prayer meetings!'

How could they know what Wesleyan revels were afoot? For inside those jam-packed halls where he flayed the Lloyd George Coalition, Churchill's economics, the betrayal of Abyssinia and Spain, the iniquities of the liquor trade or the latest menacing impertinence from the Pope of Rome, laughter always mixed with the righteous fury, whether he spoke from the platform or the pulpit; too fine a distinction, he thought, should not be drawn between the two. Men and women walked for miles and waited hours to witness the phenomenon—a full hour, maybe, of rollicking humour and invective, fifteen minutes of passionate argument and a peroration to take the roof off. On his own ground, where he knew the exact response which every reference, every inflection, could evoke, he was one of the great orators of the century, the last of the few.

He became the best-loved and the best-hated man in Devon and Cornwall, the most dashing champion West Country Nonconformity ever had, a Prince Rupert for the Roundheads. And more zealously than ever—it is hard to blame them—Tory motor-cars and brewers' money and every other resource the forces of darkness could marshal poured into the Bodmin constituency to keep Isaac Foot out. In 1935 they succeeded, with the aid of strange allies. All Liberals were invited to vote *against* my father in the name of true Liberalism, the signatories to the appeal being John Simon, Walter Runciman, and Leslie Hore-Belisha, the three Liberal-National or Simonite members of the National Government, of which my father had briefly been a member before its protectionist policies stuck in his gullet. Simon had been a close friend before the Simonite heresy; the other two he had suckled in their West Country constituencies. However, the ferocity of internal party disputes knows no limit, and my father repaid this scurvy treatment with one of the most selfless odysseys in British political history. After the election he hired halls in Spen Valley, St. Ives and Devonport, the respective constituencies of the three miscreants, and delivered to their electors elaborate, fully-authenticated indictments of their political records, worthy of any trial in Westminster Hall. Never to be forgotten was the climax in Devonport Guildhall, the immaculate timing, the deadly curse drawn from one of my father's unexpected favourites, Lord Alfred Douglas:

> Cast out, my soul, the broken covenant,
> Forget the pitiable masquerade

And then the final lines:

> Let him on graves of buried loyalty,
> Rise as he may to his desired goal;
> Ay and God speed him there, I grudge him not.
> And when all men shall sing his praise to me
> I'll not gainsay. But I shall know his soul
> Lies in the bosom of Iscariot.

It is satisfactory to recall that, after an interval, the political reputations of all these three victims *did* wither. Several years later, when I had been adopted to fight Hore-Belisha at Devonport as a Labour candidate, I reported to my father that I had met my prospective opponent at some function in London and that he didn't seem so objectionable after all. 'Oh', said my father, with a lighthearted snort; 'you didn't commit yourself to a clean fight, I hope.'

But what of my father's own career? Had that not withered too, even his glorious eloquence being washed away down the gutters of Liberal sectarianism? It may seem so from my account, but the impression is false. Of course his luckless defeat in 1935, like the earlier ones of 1924 and 1910, cheated him of the parliamentary eminence for which he was qualified; no instrument can be more merciless than the electoral guillotine. But, in personal terms, he could usually turn setbacks into conquests. An inscription in a book he gave me (a Swift first edition) indicates his mettle:

> This book (from my library at Pencrebar) is given, with my love, and some reluctance, to my son Michael, as a token of consolation on his defeat at Devonport at the General Election, May 26, 1955. I recall defeats a Totnes, Plymouth, Bodmin, St. Ives and Tavistock in the years 1910, 1918, 1924, 1935, 1937 and 1945. On the whole, these defeats were more honourable than my five victories.

At the toughest, most awkward moments my father was a Titan. He would quote Captain McWhirr from Conrad's *Typhoon*: 'Always facing it, that's the way to get through.' And that was certainly the spirit needed, following 1935, in the most shameful, perilous and epic years in our country's history. Out of office, out of Parliament, with no influence to exert except by personal inspiration and with that so-often-unheeded voice, my father's genius came to its full blossom, or so it seemed to me, since these were the years I knew him best. He grew to be what one of his chief heroes, William Tyndale, was called, an Apostle of England, seeking to rouse his countrymen to face and destroy the Nazi horror. When appeasement was still a respectable word in 1937, he fought a by-election at St. Ives against all it stood for in our age. He hung his head in shame at the news of Munich, and promptly invited a fresh flood of execrations upon it from West Country Tories with a column-long letter to the *Western Morning News* exposing the infamy done in our name. He went back to the villages, where he had once fought the brewers, to fight the Hoares and the Halifaxes, Hitler and Mussolini. His own Plymouth, he said, could suffer the fate of Guernica. Devon and Cornwall—he would never choose between his two loves—were threatened with the same desecration.

His sermon now was England Arise; and England did. As a child, my father had stood on Plymouth Hoe when the statue of Sir Francis Drake was erected, and, like Drake, had looked out across Plymouth Sound a thousand times. Now, when the little ships went to Dunkirk or when the Luftwaffe raided Plymouth, he claimed to hear Drake's Drum and, less credibly, that all other West Countrymen heard it too. Hitler, threatening invasion, standing for nothing but 'brute violence and proud tyrannic power', would have to meet much beyond his understanding; 'the land of William Tyndale and John Hampden and Oliver Cromwell and John Milton—the Britain of Marlborough (another famous Devonshireman) and John Wesley, of Chatham, and Burke and Thomas Paine and Charles James Fox.' That was my father in 1940. In 1945, when he became Lord Mayor of his shattered, bleeding City, he went to every school in the place and told the children how Francis Drake and the people of Plymouth had helped save England and freedom again, as in 1588.

His reading and his mind became even more catholic in the war years and after, as if he wished to embrace the whole of Western civilisation menaced by barbarism. He reached backwards to the Italian Renaissance and the early printers, and outward to our allies across the Atlantic; Abraham Lincoln had always been honoured as the American Cromwell but now the Library of Congress, in our attics, had to be enlarged to equal the Bodleian, down the corridor. Stricken France must be avenged, and Montaigne stepped up onto his proper pedestal. But why list the names thus? Any suggestion that my father's associaton with books was governed by a developing strategy would be a wicked deceit. Apart from my mother and his music, they were the light of his life. They were his meat and drink. They were his bulwark against the world. They became—it is almost impossible to deny—an overpowering disease.

He bought them, read them, marked them, reread them, stored them, reallocated them on the shelves, which spread like erysipelas up every available wall, knew where each precious volume of the countless thousands nestled without the aid of a catalogue. His appetite was gargantuan and insatiable. He was a bibliophilial drunkard—with the difference that the taste never palled and he never had a hangover. The only stab of remorse he ever experienced was the rare recollection of how, at one of Hodgson's sales or in one of the second-hand shops where he spent another of his lifetimes, a temptation had been cravenly resisted. He would tell me over lunch how he had been at the bookshop prompt at nine o'clock that morning to repair some cowardly error of the day before. The treasure was still there on the shelf. Who could want further proof of the intervention of Providence?

Since his house in Cornwall had still to be run as a place of human habitation my mother often found the pressure intolerable. So my father became furtive. He would get up early to waylay the postman or set off for London on a Monday morning with several empty suitcases. When he went on a lecture tour to America he returned with eleven cratefuls. When each member of the family was old enough to leave home, the parting could be borne. Valuable wall space was released. Wordsworth or Napoleon or Montaigne or Dr. Johnson could at last have a room of his own, like John Milton.

More remarkable still was the high proportion of these vast granaries of literary wealth which he had actually consumed in person without bursting. He read everything he could lay his hands on about his favourites; had, like Montaigne, 'a singular curiosity to know the soul and natural judgements of my authors'; compiled several hundreds of his own commonplace books; taught himself Greek and French; and could recite whole plays of Shakespeare and whole books of *Paradise Lost;* could indeed give his own dramatic performance on the family hearth, of Macbeth with the dagger before his eyes, or Jean Valjean escaping through the sewers of Paris, or the murder scene in A. E. W. Mason's *House of the Arrow*, or Fouché and Talleyrand arriving at the court of Louis XVIII, vice leaning on hypocrisy.

His tastes were unrestricted and unpredictable. He knew everything about John Bunyan and Johann Sebastian Bach, about Victor Hugo and Andrew Marvell, about Thomas Hardy and Thomas Carlyle, about the Massacre of St. Bartholomew and the Black Hole of Calcutta, about Blenheim and Gettysburg. He had one room full of Bibles and the next of the French Revolution, one of detective stories and another of modern poetry. He would ask fastidious guests: 'Where would you like to sleep tonight— with Lucrezia Borgia, Dorothy Wordsworth or Josephine Beauharnais?' The specially favoured might find him talking of Joseph Conrad; as my father pronounced it, was there ever such mystery and excitement compressed into a single name as *Nostromo?*

He had a whole shelf full of unwritten books which he had promised himself one day to start and complete. They would, I am sure, have been masterpieces of their own kind, like Isaac Disraeli's compilations, and a few of them did actually reach the stage of publication in the form of brilliant lectures or brief monographs. But, as one of the world's great *readers*, my father could not pause too long for the delays of *writing*; how many irrecoverable hours could be dissipated in this laborious diversion? 'In my father's house there are many mansions'; I remember as a child hearing that from the pulpit, and my father would preach sermons on the text. I never quite knew what it meant; I doubt if I do now, but I would picture in my mind whole lofts and barns and outhouses crowded with histories and autobiographies and collected works, and to each of them he applied and re-applied his Montaigne-like method.

The last time I saw him he was returning with the old zest to Oscar Wilde and Lord Alfred Douglas, the unsuspecting flail of the Simonites, a much better sonnet-writer, said my father, than the world allowed. Sonnets, indeed; they must not be overlooked. He had made his own vast private collection, all written out in his flowing, flamboyant hand. When he died, one could turn over pages of books, heavily marked, which no one would have suspected him of ever reading. How, in heaven's name, did he contrive to lead so many lives? In his seventies, he could still drive from Cornwall to London, to follow with the score that night a rare recital of the St. John Passion at the Festival Hall. He could assure Ralph Richardson from personal recollection that, of all the Macbeths of the century, he had given the best revelation of Macbeth the poet. And somehow too he spent another lifetime securing his proper peace beside his River Lynher in Cornwall; he read of all the rivers in literature, made another private anthology on the subject, knew most of those in the West Country, but loved the Lynher best.

Edmund Burke, I suppose, remained the most revered of all the gods in his teeming Valhalla, and I shall not forget him in one of his procrastinating moods when his library had once again seduced him from his Liberal duties and my mother shook her beautiful head over the dereliction. There he stood before his fireplace, extolling his men-of-action heroes, Cromwell and Lincoln, or declaiming from Burke without a hint of incongruity: 'Public life is a situation of power and energy; he trespasses against his duty who sleeps upon his watch, as well as he that goes over to the enemy.' My father could indeed be wayward in the choice of books as well as other pursuits. Across the river from us in Cornwall, in a nearby mansion, Sir Robert Abdy came as a neighbour, bringing with him a beautiful library and an even more beautiful wife. My father became a frequent visitor. Once, said the observant Lady Astor, 'it was all John Milton and Lady Astor; now its Guy de Maupassant and Lady Abdy.'

Edmund Burke also figured in one splendid scene when my father did step back into the arena of politics, and when his prodigious memory faltered. In 1925, as a leader of the Asquithian Liberals, he went on a mission to Churt to discuss with Lloyd George how to make an end of the ferocious personal quarrels which had torn the Liberal Party to fragments. After a weekend of negotiation, the compact was signed and on the Monday morning Lloyd George bade farewell to his guests with the cheerful appeal: 'Let our slogan be *Measures not Men*.' 'Edmund Burke', replied my father, 'had something to say about that. I think you'll find it on page 500 or thereabouts of that beautiful Beaconsfield edition of Burke I saw on your shelves.' On his return home he looked up his own edition, slightly anxiously, and read about 'the cant of *Not Men, but Measures*: a sort of charm by which many people get loose from every honourable engagement'. In fact, my father lived to fight several battles with Lloyd George as his leader, but he was never sure whether Lloyd George had checked the quotation.

How many battles of long ago had my father refought, and how many of the present day had he watched from his library windows? He preached of Marston Moor, and retreated with Montaigne to his tower. What excuse could a stern Puritan offer for these frivolities? Men of power have no time to read; yet the men who do not read are unfit for power. He was past answering such questions but turned aside to see if Milton or Burke or Wordsworth would answer for him. Wordsworth came nearest, I think. 'We live by admiration, hope and love,' he wrote, and that was my father's creed.

'Hope', he would whisper, and the little Cornish chapel would be utterly still. 'The gospel of hope'; he had the congregation in the hollow of his hand. Within a few sentences the language could become stirring and resonant.

> *Hope, the paramount duty*
> *that Heaven lays,*
> *For its own honour, on man's*
> *suffering heart.*

Outside, the world seemed sharply brighter than when we went in, and we would return to our Sunday dinner, the best of the week, bubbling with an unaccountable optimism, touched no doubt by the beauty of the words, the Bible's, Wordsworth's or his own, all uttered in a voice as rich and memorable as Devonshire cream.

TWO

The Shakespeare
Prose Writer

Happy are they who live in the dream of their own existence, and see all things in the light of their own minds; who walk by faith and hope; to whom the guiding star of their youth still shines from afar, and into whom the spirit of the world has not entered! They have not been 'hurt by the archers', nor has the iron entered their souls. The world has no hand on them.

From Hazlitt's essay
Mind and motive, and
occasionally repeated by
him elsewhere.

WILLIAM HAZLITT, in all his glory, at the peak of his powers, still faced a furiously hostile world. Since he would not budge an inch in his opinions, he might have become irredeemably embittered or broken altogether. Instead, he transmuted the way in which he defended his principles into a new serenity.

Born on 10 April, 1778, it was not until he was twenty years old, in the year 1798 ('the figures that compose that date are to me like "the dreaded name of Demogorgon"') that his individual spirit was truly awakened, and not until twenty-five years later again that he described that experience in *My First Acquaintance with Poets*, the greatest essay in the English language.

A year or so later he produced his best book of collected essays, *The Spirit of the Age*. Therein he pinioned, mocked, revalued or extolled some two dozen of his most famous contemporaries with an insight and wit which none of his would-be imitators have ever been able to capture. One after another he chipped away at the pedestals of popular heroes, or bestowed upon them a fresh glow of understanding, often anticipating with precision the verdicts of posterity. He was no respecter of conventional judgements from left, right or centre—crusted Tories might find themselves 'nearly' forgiven; so-called reformers were rebuked when they befuddled themselves with too much of the milk of human kindness; and those who usually came off worst of all were the whiffling moderates in the middle, 'ever strong upon the stronger side', like *The Times* newspaper (yes, even in those days). He hated the inhumanities which his fellow-citizens inflicted upon one another in the world around him; yet he loved the other worlds in which he and they lived, the world of nature, of books, of the theatre, of painting, of music; indeed the whole wide world of the imagination in which he had seen 'the prospect of human happiness and glory ascending like the steps of Jacob's ladder in a bright and never-ending succession'. All these assorted moods and aspirations and freshly-shaped nuances of judgement he poured into *The Spirit of the Age* with a newly-confident profusion.

And yet this masterpiece of a lifetime was abruptly dismissed as too pert and extravagant by the best-known, most genial, Whiggish editor of the day, Francis Jeffrey, and it is impossible to believe that Hazlitt's scorn of the Whigs was not the true cause of a disapprobation so misplaced. (Editors have never been quite the same breed since, for Hazlitt retaliated with an essay which should keep them in their place for eternity—'They are dreadfully afraid there should be anything behind the Editor's chair greater than the Editor's chair. That is a scandal to be prevented at all risk'.) Yet even before Jeffrey had rushed to the defence of his Whig dinner-friends, a printer with a fair enough record for courage thought it judicious at first to publish the volume anonymously, and the suspicion persists that either he or the author or the two together did not wish to risk immediate association on publication day with another volume which had appeared two years before, also published anonymously, but at once unmasked as something too indescribably foul to be mentioned in decent society: Hazlitt's *Liber Amoris*, the product, it was supposed, then and now, of a mind diseased, not to mention a lascivious body and soul.

But let us, for a half-moment at least, leave Hazlitt, the self-confessed fool of love, to return to his unforgettable first acquaintance with poets. Smitten though he still was by the attentions or non-attentions of Sarah Walker, and enfolded in that essay as his customary laments for her cold embraces undoubtedly were ('my heart has never found, nor will it ever find, a heart to speak to'), yet he can recall, with an exhilaration which still tingles in every sentence, all his richest memories, his youth, his father, the first books he read, the first meeting with Coleridge, the visit to Llangollen, 'the cradle of a new existence', the journey to Nether Stowey, the first hearing of the *Lyrical Ballads* from the lips of Wordsworth himself (all in that self-same sacred year of 1798), 'and the sense of a new spirit in poetry came over me'.

No man ever treasured his youth more joyously than Hazlitt did; no man ever honoured his father better; no man ever discharged with such good faith the debts of honour he owed to the favourite authors of his youth—Burke, Rousseau, Cervantes, Montaigne and a legion more. No critic (except perhaps a few fellow poets, and not many of them) ever heard the strange language of a new school of poetry with such an alert sympathy, and certainly no critic ever welcomed the innovation with greater daring and, despite all subsequent political feuds, with more persistence and warmth.

All these claims can be sustained from the evidence offered in this single essay, written when the love-diseased Hazlitt was, on his own testimony, still in a most desperate condition—'I have wanted only one thing to make me happy, but wanting that, have wanted everything!'. There he is again, in the very same essay, bewailing Sarah in one sentence and still in the next quite capable of inflicting one of his most well-considered swipes at Coleridge, and one to be upheld by the scrutiny of modern scholars. It was Hazlitt who first put his finger, without the substantial proof provided since, on Coleridge's addictive plagiarism.

Yet the attempt to rest so heavy a weight on a single essay leaves one wrong impression. It might be truer to say the opposite, as Hazlitt himself said of Burke: that the only specimen of his writing is *all that he wrote*. In literature, Hazlitt relished the old and welcomed the new. He saw how (and was one of the very first to remark how) Shakespeare achieved 'the combination of the greatest extremes'. He himself liked to see all sides of a subject, never for the purpose of searching out some muddled middle ground but rather to force an explosive fusion or an entirely new departure. One of his friends bound Burke's *Reflections on the French Revolution* and Thomas Paine's *Rights of Man* between the same covers and said that together they made a good book. A similar treatment could be applied to Hazlitt's writings. Many of his essays seem to be written in pairs, each presenting opposite aspects of the case, one, maybe, suffused with the romantic spirit unloosed by Rousseau and the other relentlessly reasserting Hazlitt's conviction that men must not only talk and dream, but act. Always he would still strive to extract the effective conclusion from the clash of contrasts. No such dreamer was ever less of a dilettante. No critic was ever more of a self-critic.

Any such claim would have provoked squeals of protest from those apostate politicians or apostate poets whom Hazlitt berated so fiercely in his lifetime. But most of them never had the chance of reading his *Conversations of Northcote* which was published in full only after his death. Many good reasons for reading the *Conversations* may be offered—their sheer readability, the individual charm of the old Plymouth painter, the wonderful assortment of irrelevancies and curiosities which both Northcote and Hazlitt contributed to the pile. But it is hard to escape the belief that Hazlitt had a deeper, if unconscious, purpose. He somehow put into Northcote's mouth most of the current criticisms or condemnations of himself, and then struggled, not always successfully, to find the right retort.

This, unconsciously also perhaps, was what Hazlitt set out to achieve on a much more spacious canvas. Ever since he had carried home in triumph from Shrewsbury to Wem his first book by Edmund Burke, he had been dazzled by that style which he revered more than any other—'His words are the most like things; his style is the most strictly suited to the subject.' Hazlitt's own style owed more to Burke's than to anybody's, but he was never primarily a student of style despite his many apposite remarks upon it. The thing mattered more than the word. Literature was not something removed from life; the two were endlessly intertwined. Books were weapons in the cause of human freedom.

How, then, could Hazlitt, the great rebel, respect Burke, the great apostate? Burke had 'stood at the prow of the vessel of state, and with his glittering, pointed spear *harpooned* the Leviathan of the French Revolution'. How could Hazlitt, the arch-champion of the French Revolution, pay such honour to him? It was not merely the magnanimous gesture of one writer to another across the gulf of politics. The kinship between the two men went much deeper. Hazlitt saw the truth and force of so much that Burke was saying; no man could write like that and tell lies. Burke's understanding of mankind, he said, was 'inexhaustible as the human heart, and various as the sources of nature'. Yet this mighty intellect had somehow been used to persuade the people of England that 'Liberty was an illiberal, hollow sound; that humanity was a barbarous modern invention; that prejudices were the test of truth, that reason was a strumpet and right a fiction'. To explain the phenomenon, the mechanism of politics must be taken to pieces. And somehow Burke must be answered. 'He presents to you', Hazlitt wrote, 'one view of the face of society. Let him who thinks he can, give the reverse side with equal force, beauty and clearness . . .' Hazlitt's life work was his great reply. He gave to the English Left a perspective and philosophy as widely ranging as Burke had given to the English Right.

Hazlitt was not content with the multitude of swift retorts provoked by Burke's *Reflections on the French Revolution*. He was one of the first to recognise that the formidable pamphleteer Thomas Paine, author of *Rights of Man*, the most famous and enduring of all the replies, was a great writer. But neither Paine nor William Godwin, nor the poets with their dreams of Utopia, less still the men of the calibre of Sir James Mackintosh, could prevail against Burke, and not all their defeats were due to the power wielded by authority. The first rebuffs made many of them abandon their creed and go over to the enemy. A tougher fibre was needed, a creed of human freedom more firmly founded on the rock. No one was ever more excited by the soaring hopes unloosed by the French Revolution than Hazlitt; he soaked himself in the romantic prophets; Rousseau's *Confessions* and *La Nouvelle Heloise* made him shed tears. He accepted to the full the reformers' doctrine that 'men do not become what by nature they are meant to be, but what society makes them'. And society could be transformed; the French Revolution looked like romance in action. But the deed would not be done by utopians who would never soil their hands, nor by an arid appeal to reason alone, nor by the economists and utilitarians who inherited the tattered mantle of the revolutionaries.

Thus, Hazlitt was a romantic in revolt against extreme romanticism; he loved the ardour of it and hated the egotism. He was an idealist who knew that present enemies must be fought here and now, tooth and nail, on their own ground; a passionate believer in man's benevolence and his perfectibility, but one who recognised as well as Burke that passion and prejudice could not easily be uprooted from the human heart. Since the passions could be good and the right traditions should be revered, why should they be? They too could be enlisted in the Good Cause. The core of his theory had been worked out in the first *Essay on the Principles of Human Action*. It was vastly illustrated in all his later writings. He tried to separate the wheat from the chaff in the bountiful harvest of new ideas which were sprouting up all around him. He searched for a synthesis between Rousseau and Burke. And they dared call him a bigot!

His politics left their brand on every aspect of his writing, just as they governed or disrupted his personal relationships. Someone said that he took his politics around with him, like a giant mastiff, and love me, love my dog was his motto. (Only Sarah was allowed a special dispensation; it is not recorded that he lectured *her* on the evils of legitimacy, although he did present her with a treasured statuette of Napoleon). But the tide of his political ideas flooded into every cove and inlet of his thought. 1798 was not only the year of the *Lyrical Ballads;* it was also the year of the Reverend Doctor Malthus's *Essay on the Principle of Population as it affects the Future Improvement of Society*. How soon Hazlitt became acquainted and obsessed with this curious literary phenomenon is not clear, but he was certainly the first reader to appreciate to the full the menacing nature of the apparition. Here, it is true, society was offered a philosophy for the rich, an economic textbook for Tories, a faith as firm as a mathematical equation which could salve their conscience and cast the cloak of religion over the whole scene of human wretchedness in the England of his time. 'Malthus,' wrote Hazlitt, 'had given to the principle of population a personal existence, conceiving of it as a sort of infant Hercules, as one of that terrific giant brood, which you can only master by strangling it in its cradle.' And that in turn was how Hazlitt set about Malthus. Without the advantage or encumbrance of expert economic knowledge, with irony and logic and passionate indignation, he exposed the moral consequences of Malthus's infamous clerical decrees.

He thereby anticipated not merely the reply of the economists decades later but the whole temper of nineteenth-century radicalism. He brushed aside the patronising charity of those who would 'take nothing from the rich and give it to the poor', and defended the right to strike with the fervour of a Chartist or a twentieth-century syndicalist. His essays on prison reform and on Benthamism raced beyond the plodding precepts of the utilitarians and came nearer to the ideas of modern psychology. 'Men act from passions, and we can only judge of passions by sympathy.' Criminals, like the world itself, could not be changed by preaching. Somehow the institutions of society must be changed, and men must show the will to do it. There Hazlitt did not differ much from his fellow-reformers, but he added his own ingredient to the reforming creed of his time. The reformers themselves needed to understand the human heart if they were to get men to move, and if they were not themselves, in the face of setbacks, to abandon or betray their cause. So many of the reformers of his time—Robert Owen, for example—who talked so much about the rights of men knew so little about the passions of men. A whole curriculum of schooling for reformers could be compiled from the writings of Hazlitt whom the nervous nineteenth century would have preferred to dismiss as a wayward romantic essayist. In his mind the interaction between words and deeds could never be severed. And the next immediate deed in the struggle, *the one that mattered*, was never long absent from his reckoning. Perhaps the most remarkable of all Hazlitt's feats in imaginative sympathy was the way he, the supreme no-com-promiser, nonetheless understood the exigencies of practical politicians.

He wrote about political ideas and political history, about the immediate controversies of the age, about the motives of politicians, about political parties and the conduct within parties, about the resolute capacity of those who hold power and the chronic failings of the reformers and revolutionaries who would seek to wrest it from them. His themes were as perennial as Burke's. Of course his own heroes both in history and in his own time were the iconoclasts, the intransigents, the rebels who would not bend with the storm or droop in the sunshine; their example suited his own situation and soothed his pride. But his under-standing of the art of politics was not limited by the experience of his own defeats. 'Ambition is in some sort genius', he said. Here is his picture of what a statesman could be. It is rarely quoted: but has it ever been bettered?

> To use means to ends, to set causes in motion, to wield the machine of society, to subject the wills of others to your own, to manage abler men than yourself by means of that which is stronger in them than their wisdom, viz, their weakness and their folly, to calculate the resistance of ignorance and prejudice to your designs, and by obviating to turn them to account, to foresee a long, obscure and complicated train of events, of chances and openings of success, to unwind the web of others' policy, and weave your own out of it, to judge the effects of things not in the abstract but with reference to all their bearings, ramifications and impediments, to understand character thoroughly, to see latent talent and lurking treachery, to know mankind for what they are, and use them as they deserve, to have a purpose steadily in view and to effect it after removing every obstacle, to master others and to be true to yourself, asks power and knowledge, both nerves and brain.

A naïve extremist, unaware of the realities of politics, could not have written that sentence.

It was not only that he could appreciate the politicians of the past—say, Cromwell, with 'his fine, frank, rough, pimply face and wily policy' (Hazlitt was accused of having a pimply face, which doubtless encouraged the show of sympathy); he looked down from the gallery of the House of Commons on the performers below, and had his own list of preferences which can scarcely have accorded with anyone else's, especially those on the left. He preferred Castlereagh to Canning ('One of those spontaneous mechanical sallies of his resembles a *voluntary* played on a barrel organ'), Burdett to Brougham ('He is not a backbone debater. He wants nerve, he wants impetuosity'), the real would-be doers to the self-conscious rhetoricians with all their finical flexibility of purpose and character.

Hazlitt exerted a comparable independence of judgement in every other field too. Naturally he liked to discern the virtues of those whose political views he shared. Not only was he the first to recognise Thomas Paine's literary qualities; he saw also, and won more jeers from fashionable critics, for recognising that William Cobbett's 'plain, broad, down-right English' made him 'one of the best writers in the language'. Of course he paid special honour to the great radical writers of the past, John Milton, Andrew Marvell and many more. But he also wrote more enthusiastically than any previous English critic on a host of others who at first sight might be imagined to have no political hold on him at all— Swift, Pope, Montaigne, Fielding, Cervantes: above all, Shakespeare. Others, like Coleridge, alongside Hazlitt (not anyone hardly *before* him), were encompassing Shakespeare in a new glory. But it was Hazlitt's criticisms which had immediate and lasting impact on two of his greatest contemporaries in Europe, Heinrich Heine and Henri Beyle, alias Stendhal, both of whom came to London and carried the new Shakespearian fashions back across the Channel.

Both Heine and Stendhal acknowledged the debt they owed to Hazlitt, which is more than can be said for Wordsworth or Coleridge. Despite his deepening political quarrels with them, Hazlitt never ceased to honour Wordsworth as the great originating poet of the age, and Coleridge still held the central place in his essay as the man who had opened his understanding, 'till the light of his genius shone into my soul, like the sun's rays glittering in the puddles of the road'.

But intertwined with the tributes—inextricably, as Hazlitt doubtless intended to make sure—were the searing, indelible invectives against those who had deserted the cause of their youth. Wordsworth and Coleridge may be forgiven if they failed to turn their Christian cheeks; what they should never be forgiven—for neither were exactly paragons of sexual virtue— were the Lakeside libels against Hazlitt's alleged sexual antics which they unloosed, not in any sudden fit of outrage at the time, but long after the unspecified exploits had supposedly occurred. However, the point concerns not the Wordsworth-cum-Coleridge intolerance, but Hazlitt's magnanimity. Long after he had plentiful evidence of the venomous gossip with which they had pursued him, even to the point of threatening his most treasured friendships with the Lambs and Leigh Hunt, he still would not be shifted from his recognition of their greatness. Literary cliques are not noted for their generosity. Hazlitt refused to be suffocated even when he had been driven, by the pressures of politics, into a clique of one.

However, for all his readiness to stand alone, for all his gift for solitude, his individuality won him some unexpected or idiosyncratic friends—John Cavanagh, the fives player, or William Bewick, the engraver, or James Northcote, the portrait painter, or William Hone, the allegedly blasphemous bookseller, or the young ex-medical student who came to his lectures, accompanied him on the journeys to Leigh Hunt in the Vale of Health on Hampstead Heath, and who had shown 'the greatest promise of genius of any poet of his day'. Hazlitt, alas, never wrote a full-scale essay on John Keats, but almost every fresh study reinforces Keats's own testimony of how intricate and all-pervasive was the Hazlitt influence upon him. 'The whole cadence of his (Keats's) prose', writes Robert Gittings, 'is that of Hazlitt whose reviews he seems to have had nearly by heart.' It was Hazlitt lecturing at the Institution across Blackfriars Bridge, or Hazlitt talking on the walk to Hampstead, or Hazlitt writing in Leigh Hunt's *Examiner*, who was responsible for most of the introductions which made Keats a poet—to Shakespeare, to Wordsworth and several more. In particular, it was Hazlitt who introduced Keats to his favourite Wordsworthian poem, *The Excursion*, at a time when Wordsworth was still rejected and neglected in fashionable quarters. Here was just another example of Hazlitt's 'disinterestedness' which Keats so much admired and emulated. Keats, of course, shared Hazlitt's political aversions, as he discovered to his disquiet when he called at Wordsworth's home in the Lakes only to find that the poet of cloud and cataract was out canvassing for the Cumberland Tories. Anyhow, thanks to modern scholarship and Mr. Gittings more especially, the truth is now established beyond challenge. Henceforth Keats and Hazlitt climb Parnassus roped together, and a terrible curse of combined Hazlittean-Keatsian power must fall upon anyone who would tear them apart.

What other critic in English literary history, or any other literary history for that matter, ever had such a pupil? And yet poetry was not Hazlitt's first love, and never even at any time his all-consuming passion. He had set out in early youth to become a painter, and he made good use of all he learnt, becoming (in the words of Lord Clark) 'the best English critic before Ruskin'. He was there at the Drury Lane theatre on the night of Edmund Kean's first appearance as Shylock, and the meeting was one of the most memorable in the history of the English theatre. He was, as Professor R. L. Brett has written, 'the first critic to take the novel seriously'. Yet none of these pursuits were the ones which touched him most closely. His pride was that he was a philosopher. In that first essay describing his meeting with the poets he tells of the tears he wept in the long, and at first vain, exertion to get words on to paper. It was nearly six years after the sacred year of 1798 before he finally succeeded in completing his little-read and not-easily-readable *Essay on the Principles of Human Action*. Like other painfully delivered first children, it remained his favourite, especially as no one else showed any liking for the brat.

He finished that first book at the age of twenty-six; he died at the age of fifty-two. What he truly wrote in that bare quarter-of-a-century interval was a vast, rambling, astringent, Montaigne-like autobiography, which abjured all the self-worshipping postures both he and Keats so much detested, but which yet succeeds in telling as much as any man ever told about his convictions, his

tastes, his emotions, his enthusiasms, and how he strove perpetually to subject them to the most severe tests at his command.
It is surely this open invitation to explore the well-nigh
inexhaustible resources, 'the whole compass and circuit of his
mind', which makes the titles 'essayist' or 'critic' such feeble
terms to describe what he sought to accomplish.

Some fine biographers have already made the exploration too,
notably P. P. Howe, the devoted and inspired editor of his
Collected Works, or Herschel Baker, author of the only volume
which deserves to be set alongside Howe's, and, on a lower shelf,
Hesketh Pearson's *The Fool of Love*, and Augustine Birrell's not-
to-be-despised pre-1914 volume. For a real addition to the
existing store of knowledge we shall have to await the forthcoming new biography by the wisest as well as the most thorough
of Hazlitt scholars, Professor Stanley Jones, whose contributions
to the learned journals have already disposed of several anti-
Hazlitt canards.

Meantime, let us return afresh to Hazlitt's evidence against
himself. Very few themes which figured prominently in his life are
left in an unfinished state in his writings. One concerns his
religion, and it is indeed surprising that one born and bred as a
Celtic dissenter, one who shared so eagerly the Puritan vision of
his country's history, one who knew every step in John Bunyan's
pilgrimage, one who would have fought and died for the true
religion's cause at Burford, one who indeed wrote about every
other subject under the sun, hardly ever made any direct reference
to any religious topic, less still any religious conviction. He
mocked the Papists, ('Nothing to be said against their religion
but that it is contrary to reason and common sense'), side-kicked
the Presbyterians ('Weighing their doubts and scruples to the
division of a hair, and shivering on the narrow brink that divides
philosophy from religion'), damned the Methodists ('They
plunge without remorse into hell's flames, soar on the wings of
divine love, are carried away with the motions of the spirit, are
lost in the abyss of unfathomable mysteries—election, repro-
bation, predestination—and revel in a sea of boundless nonsense'),
heaped secular scorn on the Laodicean Anglicans ('Satan lies in
wait for them in a pinch of snuff, in a plate of buttered toast, in

the kidney end of a loin of veal'), and extolled the true Dissenters for keeping their covenant, as the stars keep their courses. But he avoided all deep religious arguments, and one reason may be that he wished to give no open offence to his father. He himself had been intended for the Unitarian Ministry and he knew how his family were disappointed when he was seduced from that vocation by his first dream that one day he would be able to say with Correggio: 'I also am a painter', and, even more, by his later resolve to pursue the wicked trade of Swift, Defoe and such-like infidels. But the tact of father and son, towards each other if towards no one else, was such that no shadow was allowed to fall across their relationship. What would have happened if Sarah Walker had appeared on the scene while his father was still alive, none can tell.

Suddenly, when Sarah did make her first appearance, or rather when 'with a waving air she goes along the corridor', his life was transformed and he became 'the very fool of Love'. It is the only corner of his love life which Hazlitt has revealed, and the evidence has naturally been pursued by scholars with prurient dedication. He himself wrote a classic 'confession'; however, it is his reticence which may first deserve consideration.

Considering how original were Hazlitt's ideas on almost every theme which captivated him, considering how he could race ahead to anticipate the thought, in the field of psychology, say, no less than politics, of the whole ensuing century, it is the more surprising that he never seemed to turn his mind to the great question of the rights of women. He was certainly no feminist, not that the word had yet been invented nor even that the thing itself was common. He was a frequent visitor at the house of William Godwin, and one of his gleaming sentences casts a kindly ray of light across the countenance of Mary Wollstonecraft. Yet the extraordinary fact is that he did not write much more about her; seemingly, he had never read her *Vindication of the Rights of Woman* or it left no mark whatever.

For Hazlitt, as for most of his contemporaries of a similar cast of mind, the great romantic bible was Rousseau's *La Nouvelle Heloise*, which was still also a revolutionary document. Enough for the moment, enough for one century perhaps, to break the love-making conventions of polite, ruling-class society. Hazlitt's ideal of womanhood, I suspect, was Rossini's Rosina whose liberation took the form of enabling her to twist men round her little finger, without them having the foggiest notion what she was up to, and no bad choice either; who in his senses ever could resist her? However, in real life, for Hazlitt, Rosina was transformed into Sarah Walker, and she almost destroyed him with her wiles, her titillations, her prevarications and her treacheries. (Let it not be forgotten, by the way, that no one has ever told Sarah's side of the story: what a find that would be!) Yet despite the absence of the slightest touch of feminism in his make-up, Hazlitt was not a male chauvinist; more like a male pacifist indeed, and his debasement before the idol of his own creation came near to encompassing his ruin then and thereafter.

He could not keep quiet on the subject, stopping to tell everybody about his bewitchment in every tavern from Chancery Lane to Covent Garden. He unloosed a gushing flood upon her fawn-like head and upon his few especial long-suffering friends. Then he turned aside from most other labours to compile and publish anonymously the *New Pygmalion*, the *Liber Amoris*. One of his letters to Sarah—and perhaps even the most presentable—fell into the scurrilous hands of a Tory journal, *John Bull*, and was reproduced, with much sneering and snivelling, to damn him and his politics to eternity. Some of his eminent ex-friends—like Coleridge, for example—to their immortal dishonour, used the occasion to resuscitate an old unproved and unprovable charge that the young Hazlitt had been the villain in some terrible seduction scene (some have even called it 'rape', without a tincture of evidence) twenty years before. He was soon having to publish anonymously also his *Spirit of the Age* essays—some of the greatest in the English language—for fear of inviting too swift an association with 'the impotent sensualist', the lascivious author of *Liber Amoris*.

Fashions, of course, have changed altogether about the *Liber Amoris*. Robert Louis Stevenson was so shocked by it that he gave up the idea of writing Hazlitt's life. Augustine Birrell, whose biography was otherwise intelligently sympathetic, wished to consign the offending volume to 'the realms of things unspeakable, fit only for the midden'. Even the most learned and authoritative of modern biographers, Herschel Baker, turns aside in horror from Hazlitt in love, and even Professor R. L. Brett, a most eminent Coleridgean, invokes the *Liber Amoris* to justify some of the old libels on Hazlitt's youthful sex-life. How Coleridge and Wordsworth would have rubbed their pious hands at the thought. And yet in modern times too Hazlitt has been better enabled to speak for himself. In the excellent Penguin *Selected Writings* (published in 1970 and edited by Ronald Blythe), the *Liber Amoris* is printed in full but also printed where it ought to be, alongside his other writings, and Ronald Blythe also gives proper recognition to two others before him who have helped rescue the book from the midden.

It was indeed only as late as 1948—well over a hundred years after that 'sweet apparition', or, if you wish, that 'slimy, marble varnished fiend' had turned her glance so fatally upon him—that any commentator appreciated to the full the nature of Hazlitt's agony. Charles Morgan wrote in that year an entirely new kind of introduction to the despised volume in which he invoked the case-knowledge of modern psychology, partly to explain Hazlitt but, even more remarkably, to reveal how much of modern discoveries in this field Hazlitt had anticipated. Morgan also made a most discriminating comparison between Hazlitt and Stendhal, Hazlitt's contemporary whom he resembled in so many aspects, although most notably *not* in philandering bravado or technique. Just at the moment when Hazlitt was making obeisance before the statue he had erected, Stendhal was writing his own book of love, *De L'Amour*, in which the Hazlittean trauma, disease, madness, idyll, is immortally diagnosed.

Soon afterwards the two men met in Paris. Stendhal gave his book to Hazlitt who must have read it on his journey onwards towards the two mistresses they shared, Rome and Venice. I have often wondered: how Hazlitt's hair must have stood on end as he turned over those burning pages; how he must have marvelled at this French sympathiser who understood his predicament with Sarah so much better than his own countrymen; (and how he must have concealed the volume from his new sedate wife who was making part of the journey with him). 'She is dead to me, but

what she once was to me can never die.' That was Hazlitt's own
epitaph on the affair, but perhaps Stendhal and Montaigne even
helped finally to soothe his passion. And as Morgan shows, there
was one sense in which he carried the investigation further even
than these two acknowledged mentors; he 'shows'—in the words
of Morgan—'because he is a supreme realist and is unafraid to give
himself away, that the crystallising lover is by no means the blind
fool that he is traditionally supposed to be. He thus deprives
himself of the only romantic defence with which an aloof and self-
righteous world might be disposed contemptuously to cover him.
The lover, Hazlitt says in effect, is not even a dupe; he is worse, he
is a half-dupe, and yet persists'. Hazlitt made himself, again in
Morgan's memorable conclusion, 'the sane, unsparing analyst of
his own madness'. And yet Stendhal conducted the analysis
afresh, and with an even greater clinical precision, and with a sense
of humour too (and even with an invocation of the name of
Montaigne, sacred to Hazlitt certainly), to recall sexual fiascos
as remarkable as his own. Hazlitt surely must have been gratified
to be assured, after such painful torture and on such high
combined authority, that he was not so abnormal a creature after
all.

   As for Hazlitt's sanity, so often and interestedly questioned by
his political enemies, his friends may take pleasure from the fact
that plumb in the middle of the months when he obsessively and
vainly waited for a soft word from Sarah, he could still sit down
and write a five thousand word letter to his ten-year-old son
(suitable for later publication, to be sure), one of the most
civilised documents ever written by any father to any son:

> It is a good rule to hope for the best . . . Never anticipate evils . . .
> Learn never to conceive prejudice against others, because you know
> nothing of them . . . Never despise anyone for anything he cannot
> help—least of all for his poverty . . . Never despise anyone at all . . .
> True equality is the only true morality or true wisdom . . . Believe all
> the good you can of everyone . . . Envy none, and you need envy no
> one . . . Never quarrel with tried friends or those whom you wish to
> continue such . . . Be neither a martyr, nor sycophant . . . Do not
> gratify the enemies of liberty by putting yourself at their mercy . . .

So the sentences and the elaborations tumble onto the page one after another; no one could doubt the coolness and the reflective wisdom which he had achieved by sheer intellectual exertion, and yet in the midst of it he is well nigh overthrown by the tempestuous nature of his passion. And, a month or two later again, he had governed his temper afresh, and the so-called besotted bigot had returned to his favourite addiction of seeking to explain the other side of the question.

Certainly no condemnation was intended when Hazlitt, the romantic realist, insisted:

> Women have often more of what is called good sense than men. They have fewer pretensions; are less implicated in theories; and judge of objects more from their immediate and involuntary impression on the mind, and therefore more truly and naturally. They cannot reason wrong; for they do not reason at all. They do not think or speak by rule; and they have in general more eloquence and wit, as well as sense, on that account. By their wit, sense and eloquence together, they generally contrive to govern their husbands.

The compliment was barbed, but it was a compliment no less.

With or without the help of psycho-analytical treatment from 'my friend Mr. Beyle', Hazlitt did recover. The period of six or seven years, between his escape from Sarah's listless clutches and his death in 1830, is not by any reckoning a famous one in English history, and for Hazlitt especially it must have seemed craven and squalid. All his soaring political hopes had been shattered; Jacob's ladder had collapsed. No proper acclaim for his literary powers came from most of his fellow-countrymen; he was still an outcast. He embarked on what even his few remaining devoted friends considered to be a chronic wastage of his talents, a monumental Life of Napoleon, which threatened to bury him altogether. Money troubles hit him harder even than ever before; for the first time in his life he spent some months in prison for debt. Yet neither his courage nor his genius were impaired. On the contrary: made ridiculous in love, staring political defeat in the face, libelled by his enemies, harried by creditors, the Hazlitt who was often upbraided for ill-temper wrote with an ever-increasing equilibrium, almost optimism. He reasserted the convictions of his youth with something of the old exhilaration, and not only in the field of politics, and he did it with mellowness but without a hint of retreat, without a jot of weakness or cynicism.

> Really it is wonderful how little the worse I am for fifteen years wear and tear, how I came upon my legs again on the ground of truth and nature, and 'look abroad into universality', forgetting there is any such person as myself in the world.

How little diseased was that mind. T. S. Eliot wrote of Matthew Arnold that 'he had no real serenity, only an impeccable demeanour'. Hazlitt's demeanour could outrage everybody, even the long-suffering Charles Lamb. But, contrary to the impression left by his unfailing pugnacity, he had achieved a real serenity—as the later essays, one after another, prove. It was not that he had become complacent or withdrawn from the battle. He was still in the thick of it, giving blow for blow, whenever the opportunity occurred. But the poets, who in the words of his friend Keats 'pour out a balm upon the world', gave a specially healing dose to Hazlitt. He had fought a good fight; he had kept the faith. 'One source of this unbendingness (which some may call obstinacy)', he wrote in *A Farewell to Essay Writing*,

> is that, though living much alone, I have never worshipped the Echo, I see plainly enough that black is not white, that the grass is green, that kings are not their subjects; and in such self-evident cases do not think it necessary to collate my opinions with the received prejudices.

None could stop him thinking for himself; he was secure in that citadel and could survey the battlefield from its turrets. And he knew too (and who will dare deny the claim?) that 'in seeking for truth I sometimes found beauty'. Above all, he stayed young, 'kept the candid brow and elastic spring of youth'. The iron had not entered his soul although too many folk then and since thought it was uniquely constructed of nothing else.

He is, wrote William Bewick, 'the Shakespeare prose writer of our glorious century; he outdoes all in truth, style and originality'. That was the view expressed by the excited young art student who attended one of Hazlitt's lectures in the company of the equally excited John Keats. Very few agreed with them at the time, and when he died, the political furies which had beaten upon him while he lived did not quickly abate. However, through the influence of his own writings, his literary reputation has steadily increased until now, two hundred odd years after his birth, it stands higher than it ever did. William Bewick's tribute no longer looks like a youthful exaggeration.

THREE

The Good Tory

'The greatest triumph the Conservative Cause has ever had.
And yet,' Lord Buckhurst added, laughing, 'if any fellow
were to ask me what the Conservative Cause is, I am sure I
should not know what to say.'

CONINGSBY

ASK an ambitious young Tory Member of Parliament, at any
time during the past half century, which was his favourite, his
ideal, among all Tory Prime Ministers and the answer would
normally come without hesitation: Disraeli. I once put the
question to eligible candidates in the middle of the Macleod-
Maudling era, and seven out of ten said Disraeli. One said Sir
Robert Peel, but he was soon exiled to the Outer Mongolian
darkness of a provincial university. Sir Robert split his Party, the
most deadly of all political sins: no full Conservative majority in
the House of Commons was secured for twenty-eight years
thereafter. But Benjamin Disraeli was not only granted forgiveness for his part in that affair; he was apotheosised. At the
Oxford of the twenties and thirties, I recall, in the age of Baldwin
and Chamberlain, his was the name which could restore respect
and glamour to their bedraggled creed; every rising hope of the
pliant, appeasing Tories could recite his perorations. Whatever
the true nature of the man, his myth has seemed to possess an
undying magnetism.

Yet in recent times that judgement must be heavily qualified.
Few could have predicted the scale of the latest change in fashion,
and Disraeli himself would have felt most out-of-place in a world
where *laissez-faire* ideas were claimed as the essence of Conservative doctrine. He was the first to use the term 'the school of
Manchester'; it was not intended as a compliment. He satirised

those whose first allegiance was to the principles of free competition in *The Screw and Lever Review*, and would have been aghast to learn that the most likely contributors to such a journal today would be Conservative Cabinet ministers. 'To acquire, to accumulate, to plunder each other by virtue of philosophic phrases, to propose a Utopia to consist only of wealth and toil, this has been the breathless business of enfranchised England . . .' he wrote, and he wrote in derision. But today the worshippers assemble afresh round the altar of Mammon, and the philosophic chorus is conducted by Sir Keith Joseph. Such a transformation must have altered Disraeli's standing in the Tory pantheon. (Who would be the hero of the new Josephite generation? Lord Liverpool, one must suppose.)

However, even before these latest aberrations, the signs of change were detectable. The dethronement of Disraeli had started a full decade before Mrs. Margaret Thatcher was elected leader of the Conservative Party, and the hand which started the fatal work of demolition was that, not of some febrile practising politician, but of a great historian. Books may change the political climate more than politics shape books: Disraeli would at least concur with that proposition. Now, a hundred years after his death, it is a book which has knocked him off his pedestal, perhaps irretrievably.

Lord Blake's masterpiece, his eight hundred-page twentieth-century reassessment of both the man and the myth, was published in 1966, and must have required years of previous preparation and scholarship. It is a legitimate guess that he did not embark upon so prodigious an enterprise with iconoclastic intentions. Much more probably, when he set out on his journey, he too was entranced by the familiar Tory portrait of his hero, and, as publication day loomed, in the dark years of the sixties, when his beloved Party seemed condemned once more to the wilderness of opposition, how enticing it must have been to extol the leader who best taught his followers how to suffer defeat and still to triumph! Who better to reinvigorate modern Toryism than the man who, just a century before—in 1867—had laid the legislative foundation for Tory democracy in his Reform Bills, and who had synthesised word and deed into something worthy to be called a Tory philosophy? The temptation to present the prophet in this garb must have been well-nigh overpowering; a long list of writers, headed by Disraeli himself, had yielded. One measure of Lord Blake's quality as an historian is that he rejected this course, yet the tribute is absurdly insufficient. It is the scale of his renunciation which is breath-taking. No one can write anything further about Disraeli without confronting Lord Blake's lengthy charge sheet.

Disraeli was—on Lord Blake's verdict—an adventurer, impure and complex. He was, for a venial start, a born liar in the sense that he told fantastic tales about his ancestry and heritage, and stuck to them; ever afterwards the gift was vastly developed. He could mislead friends and foes alike, occasionally leaving one by the wayside or dumbfounding the other by his brazenness. He glided more or less successfully out of more verbal scrapes than any other politician of the century; he could be guilty of 'reckless mendacity'. Some of these qualities helped him to become, again to quote Lord Blake, 'the most potent myth-maker in British history,' yet previously Disraeli had used them to fabricate his own version of the past. It is this last monstrous perversion which, one feels, has irremediably offended Lord Blake's professional sense. For politicians to devise myths to help shape the future may be part of their stock-in-trade, and good luck to those who know how to work the trick; for politicians to apply comparable methods to the art of historical writing is to trespass and to vandalise. Anyhow, Disraeli resorted to this brand of devilry in a manner no one has attempted before or since. If the Whig interpretation of history was a caricature, the Disraeli re-interpretation was something much worse, much cruder still, which, apart from its intrinsic evil, has jeopardised the credibility of all subsequent and genuine Conservative essays in the same field. At the time when he did it, the attempt to make a Tory patron-saint-cum-prophet out of the free-thinking roué and rogue, Lord Bolingbroke, deeply and inevitably offended Victorian sentiment. How could anyone so intelligent contrive a theme so implausible? One is almost forced to believe he must have done it for a wager, concocted perhaps after some all-night escapade with his Young England confederates. Serious twentieth-century Tory historians cannot be expected to show patience with these aristocratic carousals.

Moreover, once the tenuous nature of Disraeli's allegiance to fact and truth is appreciated, once the grip of the legend is loosened, so much else falls into place. He was *not* a far-seeing Tory Democrat; he did *not* seek to carry into reality the dreams of Young England and his youth; he did *not* educate his Party in his own romantic ideals. He was never the towering statesman of Tory perorations. He was the inveterate opportunist, the supreme parliamentary practitioner who loved 'the high game' for its own sake, and who would rather outwit Gladstone than gain an empire. He was, as he readily admitted, and claimed every politician to be, 'a creature of his age, the child of circumstances, the creation of his times'; in short, a pragmatist, highly skilled in disguising retreat as an advance. Even when he finally achieved power, with a full parliamentary majority, he did not know what to do with it. Even, and in a sense especially, the great 'imperialist' exertions of his last few years, which previous Tory historians have trumpeted with Elgaresque assurance, may be found on examination (Lord Blake's examination, it must be reiterated) to be built on muddle and misunderstanding. He never quite abandoned the Little Englander leanings of his early years, and the theme of Empire never truly captured his imagination.

Few could discern better than Disraeli himself the test of great men. 'A great man', he wrote in *Coningsby*, 'is one who affects the mind of his generation.' And then again: 'Great minds must trust to great truths and great talents for their rise, and nothing else.' But, of course, Disraeli was never foolhardy enough to rely on his own noble prescription. So Lord Blake has his justification for denying to Disraeli his own title to the highest statesmanship. His victories were always tactical, not strategical; he did not lead, he followed. The age changed him much more than he influenced his age. In *Coningsby*, along with his heroes and heroines, he created the immortal Taper and Tadpole whose perpetual fascination was the way the political wires were pulled. Yet Disraeli lived to acquire that addiction himself. Neither Tadpole nor Taper ever despaired of the Commonwealth, it will be recalled; but Tadpole, it may not be so easily remembered, 'was of a larger grasp of mind than Taper'. And larger still was the grasp of Mr. Rigby who 'hearing that his friends had some hopes, he thought he would just come down to dash them'. Mr. Rigby is the most odious character in the whole Disraelian gallery; but Disraeli had a streak of Rigby in him too.

It would be too severe to conclude that Lord Blake reduces Disraeli to the figure of nineteenth-century Liberal lampoon, the ever-cunning, ever-cynical manipulator of the parliamentary situation, with all loftier flights reduced in proportion, or to Carlyle's 'superlative conjuror, spell-binding all the great Lords, great Parties, great interests of England, to his hand in this manner, and leading them by the nose like helpless, mesmerised somnambulant cattle . . .' But Lord Blake's aim is not so far off that target. He does not seek to withhold—who could?—the meed of praise for Disraeli's charm, his wit, above all, his courage. But how should even this combination of qualities possessed in such abundance dispel what he left behind him everywhere he went, the trail of prevarication, deceit and falsehood? And are those words too severe? They are based on the settled judgement of the man whom no Conservative can dismiss.

> He is an adventurer, and as I have good cause to know, he is without principles and honesty. You will say that I am giving great prominence to a question of mere personal esteem. It is true. But in this matter the personal question is the whole question . . . The worst alternative that can happen is his continuance in power. He is under a temptation to Radical measures to which no other Minister is subject . . . He can forward Radical changes in a way that no other Minister could do—because he alone can silence and paralyse the forces of Conservatism. And in an age of singularly reckless statesmen he is I think beyond question the one who is least restrained by fear or scruple.

Such was Lord Salisbury's (at the time he was still Lord Cranbourne) view of his colleague at a particular moment when their careers jarred, but he claimed to be writing what 'all the country gentlemen were saying in private', and a strong strand of that contempt persisted even after the two men had reached their later accommodation. No reader should suppose that he has taken the proper measure of what personal political hatred within parties can mean until he has read Lady Gwendolen Cecil's classic biography of her father, Lord Salisbury. It is Lord Salisbury's brush which has painted the dark, indelible portrait of the Disraeli whom he first despised, and then vowed never to forgive, only relenting after more than a decade—of course, in the highest interest of the Conservative Party and the English state. But the venom of that earlier time still sears Lady Gwendolen's pages, and Lord Blake does not demur. For Lord Salisbury was, he assures us, 'the most formidable intellectual figure that the Conservative party has ever produced': no mean accolade from the preeminent contemporary Conservative historian. We need be surprised no longer about the lasting injury his book has done to Disraeli's reputation, and might be content to accept the happy conclusion advanced by one of Lord Blake's most enthusiastic reviewers: 'Disraeli's usefulness to the Conservative Central Office can hardly survive this book,' wrote Professor John Vincent.

Leave aside the Central Office: good Conservatives, good Tories (Disraeli made huge exertions to draw a distinction between the two, with no real success), should have reached this conclusion for themselves a hundred years before, and if they had failed before, Lady Gwendolen's book, published in 1921, was there to guide their straying steps back into the path of Tory rectitude. She wrote:

> In all that is disputable in Mr. Disraeli's character—and there are few parts of it which have not been a subject for dispute—his lack of scruple as to the methods which he thought permissible is beyond question . . . He was always making use of convictions that he did not share, pursuing objects which he could not own, manoeuvring his party into alliances which though unobjectionable from his own standpoint were discreditable and indefensible from theirs. It was an atmosphere of pervading falseness which involved his party as well as himself and which culminated in the cynical audacities of 1867.

But could not that stricture be conceivably construed as a particular offence, a passing episode, the exception and not the rule? Not at Hatfield, for sure. Even in the later years, she insists, when 'the older man' had begun to show some glimmering of the elements of 'loyalty', he still revealed his 'inveterate *feather-headedness*', a readiness to pursue contradictory, often self-contradictory courses. 'The failing', she insists again, 'was germane to his genius. Those of his opinions which could claim the permanent quality of principles had their origin in his imagination and not in his reason. He saw visions; he did not draw conclusions.' Altogether—and this it must be repeated was the settled judgement of the brilliant father and the no less brilliant daughter who had known him in his latest and, in the Tory record, his greatest days—there was something deeply alien to the Tory mind in Disraeli's whole outlook and character. Maybe, these features in his make-up were also those which made him un-English no less than un-Tory, but that is another aspect of the tale. Frequently during his life the Tories wished to turn upon their self-appointed saviour: the clash of temperament between leader and followers became almost too painful to be borne. An observer scarcely less perspicacious than Salisbury's biographer wrote:

> No one who lived and mixed with politicians before 1874 or who has read the memoirs of that time can forget the despair and distrust with which Disraeli inspired his followers. Might not salvation be found by shelving or discarding him? by such a combination for example as making the Duke of Somerset Prime Minister, and relegating Disraeli to the serene duties of Chancellor of the Duchy, or even to complete repose? This was the project of Cairns, Disraeli's closest political ally, who nevertheless seems at that time to have had an imperfect conception of the character and aims of his friend. To such straits was the party driven. Anything, they declared, but Disraeli; under him victory was impossible. What a mere adventurer he was! What a fantastic alien! What nonsense he wrote!

Thus wrote Lord Rosebery, a Liberal observer of special acumen; the measure of Tory hatred for Disraeli should never be underrated. And even in this generation, when he was securely in his grave at Hughenden where Queen Victoria's primroses were laid on his coffin, the act of revulsion is re-enacted by his biographer and the reviewers. For Professor Vincent it is almost as if the corpse has been dug up, like Cromwell's, and thrown into a common pit.

One irony of the situation is that we have, and have always had, a better chance of dissecting the mind of Disraeli, alien or not, than that of any other Prime Minister in our history. Winston Churchill is the only conceivable rival in this claim; he poured out his thoughts, in books, letters and writings of every variety in such a superabundant profusion that we may be excused for supposing that no secrets remain. But who else? Only writers themselves, by the way, can be entered in this contest; no secretaries or officials at the great man's elbow, invaluable though their observations may be, can offer the same degree of unconscious no less than conscious revelation. And here, incontestably, Disraeli is in a class of his own. No other leading politician, let alone a Prime Minister, has left a literary treasure to compare with Disraeli's dozen or so novels. What a wonder it would be, to press the point further, if, say, Lloyd George or Charles James Fox had possessed a similar gift; if the one had used the novelist's genius to unmask the Marconi scandal or the other the Fox-North Coalition, or if each had been ready to unleash the dreams and exultations of their youth and the laments and triumphs of old age. A new aspect would be added to their political characters; we should see them full face. The miracle is that Disraeli confronts us in his novels more boldly than any other comparable figure, and yet, all too often, the world, his contemporaries, or his biographers, have turned aside. Constantly, and increasingly in the later years, he urged correspondents to look for his life in his books. A few wise men, Bismarck for one, took the hint, but a host of others resented the invocation or were too disturbed by what they read.

Lord Blake cannot be criticised on this score, for he has woven the evidence from the novels into the life-story as never before; indeed, it would scarcely be too much to say that he finds Disraeli the novelist more attractive than Disraeli the politician. And yet he offers one conclusion with shattering implications and one which he admits Disraeli would have read with incomprehension. Disraeli prided himself on this particular quality, even his enemies vouchsafed it to him, even at Hatfield, as we have seen, it was acknowledged in full measure. Yet Lord Blake dares to assert: 'The truth is that Disraeli lacked imagination.' Lord Blake's comparisons are with the great novelists of the century, and his suggestion is that Disraeli had not the full capacity to design original characters and scenes and situations of his own; he was a copyist and caricaturist, not a creative artist of the first order. Maybe. But the novels—not all, but almost all—have another dimension which has escaped Lord Blake; he has eyes but cannot see. For Disraeli, they offered an escape from the hypocrisies he detested, from Whig and Tory politics alike, from the Conservative Cause and all its squalid inadequacies, from Hatfield and kindred horrors. But let us see; the case has still to be explored. What cannot be in doubt is the gulf which exists between the Tory world, past and present, Lord Salisbury's and Lord Blake's, and the extraordinary assortment of preconceptions and prejudices, wayward hopes and aspirations, realism and romance which made up the mind of Benjamin Disraeli.

It is, paradoxically, the Tory judgement which now denies to Disraeli his greatness, but let the rest of us look afresh and see what was truly there.

Disraeli said that he was born in a library, and part of his attraction was that he never quite escaped. He lived ever afterwards this half-life of romance in his own novels and other people's, saw himself in his youth as a kind of Byronic conqueror who could make a book as great a thing as a battle, and even in his old age, as Prime Minister or ex-Prime Minister, could never resist the temptation to return to his old trade and thereby outrage his sedate contemporaries. (How lucky it was for him, as Carlyle once remarked, that most of his colleagues in the Tory Party never read anything at all.) He had acquired the addiction from his father who, however, quite outdid him in it. Isaac Disraeli never ran the risk of emerging from his library at all, unless it was for the alternative legitimate pursuit of scouring the London bookshops. Morning, noon and night, when all the rest of the candles in the house were extinguished, single or married, for better or worse, he lived, moved and had his being among his favourite authors, and those who love books everywhere (and above all those who love books about books) owe him a debt almost as heavy as the one faithfully discharged by his doting son.

Isaac Disraeli was a Tory of sorts; apart from his highly popular literary compilations which showed no special political preferences, he wrote a few little-read volumes on two Tory heroes, James I and Charles I. But these were scarcely passionate political declarations; they added little to the current orthodoxies. More surprising, for a Tory, were his enthusiasms among eighteenth-century writers. He honoured Voltaire and loved Rousseau; he became a devotee of Gibbon and a friend of William Blake. His own books (not the sycophantic obeisances before Stuart kings) drew glowing tributes from Byron, and Isaac eagerly accepted and repaid all compliments from that quarter. In his old age he contemplated a book on the history of free-thinkers ('a profound and vigorous race', the tutors of Shelley, his son called them). He was surely a dutiful upholder of the wonderful Jewish Montaigne tradition, and he became, not by sudden conversion but by steady gradations, a sceptic and a rationalist. He wished Benjamin would give up novel-writing, not because he did not like the novels but because he sensed better than his braver son how the boy's enemies would rally against him. He had some critical faculties but they were mostly softened when they were turned on Benjamin. 'Imagination only can decide on imagination', he once wrote in an essay on *The Fairie Queen*, and the point might be passed to Lord Blake. From such a father certainly Disraeli received no perceptible guidance about his political future. He was just taught to love books, the best gift of all.

Old Disraeli taught his son to love Byron too, but any paternal instruction here was superfluous. No doubt it was an added enticement that the world-famous poet bestowed such honour on his beloved father but Byron became for a while the very air the young Disraeli breathed. He responded to every various Byronic mood and placed a special Byronic mark of his own on every book he wrote. *Vivian Grey*, published two years after Byron's death, celebrated with full romantic flourish 'the most splendid character which human nature can aspire to', and some side-glances revealed a more individual appreciation: he could celebrate too the great man's 'strong, shrewd commonsense; his pure, unalloyed sagacity'. A year later *The Young Duke* caught 'Byron bending o'er his shattered lyre, with inspiration in his very rage'. *Contarini Fleming* was hailed as 'a *Childe Harolde* in prose', and so great a fellow-devotee of Byron as Heinrich Heine would not accept the general verdict that this Disraeli attempt to follow in the Byronic footsteps was so palpable a failure. Byron and his fate and his pitiless pursuit by 'the British public in one of its periodical fits of morality' continued to haunt Disraeli for a decade or more. True, the phrase and its elaboration were plagiarised from Macaulay but the theme was no less passionately felt. Indeed the young Disraeli could write on such themes with a more intimate knowledge and anxiety than Macaulay; he was truly a disciple of Byron in deed as well as word. An ambitious young politician could have been excused if he kept reasonably quiet on the subject. Instead, he wrote *Venetia*, no literary masterpiece, but a brave, reckless apologia not only for the libertine Byron but, for good measure at the same time, for the atheist and republican Shelley.

Shelley was allowed to summon to his defence a host of witnesses, Shakespeare, Dante 'and old Montaigne for me', and one other too, above all the rest, Don Quixote, 'the best man who ever lived'. Don Quixote, incidentally, was, second only to Rousseau's classic, *La Nouvelle Heloise*, a Bible among the romantics, a challenge to Toryism all on its own. 'But what do you think of the assault on the windmills?' Shelley was asked in Disraeli's account, and Shelley's answer was firm enough:

> In the outset of his adventures, as in the outset of our lives, he was misled by his enthusiasm, without which, after all, we can do nothing. But the result is, Don Quixote was a redresser of wrongs, and therefore the world esteemed him mad.

Such were the rough lines which the now not-quite-so-young Disraeli was scratching out at top speed in the winter of 1837. *Venetia* was published in May, 1837: one month later he was elected to the House of Commons as the Tory M.P. for Maidstone.

Why did he do it? Why become a Tory? Why not let some woman make him a Whig—as one woman had already boasted she had succeeded with his hero Byron? He had indeed posed the dilemma wondrously ten years before in *The Young Duke*, so wondrously indeed that the satire was softened and censored by the author in later editions:

> I must be consistent, and not compromise my principles which will never do in England—more than once a year. Let me see: what are they? Am I a Whig or a Tory? I forget. As for the Tories, I admire antiquity, particularly a ruin; even the relics of the Temple of Intolerance have a charm. I think I am a Tory. But then the Whigs give such good dinners, and are the most amusing. I think I am a Whig: but then the Tories are so moral and morality is my forte: I must be a Tory. But the Whigs dress so much better; and an ill-dressed party, like an ill-dressed man, must be wrong. Yes! I am a decided Whig. And yet—I feel like Garrick between Tragedy and Comedy. I think I will be a Whig and a Tory alternate nights, and then both will be pleased: I have no objection, according to the fashion of the day, to take a place under a Tory ministry, provided I may vote against them.

This was not the candid tone of an unprincipled adventurer, as Professor Jerman who first unearthed and displayed them has remarked. And if he was an adventurer, as he further remarks, why not indeed join the Whigs, if not at that precise moment, then soon after?

The answer is: he was a Radical, and *The Young Duke* was the satire of an incipient Radical. The Upper House was put in its subordinate place; the Lower House was patronised; both were warned of what might occur when the young Disraeli turned his oratorical powers in their direction, and meantime the country gentlemen were put in their place too, Sir Chetwode Chetwode of Chetwode, and Sir Tichborne Tichborne of Tichborne:

> Sir Chetwode's hair was straight and white; Sir Tichborne's brown and curly, Sir Chetwode's eyes were blue; Sir Tichborne's grey. Sir Chetwode's nose was perhaps a snub; Sir Tichborne's was certainly a bottle! Sir Chetwode was somewhat garrulous, and was often like a man at play in the wrong box! Sir Tichborne was somewhat taciturn; but when he spoke it was always to the purpose, and made an impression, even if it were not new. Both were kind hearts, but Sir Chetwode was jovial, Sir Tichborne rather stern. Sir Chetwode often broke into a joke; Sir Tichborne sometimes backed into a sneer.

Sir Chetwode and Sir Tichborne were two inoffensive Catholic Baronets and were treated most leniently. A multitude of others in all ranges of the aristocracy he was supposed to revere were given their deserts, astringently or laughingly: the Dukes of Twaddle and Ego and various other exponents of Dukism, those mitred nullities, the Bishops, the Lords Dunderhead, Grubminster and Grouse and Squib, the Lords Fitz-Booby and Fitz-Pompey, the Lords Protest, Content and Proxy, and more besides, not forgetting many who were just content to sink into 'ermined insignificance', or Lord Loraine, in particular, 'a mild, middle-aged, lounging, languid man, who passed his life in crossing from Brooks to Boodles, and from Boodles to Brooks, and testing the comparable intelligence of these two celebrated bodies'. Strong premonitions of Oscar Wilde are evident in many of Disraeli's novels, and this feature has sometimes been noticed; it is the full P. G. Wodehouse strain which has been underestimated. He was, without any rival whatever, the first comic genius who ever installed himself in Downing Street.

However, long before he achieved the feat, this and some kindred gifts of temperament well-nigh crushed him altogether. It was in the decade of the 1830s that by a series of misadventures and misdemeanours, false starts and hair-raising retreats, he imprinted on the mind of his countrymen that reputation for slipperiness, for downright double-dealing, from which he could never quite escape. He fought High Wycombe as a Radical in 1832 and was elected as a Tory for Maidstone in 1837 and for the even safer Tory stronghold of Shrewsbury a year later. Between the two events he twisted and turned and prevaricated and engaged in every form and degree of political tergiversation, to use his own favourite word later hurled at Sir Robert Peel, thereby inviting on his head Daniel O'Connell's famous and terrible curse which traced his ancestry to the impenitent thief on the cross. It was during this period too that his financial and emotional affairs mounted to a climax, or rather a series of overwhelming climaxes which even the most devoted historical inquiries have not finally unravelled. He was thrown ever deeper upon the mercy of the moneylenders, and the last few scenes of his great love-affair with Henrietta are still not finally delineated.

Did he incite or at least encourage his mistress to share her favours with the lascivious ex-Lord Chancellor Lyndhurst and thereby secure the essential backing for his own political advancement? It looks likely. During these years a frenetic, impatient tone creeps into his controversial writings. He wrote a hideous, hopeless poem called *Revolutionary Epick*; and in a strangely rambling diary which he kept at the time he himself noted: 'My mind is a continental mind. It is a revolutionary mind . . .' He had something to say but had not found the means to say it; he could impose no sense of order on the revolutionary passions, the spirit of the age, which stirred within him. So 'without a pang', as he claimed falsely, he 'hurled his lyre to Limbo'. He seems momentarily to have lost his marvellous poise: the combined coolness and courtesy in the teeth of all trials which helped to shape his greatest gift of all, his courage. Perhaps he started to recover this most precious possession in *Henrietta Temple, A Love Story*; it certainly did not tell all, but perhaps it told more than the cynics have allowed and, of course, it concluded with a triumph for the hero. It was written, incredibly, in the hundred odd days of the summer and autumn of 1836 when both his love life and his financial affairs were collapsing into fiasco, but he somehow created for himself a world of hope and composure.

Yet it is another event altogether which truly heralds his recovery from the tribulations of the 1830s, a deed to wipe away all stains. Disraeli's maiden speech in the House of Commons, as every schoolchild is instructed, had been a disaster, and there-after he was forced to make painful and humiliating efforts to rehabilitate himself in what can be the most unforgiving and ungenerous assembly in the world. But then, at the most unpropitious moment for him, came another test. Outside the walls of Westminster, the great Chartist revolt was mounting to its fullest fury, and inside, all parties, Whigs and Tories alike, Conservatives, Liberals, even several of the self-styled Radicals, huddled together to protect Church and State in panic-stricken unity. Disraeli would not bow to the House of Commons in one of those swelling tempers when it converts itself into a mob. He was one of only three who voted against a Bill advancing money for the Birmingham police where the Chartist Convention was sitting; one of only five who opposed the fierce sentences imposed on Chartist leaders. 'Nobody can deny,' he told the House in that full Petition debate:

> that the Chartists labour under great grievances. Look at the House; it has been sitting now for five months. What has it done for the people? Nothing. The Government sees everything in the brightest colours; everything is the best in the best of worlds. The Government is busy making peers, creating baronets, at the very moment when a social insurrection is at the threshold . . .

He drew upon himself a rebuke from the Chancellor of the Exchequer of the day, and a junior member of the Government rushed in to call him 'an advocate of riot and disorder'. He yielded not an inch to either. It was a proud moment in his life, and he never forgot. When one of the leaders involved in these tumults who had had a spell in Leicester gaol knocked at the door of Disraeli's house in Grosvenor Gate, he was offered exquisite courtesy and excellent advice. Thanks to the guidance received there, the prison-poem, *The Purgatory of Suicides*, by Thomas Cooper, the Chartist, was properly printed. 'Nay Sir', said Cooper to his sceptical publisher, 'I shall not strike "the Chartist" out. Mr. Disraeli advised me not to let anyone persuade me to strike it out, and I mean to abide by his advice.'

Just a few years later again in *Sybil* he was entitled to exult:

> Yes! there was one voice that had sounded in that proud Parliament, that free, from the slang of faction, had dared to express immortal truths . . . that the rights of labour were as sacred as those of property; that if a difference were to be established, the interests of the living ought to be preferred . . .

Years later—in 1870—he wrote that 'the Chartists formed a popular organisation which in its extent and completeness has perhaps never been equalled'. Most of Disraeli's biographers confine the story of his Chartist speeches to a few casual sentences. Disraeli himself saw them in different and wiser proportions. He had no real sense of history, says Lord Blake; he was for ever the propagandist. True, perhaps: but he was the only leading political figure in the Parliament of the 1830s and the 1840s who recognised Chartism for what it was, the stirring of a new class, the movement of the future.

Moreover, Disraeli's sense of history, his comprehension of the revolutionary state of England, so much sharper than that of most of his contemporary politicians, became sharper still when he looked across the Irish sea. A few years later, in February 1844, he delivered in the House of Commons a speech which seems to have compressed into it something of the whole ensuing century of Irish history, a foretaste of the famine, the Fenians, Parnell, 1916, the founding of the Republic and more modern events still:

> I want to see a public man come forward and say what the Irish question is. One says that it is a physical question: another a spiritual. Now it is the absence of the aristocracy; now the absence of railways. It is the Pope one day and potatoes the next . . . A starving population, an alien Church, and in addition the weakest executive in the world. Well, what then would gentlemen say if they were reading of a country in that position? They would say at once, 'The remedy is revolution'. But the Irish could not have a revolution and why? Because Ireland is connected with another and a more powerful country. Then what is the consequence? The connection with England became the cause of the present state of Ireland. If the connection with England prevented a revolution and a revolution was the only remedy, England logically is in the odious position of being the cause of all the misery of Ireland. What then is the duty of an English Minister? To effect by his policy all those changes which a revolution would affect by force. That is the Irish question in its integrity.

No clearer voice than that had ever been addressed to the Irish question. He had never been to Ireland. He relied on his incomparable political imagination, shaken perhaps by the invectives which Daniel O'Connell had directed especially at himself.

When Sir Robert Peel formed his Conservative administration in 1841, he could find no Ministerial place for the young Disraeli, despite the sycophantic, appealing letters which he had demeaned himself to write to his leader. It was an error on Peel's

part, as even the most high-minded Peelite might later have been
ready to admit. But if the importunate upstart had been given the
advancement he craved, would Young England never have been
immortalised, would the great contest of the Two Nations never
have been unmasked: what would have become of *Coningsby,
Sybil* and *Tancred*, the trilogy which must certainly form the
chief Disraeli claim to literary achievement? The so-called 'ifs' of
history can be just tedious. But the whole suggestion that, if the
necessary office and cash had been forthcoming, he would never
have embarked on these works of imagination, is to depreciate
the books themselves. Two of them at least were written long
before the Corn Law crisis reached the point of breaking the
Peelite administration. None of them, as it happens, ever
touched upon the Protectionist issue, except in the most
glancing terms. The great themes were quite different which is
why the books are so readable—the social disturbances which
were threatening all the old landmarks, the argument about what
should be cast aside and what preserved, the true place of
Parliament in the life of the nation, indeed the future of the two
nations, and the role of great and little men within Parliament,
but, above all, swallowing up all other themes whatever, the
perpetually recurring one of how the world could be reshaped,
how England could be saved by the young heroes who understood the age in which they lived. *Contarini Fleming*, Childe
Harolde in prose, had already set the tone: 'In imagination I
shook thrones and founded empires. I felt myself a being born to
breathe in an atmosphere of revolution.' Henry Coningsby and
Charles Egremont were Contarini transformed into an English
context. Allegedly these characters were intended to portray the
now-forgotten figures of the Young England aristocracy but,
however true that may be, the words they uttered were drawn
from Disraeli's own romantic political philosophy. Bashfulness
was never prominent in the author's character; long before the
end of each volume he had made himself the hero, and a hero
whose whole instinct was to join, indeed to command, the revolt
against the existing order.

'I have been of opinion that revolutions are not to be evaded',
said Sidonia, and the fact that Disraeli put this remark into the

nearly-always wise Rothschild-Solomon figure is the most significant. Not many could be expected to share his wisdom. The more general view of those who so much despised the visionaries was that the great issues could be skirted and sidestepped. *Coningsby* described the unawaredness among those inside the Westminster walls: 'they knew as little of the real state of their own country as savages of an approaching eclipse.' *Sybil* described the brewing storm outside. It was no mean or merely egotistical vision. For all the melodrama, even the hero could be pushed aside; it was Sybil who first told Egremont that 'the conquerors will never rescue the conquered'. The salvation of working people would not come from on high, from a supposed superior class. So how was the resistance to be roused and directed? The great Chartist debate, the strategical argument within their own ranks, was not dodged or debased by Disraeli. 'I never heard that moral force won the battle of Waterloo', said Devildust. 'I wish the capitalists would try moral force a little, and see whether it would keep the thing going. If the capitalists will give up the red-coats, I would be a moral force man to-morrow.' Since Julian Harney, the chief spokesman of the physical-force Chartists, lived to pay the highest honour to William Lovett, the chief spokesman of the moral-force Char-tists, it is fitting that the author of *Sybil* should have kept the balance between them so delicately. 'The people must have leaders', said one noble Lord. 'And they have found them', replied one Chartist delegate. Disraeli saw that 'the claims of the future are represented by suffering millions', but many others saw that too. He was the first practising parliamentary politician of the age to recognise further that those suffering millions had already found leaders of their own, from their own class, who could speak for them in an accent more authentic and vibrant than any heard before. Sometimes in his pages a false sentiment or nostalgia for ancient times was allowed to mix with the realist assault, but this objection is trivial. His Chartist leader, Walter Gerard, could speak like William Cobbett. 'Half lamentation, half lampoon; half echo of the past; half menace of the future; at times by its witty and incisive criticism, striking the bourgeoisie to the very heart's core . . .' Thus Karl Marx made his comment on the programme of Young England, drawn to Disraeli's design. True, he added (the sentence appears in the Communist Manifesto) that the criticism was always 'ludicrous in its effect through total incapacity to comprehend the march of history', but the first half of the judgement does not thereby lose its force.

But the prophecy was not fulfilled; the march of history took a detour. The revolution did not happen, neither in Ireland nor in England; the Chartist hurricane of 1839 subsided, stirring again a few years later but never recovering its original force. For the next quarter of a century Disraeli concentrated on the necessities and enticements of the parliamentary game: the overthrow of Peel, the outwitting of Lord John Russell, the uneasy alliance with Derby and the mock challenge to Palmerston, the rivalry with Gladstone, above all his own survival among colleagues who could eye him with envy and even hatred. He had descended from the intellectual heights, and that at least helped to put his colleagues more at ease. He finished *Tancred* in 1847 and published no novel until 1870. Like Edmund Burke before him, he could be accused of giving to Party what was meant for mankind. The visionary had become the pragmatist. Certainly Young England and all its romantic imbecilities had been scattered to oblivion, and 'good riddance' muttered many gruff old Tories at the time, with Tory historians more recently renewing the applause. However the outcome was not quite as they may have wished or as we have been latterly assured. Disraeli was resolved to lead the Tories but he was not required to love them. He felt compelled to adopt the Conservative Cause but he retained his private opinion about it, an ineradicable spirit of mockery. Byron's disciple was not dead yet.

One sign of how perpetually irksome he found his captivity within the Conservative hierarchy—self-imposed, but none the less oppressive—was the link he sought to keep with men of other ideas and allegiances—or, more accurately in Disraeli's case, with men and women, or rather, women and men. His strong preference for the society of women grew stronger still, if anything, as he grew older. Women played a major role in most of his novels not only as heroines or lovers but as individual characters differentiated one from another as much or even more meticulously than the men. The Whig ladies were given their chance no less than the Tories (indeed a wittier and more winning lot on the whole), and the Chartists had their individual wives and daughters too who would only flirt with true suffrage men. Not surprisingly at all Disraeli favoured giving women the vote*—while Gladstone was still being denounced by the earliest advocates of votes for women as 'the woman-hater'.

Moncure Conway, the American free-thinker and biographer of Thomas Paine, who came to London, and, incidentally, gave his name to the Conway Hall, Red Lion Square, has left in his autobiography clear evidence of how widely in the 1860s

---

*Indeed, thanks to the recent discovery of the new Disraeli novel, *A Year at Hartlebury or the Election*, (published in 1834, and written, it is supposed, in association with his sister Sarah), his interest in women's questions is found to go back a good deal longer and deeper. That volume has upon it his distinctive literary trade mark: the Disraeli attitude to women, a combination peculiarly his own. The influence, explicit or implicit, of influential women, runs back and forth, but that on its own is not so remarkable. More striking—and much deplored on moral grounds by a contemporary reviewer—are the rousing cheers (and the kindly salutations from the author) accorded the Amazonian Kitty.
  'I'll never kiss the lips that don't shout Bohun', cried out a beautiful, bold girl, the leader of those unhappy victims of our virtue who in moments of popular excitement generally distinguish themselves and it is curious are then only treated with consideration.
Defoe might have written that tribute too. But then comes an original scene outside the almshouse where Dame Harrald is 'surrounded by the petticoats.'
  'I wish I had a vote,' said Dame Harrald.
  'The women have no votes,' said Mrs. Collins mournfully.
  'The more's the shame,' said gossip Faddle.
  'In this world the men have it all their own way,'
remarked Dame Harrald, pensively.
And that was written not quite ninety years before women in Wycombe *did* get the vote. And it was written, too, just a few months after Disraeli recorded in a letter to Sarah on January 29, 1833:
  I dined with Bulwer *en famille* on Sunday 'to meet some truffles'—very agreeable company. His mother-in-law, Mrs. Wheeler, was there; not so pleasant, something between Jeremy Bentham and Meg Merrilies, very clever, but awfully revolutionary. She poured forth all her systems upon my novitiate ear, and while she advocated the rights of woman, Bulwer abused system-mongers and the sex, and Rosina played with her dog.
Anna Wheeler looks like the model for a Dame Harrald. (See page 187.)

Disraeli's feminist sympathies were recognised. It was part of his temperament and creed; with Disraeli no sharp distinction could be drawn between the two. 'Talk to women, talk to women as much as you can. This is the best schooling': that had been the advice given to the young Contarini Fleming. Disraeli followed it whenever he could. 'I owe all to women', he wrote to Lady Bradford nearly half a century later; no one could question his consistency on this theme. After some of his parliamentary debating triumphs, rather than waste time celebrating with the Tadpoles and the Tapers he would hasten home to his wife and the champagne supper she had ready. Perhaps he made platonic love to Queen Victoria because in the end he found Tory hosts so boring. He came to detest the society he had conquered, especially male society. Not enough consideration has been accorded to this aspect of the aristocratic world which he loved to inhabit and to delineate and to satirise: a few dashing heroes, several lovely heroines, a good number of scheming politicians of every rank and sex but then also solid phalanxes of bores, intentionally paraded and soon despatched back to the bosoms of their proud and obtuse families. He was supposed to adore the English aristocracy and certainly he gave them a new lease of life in fiction and perhaps in fact. But the whole class, more or less, was, with a show of old-fashioned politeness, put in its place. Once the point was presented to Coningsby in a tone which the author did not entirely disown:

> We owe the English peerage to three sources: the spoliation of the Church; the open and flagrant sale of honours by the elder Stuarts; and the borough-mongering of our own times. Those are the three main sources of the existing peerage of England, and, in my opinion, disgraceful ones.

If necessary Sidonia would make an appearance to remind us that one ancient race had a wisdom which no other could match. How often did Disraeli feel it desirable to mention that he traced his ancestry to Solomon in all his glory and, for better measure still, to the Queen of Sheba too.

However, to descend, alas, from these heights, the House of

Commons offered nothing but male companionship, and perhaps this is one of the reasons why he formed few of his most intimate friendships there. So the one or two exceptions to the rule become the more instructive. For nearly two decades he fostered, across the gulf of party, a special relationship with John Bright which was certainly not due to the enforced proximities of the House of Commons or anything deriving from the fashionable manners of the time. Lord John Russell, Bright's own leader, sometimes found himself in trouble for tolerating the treacherous demagogue at his dinner table. John Bright was the stern upholder of nonconformist morality, the arch-champion of free trade and Little England pacifism; how could he and Disraeli discover any bond of political sympathy? Most of the cultivation of it came from Disraeli's side; he would happily have sought an alliance with Bright and Richard Cobden too, or at least wanted to ensure that this labyrinthine channel was kept open; could they not together get rid of the 'old stagers' and the 'red tapists'? Disraeli did indeed recognise and respect the mighty democratic force in British politics which the two men represented and which Bright clothed in a language never surpassed in the records of English oratory. Disraeli was one of the great listeners in our parliamentary records; he was there all the time. At the supreme moment of crisis in the Second Reform Bill agitation it was the hidden unspoken understanding between them which tipped the balance. Benjamin Disraeli secured the passage of John Bright's Radical conception through the Commons and, more important still, the Lords. Hatfield and the Tory historians are entitled to their scream of outrage. Such consequences, the next great stride forward towards British democracy, could indeed be partly traced to Disraeli's devilry. It was due more to the affinity he would never disown with the radicalism of his youth. Younger Radical members—Professor Fawcett, for example—testified that Disraeli was the first person in the place to extend a hand of welcome. John Bright wrote to his sister in December 1851:

> Disraeli never denies any merit his opponents may possess; speaking of W. J. Fox to me one evening, he said: 'We must go in to hear Fox; I have a great regard for Fox; Fox is a man of genius.'

William Johnson Fox was a famous nonconformist preacher who turned to Radical politics; he was also, a great admirer of Disraeli's novels, and it was to him also that Disraeli confided or boasted: 'I am much misunderstood; my forte is revolution.'

Years later, on what proved to be his deathbed, he was interviewed by, or rather—it must be said, if the authentic atmosphere is to be revived—gave an audience to Henry Mayers Hyndman, then at the top of his influence and powers, as the guiding light of the Social Democratic Federation and the exponent of his own special brand of British Marxism. Maybe Hyndman's detestation of mid-Victorian Liberal hypocrisy established for him a peculiar sense of kinship with Gladstone's great antagonist, and this instinct had been fortified by the views of a Radical friend. Disraeli, he suggested,

> owed something of his success to the fact that he was a foreigner who regarded all the problems of English society from the outside with a detachment of coolness impossible for a native. Thus, said his friend, when he looked round the House of Commons, after he had definitely taken the Conservative side, he saw himself surrounded by men who did not understand him, who were bitterly prejudiced against him, who cordially disliked him indeed as much for his good as for his bad qualities. 'That damned Jew' had therefore a hard time on his way to the leadership, and he needed a set of people who, like himself, were divorced from English politics proper, in order to form a praetorian guard for him, and protect him from the intrigues of the Cecils and the cavils of the Carlton Club.

Alas, due to these supposed necessities, the Conservative leader, despite his instinctive support for Home Rule for Ireland, had allowed himself to fall into the hands of 'the North of Ireland combination'; alas too, 'compelled by the exigencies of an inferior profession', he had been unable to carry further his sympathies with the Chartists. Yet to mark the mood in which the young Hyndman, a man by no means known for his reticence or deference, knocked on the door of Lord Beaconsfield's house in Curzon Street in the year 1881 is to have proof of how startlingly different from the figure revered in Primrose Day perorations was the impression he could leave on an astringent observer. The two men talked for hours, or to be more precise, as Hyndman has the candour to acknowledge, Disraeli listened while he turned to one theme after another, starting with some diplomatically contrived references to Disraeli's recent anti-Russian policy which happened to be partially shared by Hyndman (and Karl Marx, too, for that matter) and moving at last to a grand exposition of the full Hyndman-Marxist case for the damnation of *laissez-faire* and for collective action as the only means to extend and secure democracy itself. 'Why not say Socialist movement? That is what you mean', interposed the old man at one point. And then '. . . private property which you hope to communise, and vested interests which you openly threaten have a great many to speak up for them still.' And then again, 'It is a very difficult country to move, Mr. Hyndman, a very difficult country indeed . . .' But Mr. Hyndman came away believing that he had made a mark, that his audience had been deeply comprehending, that he had in a sense been incited to proceed with all possible speed with his great Socialist campaign. Perhaps the exchange reveals afresh little more than the courtesy of which Disraeli was always capable, but it may be imagined how different would have been the outcome if Mr. Hyndman had had the chance to unleash his eloquence on the head of Lord Salisbury at Hatfield or the Grand Old Man himself at Hawarden. Lord Beaconsfield, like the young Disraeli, was fascinated by political ideas in a way practising politicians usually find to be beyond their grasp.

But the place to look for any clue to Disraeli's inner mind in his old age is not in casual conversations but where he had always offered it before, in his novels. 'My works are my life', he wrote (significantly from No. 10 Downing Street at the reckless age of seventy-one) at the height of his infatuation with Lady Bradford excepting only 'the somewhat puerile frivolity', *Vivian Grey*, which she happened to have hit on first. Her interest in his writing clearly added, if anything could, to her charm. In his last period, he wrote two more novels, one in his sixties, *Lothair*, and another in his seventies, *Endymion*, and left a further fragment, *Falconet*, unfinished when he died. Since he had written no other work of fiction for more than a quarter of a century, since in the interim all his ambitions of political fame had been filled to overflowing, since he had become the revered Prime Minister of his Party and his sovereign, since even the animosities of Hatfield had abated, he might be expected to present an altogether softer, mellower picture of his England and his world. However, the outcome is somewhat different.

One feature common to both *Lothair* and *Endymion*— unwittingly so perhaps, and the more significant on that account —is the transformation to be noted in the character and calibre of his leading figures. Lothair and Endymion are romantic enough names by any reckoning; golden spoons and great estates and glittering political opportunities were at one stage or another in their careers showered upon them; princes and peers and prelates and politicians of every degree were paraded to do their bidding; the general background was more splendid and sumptuous than ever; by every outward sign both of them could be regarded as reincarnations of Disraeli's former Young England heroes. But sharper inspection is required. Neither Lothair nor Endymion had much of Coningsby or Egremont in them, and what was lacking in each was the youthful dynamism, the quick imaginative sympathy, the individual zest to master the world around them, all the special qualities which were the young Disraeli's own.

Less still even were they worthy exponents of Disraeli's dream of love at first sight, the only true love, to which his novel *Henrietta Temple* had been dedicated. True, Lothair did return after much circumambulance and circumspection to the same Corisande upon whom his first tender glance had chanced to fall; but compared with the tempestuous affair with Henrietta Temple it was a marriage of political convenience. As for Endymion, he stifled the first promptings of his passion and never blurted them out thereafter; political caution and sisterly admonitions cut him short at almost every turn. In the end, he, like Lothair, was married off to the most gorgeous and eligible among the great Whig ladies. Not, be it hastily noted, that this was presented as in any sense a slight by the Tory-Prime-Minister-novelist; rather he magnanimously saw them scaling the highest pinnacle and living happily ever after.

Despite their dashing good looks and good manners, despite

the pivotal role in the story which they appeared to be allocated, both Lothair and Endymion were pushed aside to make room for more formidable characters, indeed to let the political world itself assume its rightful, governing pride of place. Byron's heroes would never have tolerated such disrespect, and nor would Disraeli's own Byronic heroes of a quarter of a century earlier. 'You must choose, my lord', he has someone say in *Endymion*, 'I cannot send you out looking like Byron if you mean to be a Canning or a Pitt.' But that, of course, was just how he did send himself and many others out in the 1820s; his wit now made mock obeisance to the different tone of the late 1860s. But it was not just old age which caused the change; by almost any test *Lothair* and *Endymion* were as lively as anything he had ever written. He had new insights, interests and enthusiasms which filled the arena once occupied by the Young England myth, and these required that both Lothair and Endymion should be gracefully put in their subordinate place. So they were both made plastic characters, clay in the hands of the potter or, rather, the potter's wives.

Lothair, it must be noted in passing, was not ostensibly a political novel; its supposed theme was religion. Rome, Canterbury, even Calvinistic Scotland battled for the hero's soul and he finished up, as we have seen, in the Erastian arms of a wonderful Whig beauty and patriot whose faith was embalmed more in the Church of England than the Church of Christ. Considering how deeply religious our Victorian great grandfathers were, it is surprising that the sense of outrage against the book was not expressed infinitely more strongly than it was. Once upon a time he had written of Roman Catholicism with sympathy and appreciation; Sybil after all and her Chartist father were of the old faith. But *Lothair* is a furious and deadly indictment of the Church which set its face against political liberty, of the Scarlet Lady, of a system of sorcery, which 'to save itself would put poison in the Eucharist'.* No comparable invectives are directed

---

*Even sharper is the picture of Cardinal Grandison which Disraeli drew elsewhere:

The Cardinal was an entire believer in female influence, and a considerable believer in his influence over females; and he had good cause for his

against any other creed, but few Anglican Bishops make even a momentary appearance without receiving a faintly supercilious greeting, whether from the forthright Lord St. Aldegonde ('I do not like Bishops; I think there is no use in them') or his kindred spirit unmasking the celebrated preacher 'who in a sweet, silky voice, quoted Socrates instead of St. Paul.' Even the most devoted of Disraeli's followers had to admit that 'the Church of England was not his strong point'; he never appreciated its spiritual quality. Even in the late 1870s Dean Wellesley was warning Queen Victoria that he just regarded the Church as 'the great state-engine of the Conservatives'. And even when he made his famous pronouncement on the Darwinian theory, professing himself on the side of the angels, not the apes, Conservative congregations, at their prayers, shuddered at his flippancy.

The truth is, Disraeli's mind was rootedly irreligious. He had attempted to frame a religion of his own in *Tancred*, a sort of amalgam of Judaism and Christianity with more than a dash of Mahomet thrown in for makeweight; it was a ridiculous failure, and he privately knew it. He could laugh at others who set out on the same quest and were no more successful than himself—for example, 'Goethe, a Spinozist who did not believe in Spinoza', or 'one of those distinguished divines who do not believe in divinity.' He had found his own resting place in the end, not that the journey had needed to be lengthy, in his father Isaac's free-thinking bosom. 'The time is now ripe for terminating the infidelity of the world', the Cardinal had said to Lothair in Rome. 'I look to the alienation of England as virtually over. I am panting to see you return to the home of your fathers and reconquer it for the Church in the name of the Lord God of Sabaoth. Never was a man in a greater position since Godfrey or Ignatius. The eyes of

---

convictions. The catalogue of his proselytes were numerous and distinguished. He had not only converted a duchess and several countesses, but he had fathered into his fold a real Mary Magdalen.

In the height of her beauty and fame (added Wilfrid Meynell in his book *The Man Disraeli*) 'she had suddenly thrown up her golden whip and jingling reins, and cast herself at the feet of the Cardinal.' This passage offended the taste of the Cardinal.

Christendom are upon you as the most favoured of men, and you stand there like Saint Thomas.' To which Lothair made the reply: 'Perhaps he was as bewildered as I am.' Montaigne himself could not have improved upon it.

But, if *Lothair* has no hero, it has a heroine; as it bows the knee to no particular religion, so it offers the highest honour to a political religion. It is Theodora, 'the divine Theodora' with the look of a Maenad and a voice vibrant with the Marseillaise, the champion of a doctrine which knows that 'the necessities of things are sterner stuff than the hopes of men', who speaks of another Rome, 'that country which first impressed upon the world a general and enduring form of masculine virtue; the land of liberty, and law, and eloquence, and military genius, now garrisoned by monks and governed by a doting priest'. No chink of doubt is left by the author (the sixty-six year old gout-ridden, asthmatic Tory Premier, let it not be forgotten) about Theodora's pre-eminence and glory. She shapes the plot; she directs Lothair's destiny; she stirs from him the ecstatic confession: 'Had it not been for you, I should have remained what I was when we first met, a prejudiced, narrow-minded being, with contracted sympathies and false knowledge, wasting my life on obsolete trifles, and utterly insensible to the privilege of living in this wondrous age of change and progress.' *Lothair*, or *Theodora*, as it might better have been titled, is an anthem of the Roman Republic, not of ancient times, but the Republic of Mazzini and Garibaldi, of the Italian Risorgimento, presented with an exhilaration and richness worthy of Rossini himself:

She spoke to the men in all the dialects of that land of many languages. The men of the Gulf, in general of gigantic stature, dropped their merry Venetian stories and fell down on their knees and kissed the hem of her garment; the Scaramouch forgot his tricks, and wept as he would to the Madonna; Tuscany and Rome made speeches worthy of the Arno and the Forum; and the Corsicans and the islanders unsheathed their poniards and brandished them in the air, which is their mode of denoting affectionate devotion. As the night advanced, the crescent moon glittering above the Apennines, Theodora attended by the whole staff, having visited all the troops, stopped at the chief fire of the camp, and in a voice which might have maddened nations sang the hymn of Roman liberty, the whole army ranged in ranks along the valley joining in the solemn and triumphant chorus.'

And who else would thus have spoken or sung? Who else would have so joyously led that chorus, with Rossini and Verdi? Byron himself, the fellow-conspirator of the Carbonari, the herald of the Risorgimento, the man who wrote of 'a free Italy, the poetry of politics'.

Lothair has other implications too; maybe it contains premonitions of how forces were gathering, strange forces of revolutionary strength, to shake Victorian blandness and power. Apart from the Risorgimento heroes and heroines whom the Tory Disraeli has extolled so incongruously, one other who flitted across the pages was a Fenian leader. Disraeli never lost the imaginative capacity of his youth which enabled him to comprehend the ways and wiles of those who championed political ideas quite different from his own. He would not dismiss them as devils; he wanted instead to explore how their minds worked. So suddenly an Irish cut-throat or terrorist would turn up in his novel as a liberal chieftain, and no one could be more aghast at the apparition than the great Liberal leaders. But *Lothair* laid itself open to much wider misapprehensions. 'It was supposed, on its first appearance', wrote J. A. Froude, 'to be a vulgar glorification of the splendours of the great English nobles into whose society he had been admitted as a *parvenu*, and whose condescension he rewarded by painting them in their indolent magnificence.' But it was nothing of the kind. Froude was one of the few who read and reread the masterpiece, ever more startled by his discoveries. 'The true value of the book', he wrote at the end (in the year 1890, ten years after Disraeli's death):

> is the perfect representation of patrician society in England in the year which was then passing over; the full appreciation of all that was good and noble in it; yet the recognition, also, that it was a society without a purpose, and with no claim to endurance.

But Froude was one of the few of Disraeli's contemporaries who would exert his imagination to understand. Mostly, on the publication of *Lothair*, his political friends trembled and his enemies gloated. Whatever else the book was, it was not the proper work of a Tory Prime Minister, past or present.

Endymion, it seems, was a slighter work altogether; neither on the surface nor beneath did it purport to touch on such mighty themes as those which had befuddled the none-too-brilliant Lothair. Disraeli started writing it just before he was launched upon his final Premiership in 1874, laid it aside, supposedly, while distracted by crises ranging from Suez Canal shares to the Congress of Berlin, and returned to complete it a few months after his defeat in the election of 1880. Even a Flaubert might have found his concentration affected by such intrusions; even so friendly a critic as Froude was inclined to depreciate *Endymion*. Yet considering all the circumstances in which he wrote, considering how asthma had finally fixed its grip upon him, considering how he had led his Party to electoral defeat and how the Tory gentlemen, according to their custom, were turning upon their leader, the equable, light-hearted tone of the book is all the more astonishing. A fresh judgement upon it is required, and a hint of *Endymion's* true novelty is forthcoming from the most unlikely quarter. Queen Victoria read it with a rising disquiet: she was not at all amused to discover that it was all about the Whigs. She had been justly dubious about *Lothair* too, and when some Duchess at dinner had asked her whether Theodora was not a divine character, she had looked 'a little perplexed and grave'.

In *Endymion* the Tory Prime Minister set out to describe the parliamentary history of England from the late 1820s when he had first arrived on the scene, and he chose to tell it almost entirely through the eyes of the great Whig houses which were once the victims of his invective and, in particular, through the eyes of Lord Palmerston whom the young Disraeli had variously pilloried as 'the great Apollo of aspiring under-strappers, the Lord Fanny of diplomacy, the Sporus of politics, cajoling France with an airy compliment, and menacing Russia with a perfumed cane'. Lord Palmerston, Lord Roehampton, is, if not the hero, at least the most appealing figure in the whole book. It is a glowing, laughing portrait of the old rapscallion; small wonder Queen

Victoria was outraged. Around him cluster all the adoring Whig beauties of the day—'all the ladies admire him and he admires all the ladies'; indeed, so evidently was he stealing all comers, duchesses and diplomats and dowagers and everyone else, and the book itself, that he had to be struck down before his prime, prematurely and quite unhistorically consigned to an early and chaste grave. Perhaps this was the author's necessary gesture to secure convenient reconciliation with his Queen.

Not, however, let it be insisted at once, that Disraeli would ever allow his women to be reduced to the status of subordinate creatures, even in this extremity and even by the roving Lord Roehampton. 'What women!' exclaimed another of the book's secondary heroes, young Louis Napoleon, 'What women! Not to be rivalled in this city (Paris), and yet quite unlike each other.' It was true enough. Two splendid women mould the book to their design as surely as they moulded Endymion himself. So much so that Froude, so often Disraeli's most perspicacious reader, suggests that Myra, Endymion's sister, may have been intended as the author's attempt to create a female young Disraeli. Endymion himself could never quite screw his courage to the sticking place; Myra always could. 'Power, and power alone, should be your absorbing object', she upbraided him, and when he pathetically protested that he (and she too) was only twenty-five: 'Great men should think of opportunity, and not of time. Time is the excuse of feeble and puzzled spirits.' His Shavian sister knew him so well. 'Give *me* the daggers', was the cry so near her lips. Just as *Lothair* should have been rechristened *Theodora*, so *Endymion* should have given the title of honour to *Myra*. It would have been a just recognition of the role which women played in Disraeli's mind.

However, there is another element in *Endymion*, a strong strand of satire inextricably interwoven in almost every chapter, which must be accorded its pre-eminence in the whole Disraeli saga. One of his most attractive characteristics was his capacity to honour an opponent, his freedom from malice, his readiness to forgive insults and injuries done to himself, his name, his race even. He had plenty to avenge but he would not waste his spirit in such self-destructive pursuits. But he could not be expected to forget, and mockery was an instrument which his good nature did not require him to discard. It is poured forth in *Endymion* in a ceaseless flow on the unsuspecting head of one particular victim. Little doubt is possible about Disraeli's last combined testament of heart and head.

The woman who is given the position of misleading dominance in the early chapters of *Endymion* is not at all one of the upstart Whigs, but Zenobia, the ample, still-utterly-self-confident Queen of London, of fashion, and of the Tory Party, just in those tremulous years when Toryism itself was being ineffably transmuted into the Conservative Cause. 'I shall always think', she said, 'that Lord Liverpool went much too far, though I never said so in his time, for I always uphold my friends.' And she always did. 'I have some good news for you', said one of her young favourites at one of her receptions. 'We have prevented this morning the lighting of Grosvenor Square by gas by a large majority.' 'I felt confident that disgrace would never occur', said Zenobia, triumphant. And her triumphs followed thick and fast, in the last few months before 1830. 'We shall now have a Cabinet of our own. We shall now begin to reign . . . I think now we have got rid of Liberalism for ever.' A little while later the Reform Bill of 1832 was passed over the live body of Zenobia and the House of Lords, and quite contrary to all her expectations and incitements. Momentarily, even she was abashed, yielding to 'that increasing feeling of terror and despair which then was deemed necessary to the advancement of Conservative opinions'. As the years passed, Zenobia recovered a little of her illusive nerve, but it was never a complete rehabilitation, and at the most perilous hour of crisis when the great stake of Church and Constitution had to be defended with every resource which valour and intellect could command, the task was reposed in the hands of an aspiring and newly-respectable Mr. Tadpole. And since Mr. Tadpole did contrive to snatch some temporary electoral success, it was to his towering philosophy that the Tories increasingly turned, in so far as they would ever turn to politics at all. Most of them had other pastimes which they practised more skilfully. Disraeli never ceased to be entranced by the combined phenomenon, the diligence with which the aristocracy he was presumed to adore pursued animals and birds of every size and species, and the determination with which they recounted their feats of the day at interminable, excruciating male dinner tables. 'Jerusalem! What on earth could they go to Jerusalem for?' said Lord Carisbrooke (a real Tory). 'I am told there is no sort of sport there. They say, in the Upper Nile, there is good real shooting.' St. Aldegone (a good Whig) was disappointed. 'I suppose our countrymen have disturbed the crocodiles and frightened away the pelicans?' Then again:

> The general conversation did not flag; they talked of the sport in the morning, and then, by association of ideas, of every other sport. And then from the sports of England they ranged to the sports of every other country. There were several there who had caught salmon in Norway and killed tigers in Bengal, and visited those countries only for that purpose. And then they talked of horses, and then they talked of women.

This, incidentally, was an exchange which occurred in *Lothair*; it was little more than a sideglance. In *Endymion*, the contrast between the Whig and Tory Lords became almost as sharp as that between the Whig and Tory ladies. Lord Roehampton would read French novels, although he happily confessed his inability to spend all his time doing so. Lord Montfort, another Whig, would furtively retreat to his country seat to get back to Don Quixote. But Tory tastes and priorities were inclined not to waver. Lady Beaumaris, inheriting Zenobia's mantle so gracefully, understood: 'It will never do to interfere with my lord's hunting—and when hunting is over there is always something else—Newmarket, or the House of Lords, or rook-shooting.'

Yet *Endymion*, after all, was not quite the last word of Disraeli, the novelist. Perhaps the old man had a slight twitch of alarm lest his Tory colleagues, like Queen Victoria, would understand all too well. So he hastened to make some ostensible amends: not to alter the verdict, but to offer a diversion. Even before *Endymion* was published, he was at work on Joseph Toplady Falconet, what could only be a full-length elaborate portrait of Gladstone. If *Endymion* had bestowed such gratuitous glory on the Whigs, if it had achieved its dangerous object of inflicting sweet vengeance on Hatfield and all such Tory presumptions, might not *Falconet* help to restore him to favour and kill another bird with the same stone? He set to work with a splendid relish and soon everyone was overwhelmed by the Gladstonian rhetoric, even the women, or at any rate one of them, who listened in 'veiled ecstasy as she would to a cataract in the Alps'. Alas, the author had completed only a few chapters of the likely new masterpiece when he died. Alas, too, if reconciliation to the bosom of the Conservative Church and Cause was ever his fleeting aim, the old Byronic scepticism would persist in breaking through. Once religion became the topic, a legion of devils was unloosed within him and he would zestfully return to his old pastime of denouncing all other religions and creating in their place his own secular, humanitarian idols which bore so little likeness to anything in heaven above, or in earth below or in the waters under the earth.

The fragment of *Falconet* left to us suggests that he would have flayed Gladstonian Anglicanism and Non-conformity, all rolled into one evangelical whole, with the same fury with which in *Lothair* he had pursued Rome and the Jesuits. What would be left? 'So they call him a visionary?' one seer-like character says to his disciple in *Falconet*. The word must put us on guard: it was the old charge against the young Disraeli which he took to heart and treasured.

> A visionary! So are you a visionary; so am I; so was Mahomet; so was Columbus. If anything is to be really done in the world, it must be done by visionaries; men who see the future, and make the future because they see it.

It would be tempting to end on that true Disraelian note: that was Disraeli, the revolutionist, as he had claimed to W. J. Fox or half-hinted to Hyndman.

But there are some other words added: 'What I really feared about him (the man damned as "the visionary") was that he had the weakness of believing in politics, of supposing that the pessimism of the universe could be changed or even modified by human arrangements.' Did Disraeli join in delivering that condemnation? If alas so, it must be just about his only utterance which would have won, and deserved, the unqualified approval of Lord Salisbury. But there are other words added too in the same context. 'I heard he was a Communist', interrupts the other party to the conversation, to which the wise man replies: 'He might as well be a Liberal or a Conservative—mere jargon; different names for the same thing . . .' It is not sure from the later exchange in which direction Disraeli's philosophical judgement was moving: was he a Malthusian who did not believe in Malthus, a Marxist who did not believe in Marx, as he had been a Jew who could not worship Jehovah? In his novels at least he always had the courage to follow where his imagination would beckon him, and, whatever else developed, it is legitimate to believe that, if he had been able to complete *Falconet*, the good Tory would have mustered afresh all his derisive strength and left the Conservative Cause, beaten so hard in *Lothair* and *Endymion*, a thing of shreds and tatters. Once, not in a novel, but in his biography of Lord George Bentinck, he wrote of 'the great conservative party that destroyed everything . . .' He knew that party so well; he knew how cold could be its heart and imagination; he had a taste in the last year of his life how defeated Tories can treat a defeated leader, and in his last book he would not have refrained from settling that old score.

Lord Rosebery,* I believe, spoke one last word better than anybody else: 'Disraeli died; and the Tadpoles and Tapers were left wondering what Toryism was next to be. The prophet had vanished and had left not a shred of his mantle behind.' But he had, after all; he had left his shelf-ful of novels to befuddle the Conservative, or the Tory, mind for ever more.

---

*In his essay on Lord Randolph Churchill.

FOUR

The Case for Beelzebub

My son, if thou come to serve the Lord, prepare thy soul for
temptation.

> 'Ecclesiasticus', quoted by
> Arnold Bennett, *Books and
> Persons*, 1930

LEGENDS ARE CREATED, as every journalist knows, in the
cuttings libraries at the newspaper offices; no sooner are a man's
or a woman's eccentricities established there than they become
embalmed, and may be disinterred, in every plausible detail, until
the last trump is sounded. But history, against the odds, must
attempt some readjustments.

'You Bollinger Bolshevik, you ritzy Robespierre, you lounge-
lizard Lenin', Brendan Bracken is alleged to have roared, as he
strode up and down the drawing room of Lord Beaverbrook's
Stornoway House, gesturing as he went somewhat in the manner
of a domesticated orang-outang, and his victim was Aneurin
Bevan. 'Look at you, swilling Max's champagne and calling
yourself a Socialist.' The assembled company, including Bevan,
listened with delight. Or so the tale has been recounted by
Brendan Bracken's latest biographer, but his recital is based on a
first report, presumably from Bracken himself, as relayed by
Randolph Churchill in a newspaper article dated 8 August 1958,
and the emphasis must be examined. Certainly Bracken had a gift
of invention, if not of the gab, but his conversational assaults
were rarely delivered with such alliterative polish, and who can
believe that Aneurin Bevan sat silent beneath the downpour? The
story I was told by another eye-witness, Frank Owen, a qualified
reporter, was that Aneurin Bevan claimed his right to like good
wine, adding with the approval of the whole company: 'The best I

ever had from you, by the way, Brendan, I'd call bottom lower-class *Bolshevik* Bollinger.' The mysterious Brendan was not in the habit of offering us working journalists liquor of any brand; he supplied instead a steady flow of fanciful news stories which had to be laboriously checked the morning after. For the rest, however, the scene is authentic: the assorted company, the polemical free-for-all, the deluge of drink and journalism and politics, the orang-outang manner, the absolute rule that no holds were barred; indeed, customarily, an incitement from the host that the more eminent his guests, the more ferocious should be the cross-examination or the raillery.

I made my timorous entry into this unimaginable world, thanks to a word to Beaverbrook from Aneurin Bevan. Here was the origin, or rather in the earlier social exchanges between Bevan and Beaverbrook was the origin, of all the tales of a sinister Bevanite-Beaverbrookian conspiracy which historians of the Nuffield School—notably Mr. Philip Williams, the official biographer of Hugh Gaitskell—have now sought to erect into a major theme of vilification. I hope to show that there are more things in heaven and earth than the Nuffield School may include in its curriculum. However, back to 1938: at the time Aneurin Bevan was on the board of the recently founded, but already financially-ailing weekly *Tribune* where I had worked as assistant-editor and with whom I had quarrelled over the sacking of its first editor, William Mellor. I was a journalist-innocent, innocent in most other ways too, having spent as a journalist only one year of semi-freelance penury on the *New Statesman* under Kingsley Martin's critical eye, a few odd months learning typography from the master, Allen Hutt of the *Daily Worker*, and nearly two years of elation and occasional dejection on *Tribune*. I was not exactly equipped with the suit of armour recommended for those summoned to Lord Beaverbrook's Stornoway House or his country house, Cherkley, but that is where I turned up one Saturday evening, after a first peremptory phone-call. I cannot recall too precisely what happened at the dinner table that night; I was tongue-tied by the general company and atmosphere but also by the apparition who sat at my side, an exquisitely beautiful girl who had some trouble with her English, but who seemed otherwise at ease and whom I took to be an Hungarian countess or something of that sort. Next day also she was floating through the house; her disturbing presence seemed to be everywhere. But immediately I had other matters pressing for attention. Beaver-brook came downstairs in his riding-attire and asked whether I had read the newspapers. When I replied, 'Yes a few', he insisted: 'Read them *all*. Albert, see that Mr. Foot is supplied with all the newspapers in the library. I will return in an hour or two, Mr. Foot, and perhaps you will be good enough to tell me then what is in the newspapers.' When he did return, he made a bolt for the swimming pool, calling me to follow, and prepared to plunge, naked-ape like, into the water. 'You've brought your notes with you, Mr. Foot; now let me hear what is in *all* those newspapers.' But I had no notes, instead what might have just passed muster as a photographic memory. I had memorised the Sunday news-papers as no one, I trust, has felt required to do before or since. 'Come with me with no delay', he said as the recital concluded, and he led me where the assembled score of house guests, one of his usual congregations of the incongruous, were drinking their pre-lunch drinks on the spacious porch overlooking the Surrey woodlands. 'Mr. Foot will now tell you what most of you no doubt have been too damned lazy to read for yourselves.' I got the offer of a job and started immediately on the *Evening Standard*, at what was then the union minimum of £9 per week which however was exactly double my salary of £4 10s. on *Tribune* (cut from the original figure of £5, to help meet the first of *Tribune's* series of financial crises).

For the next twenty-five years of my life I knew Beaverbrook until the day of his death as well, I believe, as almost any man did (not attempting for the moment to compete with the women), and for all that time, with occasional spasms of fury or hatred and one of four years of something worse, I loved him, not merely as a friend but as a second father, even though throughout I had, as I have earlier indicated, the most excellent of fathers of my own. Many other friends found this friendship absurd, inexplicable, discreditable, scandalous, evil; for, the simple, widely-dissemin-ated view of Beaverbrook was that he was a kind of Dracula, Svengali, Iago and Mephistopheles rolled into one. Anyone who crossed his threshold, anyone who took his shilling or the larger sums soon on offer (my £9 was increased to a munificent £12 within months and much more later on) was jeopardising his immortal soul. 'Well, how was it in the House of Rimmon?' my real father would ask when I returned to his chaste, puritan, teetotal hearth. He at least cheerfully accepted my discriminating reports.

When I first set eyes on the monster he was sixty years old; everyone working at close quarters talked of 'the old man' (no one called him 'the Beaver'), but, apart from lapses into hypochondria, chiefly on account of his asthma, he showed no signs of age or decline in any of his faculties. Mind and body could move with an electric alertness. The first impression also was sharply different from that conveyed by the cartoonists, Low and Strube and Vicky, who, doubtless for their own good reasons, made him gnomelike, too squat, too much dominated by the big head and the big smile. He liked to dress with a careless elegance and was positively vain about the delicacy of his hands and the meticulously-well-shod feet. His strong Canadian accent which he himself fostered and exploited, and which so many who came in contact with him found it tempting to imitate, was more likely to surprise by its softness than the calculated bursts of power. And most remarkable of all, in this general physiognomy which was somehow shifted from the expected focus, were his ears, and the purpose to which he put them. He *listened*. He took in everything said to him, everything he overheard. No use to give *him* false scents, misleading hints, half-baked suggestions; he could always remember. Nothing but candour could survive his sensitive powers of cross-examination and recollection. Yet on this same level of personal exchange there was no cant, no personal pretension, no side, no snobbery, not the smallest tincture of it. I soon discovered I could say anything to him. No sacred topics, political or otherwise, had to be skirted. Indeed, many of the public crusades which he espoused could be quite safely derided in private, and he had quite unexpected sympathies in personal dealings and a political imagination which could be convulsively stirred. The private 'old man' I met in the autumn of 1938 remained for me ever afterwards a figure of bewitching interest.

Nothing the public man did could kill it, and truly the public Beaverbrook, I believe, has not received his due honour.

One partial explanation of the devotion he could excite in the most unlikely quarters derived from the nature and scale of his emotional radicalism. Observers whose first or lasting impression of him was imprinted by the *Daily Express* of the thirties ('No war this year or next') or even by that journal in its last great decade of the fifties may rub their eyes in bewilderment at any such claim; but here was always one clue to the mystery, evident to anyone who saw the man himself instead of the varying portraits which, for whatever recondite purpose, he sought to present to the outside world. When he had arrived in London in 1910 he had at once become encoiled in the dismal politics of the Conservative Party, and the rest of his life might be construed as a prolonged exertion to break loose. He was a rampaging individualist—no one could ever question that—and he always favoured the rumbustious, marauding private enterprise system which had enabled him to become a multi- or, as he would call it, a Maxi-millionaire.

But he brought with him too, in those pre-1914 days, inherited from his Covenanting Scottish ancestors or blown across to him in the continent of his birth from the tradition of American populism, a detestation for the stuffiness and stupidities and snobberies of the English Establishment. He was an instinctive radical—not as the word may be risibly applied nowadays, say to Mr. Jo Grimond or Mr. Roy Jenkins—but in the true sense that he had an urge to get to the roots of the question and the will to wrench them up with both hands. This is what he did at his greatest moments, in 1916 and 1940, and at several other dates less famous in our history. His paradox-loving biographer, A. J. P. Taylor, has even gone so far to see Beaverbrook as a reincarnation of another radical hero, Richard Cobden, but that cap will never fit on this unique skull. For Beaverbrook was interested in political moods and intrigues, not theories or principles, and Cobden, unlike Beaverbrook, was a born and dedicated leader and organiser. Nonetheless, Beaverbrook's radicalism was deep and abiding and would break out when least expected, and was often active behind the scenes, it appeared to me, in his approach to journalism and indeed to politics too. Seemingly, and according to his own later reiterations, the rich, young pre-1914 Max Aitken-on-the-make had selected Bonar Law as his man of destiny. But, of course, that was ridiculous; it was a simple case of mistaken identity. Lloyd George was his true and natural hero, and nor was it a matter of mere temperamental affinity. Beaverbrook engaged in 'the honest intrigue' to make Lloyd George Prime Minister in 1916 and to sustain him thereafter since he was convinced that incompetent generals and an irresponsible War Office, shielded by the monarchy, must be brought under masterful civilian control. To tackle that root question was necessary for victory. Doubtless too he was dazzled by the sheer power and glory of Lloyd George at the peak; Lloyd George in 1918 was a spectacle which entranced him then and thereafter:

> He dictated to Europe; he flung out great dynasties with a gesture; he parcelled out the frontiers of races; everything was in his hands and his hands showed that they had the power to use everything.

And yet with a subtlety of perception for which his contemporaries rarely gave him credit, Beaverbrook also saw the weakness of his idol—'the glitter of his supreme office held him in chains'. Certainly it was the native radicalism of the two men which provided the blood bond, and was, incidentally, one of the reasons why neither could establish the same intellectual intimacy with the traditionalist Churchill.

Together, too, this couple of prophetic adventurers, Lloyd George and Beaverbrook, joined in vehement protest—and again with no assistance from the orthodox Churchill—against the long agonies which the bankers and the City inflicted on their fellow countrymen but here the primacy could be claimed for Beaverbrook (—'when it comes to Finance, I am a tub which stands on its own bottom'; he could teach both Lloyd George and Churchill how to keep out of financial scrapes). 'The power of the bankers must be wiped out', he wrote in 1932, although the same theme might be quoted from his utterances consistently, from the deflationist twenties to the squeezes of the sixties. 'They have used their powers so badly that they have shown they are not safe custodians of the money and credit of the country.' That was the flavour of Beaverbrook's iconoclasm which could make his judgements truly original. Since 1918 he had favoured the Government controlling the banks and not the other way round. The radical temper of the man had sure foundations.

Constantly through his life he sought friendships which seemed to conflict with his public professions or allegiances, and once formed they were not easily broken. The case of Lloyd George was only the most spectacular; more acutely than almost any other associate he saw the nature of Ll. G.'s genius and the moment when he must strike; that was 1916. But there was another date and another drama of personal perception with immense consequences a few years later. Incongruously again the up-and-thrusting Canadian adventurer had formed one of his closest friendships in the House of Commons with Tim Healy, the wily Catholic spokesman of Irish independence, once the flail of Parnell. The friendship governed him so powerfully that in 1920, when the Treaty to establish the Irish Republic was being negotiated, he used all his influence to reach the settlement which some have said since, and some suggested at the time, led to the eventual break-up of the British Empire; yet in 1920 Beaverbrook broke one friendship with Rudyard Kipling, risked another even with Bonar Law and successfully beguiled the arch-beguiler, Lloyd George. The radical recognised the roots of that question too.

Yet were these not battles fought and victories won long since? In the autumn of 1938, just after Munich, when I arrived on Beaverbrook's scene, had he not become an arch-appeaser, the prophet of peace when there was no peace, the defender of Neville Chamberlain and Samuel Hoare, even enduring their presence at his dinner table? He had indeed, and may his Presbyterian God forgive him this sin more scarlet than all the others. But the Cherkley atmosphere, or Stornoway House where the rhetorical prize-fights were staged throughout the week, bore, I swear, little relation to the suffocations perpetrated in Fleet Street and beyond. Robert Vansittart would be there to put his case and he could charm and persuade in the same sentence; Randolph Churchill lashed out at any Munichite in range; Brendan Bracken would aver that Hitler was bluffing and that the bluff must be called; Aneurin Bevan was not likely to be silent for long, and most of Beaverbrook's leading journalists, headed by Frank Owen, were moving into the anti-Munich camp. Beaverbrook remained unconvinced; he still clung wretchedly to his dream of splendid isolation, but he would never bring the shutters down on the debate. And he listened; always listened.

He loved good talkers, good reporters, keeping a strict ration on the monologuists, even if the offender happened to be Winston Churchill. Beaverbrook was a good talker himself; Arnold Bennett, no mean judge surely, called him the best dramatic raconteur he ever heard. Exaggerated or not, he certainly knew what good talk was, and had assembled around him no conventional crew. Viscount Castlerosse could talk; no one who ever heard him doubted that he was one of the real wits, but the difficulty of proving the claim is that he relied very little on his considerable powers as a story-teller; his forte was the sudden audacious blow between the wind and the water which could convulse the whole company and send his victim—usually one who richly deserved it—reeling through the ropes. Everything depended on his exquisite timing, or rather the timing plus the presence; it was incomprehensible how this grotesque elephant of a man could deliver his thrusts with such feline precision. As a ne'er-do-well Irish Catholic peer, dependent on the Calvinist Beaverbrook to keep him in cigars and mistresses, he might have cut a pitiful as well as a ridiculous figure, but by sheer nerve and talk he carried off the whole performance. 'And how is the old bucket shop today?' he was reputed to have asked as he entered the banking sanctum of his Baring-Brothers relation, Lord Revelstoke, who had tried to find him a niche in the city. That stroke helped to end his career as a financier, and he was soon back at Beaverbrook's for board and bed.

Robert Bruce-Lockhart was another in the company, the dashing, handsome author of the *Memoirs of a British Agent*, once the friend of Trotsky and the suitor of 'the big-minded, big-hearted', wise and beautiful Moura Budberg who had understood him so well and some others too, from Maxim Gorky to H. G. Wells. 'Moura says', Bruce faithfully reported, 'I am a little strong but not strong enough, a little clever, but not clever enough, and a little weak but not weak enough.' Moura knew. And Moura also was there on one of the very first weekends I spent at the house of ill-fame, not with Bruce or Gorky or even Budberg, but with her later lover, H. G. Wells, and I heard H. G. in person protesting against the playing of the national anthem 'and all that Hanoverian stuff' in a fine republican squeak which the near-republican Beaverbrook was happy to applaud.

H. G. Wells had the distinction of being re-invited even though he had committed the unforgivable solecism of satirising in a book 'one of those crude plutocrats with whom men of commanding intelligence, if they have the slightest ambition to be more than lookers-on at the spectacle of life, are obliged to associate nowadays'. Of course, the villain of *The Autocracy of Mr. Parham*, Sir Blasted Bussy Bussy Buy-up-the-Universe Woodcock, was a composite figure:

> He's the sort of man who buys up everything. Shops and houses and factories. Estates and pot houses. Quarries. Whole trades. Buys things on the way to you. Fiddles about with them a bit before you get 'em. You can't eat a pat of butter now in London before he's bought and sold it. Railways he buys, hotels, cinemas and suburbs, men and women, soul and body. Mind he doesn't buy you.

Beaverbrook was not quite engaged in that scale of business, but there was the popular suspicion, and Sir Bussy was also 'a short ruddy man', with 'a mouth like a careless gash', and, more precisely incriminating still, the book also contained a cartoon by David Low in which the Cherkley luncheon party was indelibly portrayed. There, in the corner, was Castlerosse, flirting with two flappers of the thirties; 'hangers on and parasites of the worst description', calling Sir Bussy Woodcock, 'Bussy dear'. The whole scene could have ensured that neither H. G. Wells himself nor David Low nor even the still radiantly composed Moura Budberg would ever darken his doors again. But there they all were, graciously invited back for more; the magnet was irresistible. And H. G. Wells was one of the heroes of my youth. I had devoured *Kipps* and *Mr. Polly* and *Marriage* and all the rest, and when it came to *Tono-Bungay* had rationed the reading to twenty pages a day so that paradise should not come to an end too abruptly. Beaverbrook had devoured those same pages too twenty years before, not quite in the same spirit of Socialist excitement, but with all his own discernment. So he managed his *ménage* not quite in the manner of Sir Bussy Woodcock after all. Souls and bodies might be in peril in his household; but the atmosphere was subtler than any caricature.

The morning after my own Cherkley hiring, I was instructed to report to Frank Owen, editor of the *Evening Standard*; we became from that moment onwards bosom companions, night and day, if such terms may be used without giving any misleading notion about one so spectacularly heterosexual. During those next months, indeed the next year or two, he gave me an intensive pressure-course introduction to the world, the flesh, the devil, and his notion of Beaverbrook, not troubling always to draw too sharp a distinction between the last two on the list. He was himself a superlative journalist and editor, being capable of enlisting an incomparable allegiance from those who worked for him. But the man was even more appealing than the journalist. His high spirits had a God-like quality. His physical capacity was such that he could drink all night everything and anything set before him, and be hard at work at his desk, after a couple of Coca-Colas, at seven o'clock next morning; so he continued for some twenty years, with suitable recuperations at weekends, until tragically that physical apparatus suddenly snapped, never to be restored to full working order again. Women fell for him in droves, at a glance; no one else I ever saw was ever in the same competition. Yet he did not treat the matter offensively or vaingloriously but rather as if this triumphant promiscuity had been the natural lot of man (and woman) since Adam or soon after. More than any other human specimen I have ever known, he was utterly absorbed by the pressing moment. He could forget everything except the article he was writing, the next edition to catch, the next round of drinks, the girl in hand. He had a first-rate mind, according to the tests they make at Cambridge University, and would sit up all night devouring some new book when not otherwise preoccupied. He liked to call himself a Trotskyite, partly because he was steeped in Trotsky's writing but partly also to disown the current Stalinite vogue which he abhorred. He was then (as he had been as the youngest M.P. in the 1929–31 Parliament) a Lloyd George Liberal, and he remained such till his dying day. He had already experienced eight years of Beaverbrook, and had touched the heights and the depths. When in the first year or so of their acquaintance, Frank's lover had literally died in his arms, it was Beaverbrook who knew best how to help him at the moment of human crisis, and when six years later he went off in pursuit of Grace who became his wife, it was the possessive Beaverbrook who—along with several others—felt himself to be mistakenly abandoned. Frank viewed Beaverbrook with a finely balanced scepticism and admiration, a kind of adoring fury; it lasted for nearly two decades.

Anyhow, in the autumn of 1938 he was just the man who might be expected to take the *Evening Standard* by the scruff of the neck, and transform it from what it was, the house-journal of the exclusive London West End, into a real rival of the *Star* and the *Evening News* with their larger circulations. Not that the characters of newspapers can be subjected successfully to such revolutionary seizures, to coups-d'état. They must be moulded, re-shaped by organic methods and loving hands, applied softly day by day. That autumn, it was Frank more than most rivals who discovered first how Hitler's awful name sold newspapers. He started, just for one week at first, to write a serial on Hitler's *Mein Kampf*, a work little studied before in the England of the Chamberlain appeasement epoch. Then, when sales soared, he continued the enterprise for weeks on end. Two or three times a week each night, after the paper had been put to bed, he would attend a session at Stornoway House where the successes and failures of the day and the prospects for the next day were compared with those of our rivals by our most relentless reader. Soon I was attending these meetings too, and would sit enthralled as managerial and editorial heads were knocked together. Why did the *News* and the *Star* seem to have more space available for real news? One answer supplied by Frank, much to the horror of Captain Wardell, the manager, was suggested by the columns of advertising puffs, 'musts' which the management required to be printed. One night Frank supplied a stack of this scandalous material to prove his charges; Captain Wardell received his instructions; and the victory was celebrated long before we returned to Shoe Lane.

Not so long after my arrival at the *Standard* I was whisked away on a travel jaunt with Beaverbook himself alone, apart from valets and secretaries, on the blue train to Cannes, to Monte Carlo, and back to the Ritz in Paris; I could hardly have been more surprised if Aladdin had turned up with his lamp and put me on a magic carpet to Baghdad. The idea was, apart from telling him what was in the newspapers, that I should be instructed in the business or art of writing a column. I was told to study the modern American masters of the craft, Arthur Brisbane, Heywood Broun and Westbrook Pegler. Soon some specimens were being despatched back to the *Standard* office and the row which one of them provoked started to endear my new master to me more even than the introduction to the delights of Heywood Broun. In pursuit of our belated aim of transforming the *Standard*, one idea was to provide a real *London* paper, and our leader column was to be freshly directed to that purpose. 'PULL DOWN THE RAIL-INGS', was the headline I had produced for a column and the proposed text began:

> Henry VIII built a fence round Hyde Park. The fence was changed to a wall and the wall to railings. And there those railings stand to-day, ugly iron monuments to the tyranny of a rapacious monarch. Someone ought to pull them down.

But, in the sedate Shoe Lane of those times, this smacked of the tumbrils. Captain Wardell, a constant attender at Cherkley, a passionate Munichite, and a scarcely less passionate philanderer, an admirer even of 'Tom' Mosley, a stern protector of the *Standard*'s elitist appeal but no equally successful protector of its finances, was shocked, deeply shocked. He knew, and also took the precaution to check, the long-standing objection of the police to the removal of Hyde Park railings; it was hard enough to guard against the spread of vice in any case, but, with the railings down, the task would become hopeless. However, Beaverbrook would have none of it, and his message was conveyed to the pious and passionate Captain in his presence and in a manner not calculated to advance my popularity in the office. 'No more of it, Captain Wardell; you have beautiful beds in Claridges and all over London where you can do your fucking; what about the rest of us?' The column was printed without amendment, and indeed with a mischievous reference to the expected protests from the moralists, on 2 March, 1939.

Within a year or so, I had become, I suppose, one of the family, a favoured son, and the real sons and daughter showed not a twinge of enmity or jealousy. Max and Janet and Peter all had strong streaks of the Beaverbrook charm but none of them possessed their father's devotion to politics and journalism, the two inextricably mixed together in one tempestuous passion. Each had other pursuits: apart from romantic explorations, Max was off driving passenger planes in America or delivering war planes to Republican Spain and acquiring the exceptional experience which made him the best-equipped pilot in the world when the catastrophe finally came. He was handsome as Apollo, as swiftly-moving as Mercury, but newspapers would have to wait for his attention until after he had helped win the Second World War. Janet had a streak too of the old man's guile to add to the charm, but she was still no politician. Only one member of the family, so far, has inherited the golden journalistic talent. She was Jean Campbell, daughter of Janet, and when I first went to Cherkley she and her brother were seven and five years old respectively, and I played with them around the porch where I had once recapitulated the contents of the Sunday newspapers; her Beaverbrook smile was already the most bewitching of the lot. (Read the Jean Campbell reports from Chippaquidick, 1969, if anyone wants to know how a true Beaverbrook can report.)

The word *charm* keeps intruding, and may seem quite out of place in the light, say, of the H. G. Wells caricature and many others besides. But, as with Charles James Fox, it is his charm that lives even if the debased word is insufficient for the purpose. Beaverbrook's charm was more like the secret potions used in *A Midsummer Night's Dream*, and he could apply them, seemingly at will, to men and women alike. So, sharply contrasting with the harsh or even crude appearance which readers of his newspapers might deduce, he fitted regularly into no definable category, political or personal. He was wary, high-spirited, erratic, cunning, calculating, passionate, sentimental, restless, impulsive; he could be mean and magnanimous; he had the most perfect manners, and he could turn savage. If intuition is a feminine characteristic, he was at least half feminine. It was the perpetual interplay of temperament and character all around him, in politics, in Fleet Street, and in his own circle which fascinated him and which doubtless gave rise to the notion that he was engaged in some vast Faustian conspiracy against the human race. But most of his critics knew barely one per cent of the story, and the nearer one approaches the whole truth, the more necessary it is to speak in nuances and to search for qualified judgements. He could combine—almost in the same deed, on the same day—the most staggering misjudgements and the most piercing insights. He had many of the visions or far-seeing appreciations of greatness but he could also feel his way round the furniture of the English political workshop like a blind man.

So the respectable Stanley Baldwin outmanoeuvred this would-be master manoeuvrer, once in the battle over Empire Free Trade and once again in the Abdication crisis. In the late thirties, it might seem his star, especially any radical star, had set for ever. He became for a moment an aggressive defender of Munich and all it stood for, and it would have been a wretched irony indeed if his fame had come to rest on his championship of the Chamberlains and the Halifaxes, the Simons and the Hoares, the English Establishment which he despised, at its most ignoble and defeatist. But, fortunately for his adopted England, which he loved but never comprehended, he would not break his other associations. He kept open his line with the Churchillites, I felt, in much the same way he retained his interest in the hereafter; it might be true after all. How foolish to foreclose the chance of reversion in the skies by some premature and quite uncharacteristic descent into dogma.

Yet the truth, or rather another truth, was that nothing could subdue him for long. Night and day, day and night, there were editions to be caught, stories to be pursued, editors to be whipped from their conjugal relaxations, fellow proprietors to be baited, fresh young talent to be hired, a world to be ransacked for every curious proof of human frailty and courage. He was truly a born editor, and not a manager or financier; for each hour he devoted to his business interests he would give ten to every detail of each issue of every paper, stopping only at the sports pages in which he had no interest whatever; there the Christiansens and John Gordons were free to print what they liked. I went on many strange expeditions with him in those years, apart from the trips on the magic carpet; to a theatre in Brighton, for example, where he had been told how, in the interval between acts, a young man called Godfrey Winn could hold the audience spell-bound, just talking. The report was true, and Godfrey Winn was soon on the pay-roll. But, wherever we went, some of the best explorations were into his peculiar realm of books, starting where he had started at his father's knee. If you wanted Bible stories you'd never heard before, Beaverbrook was the man. He had a full repertoire of the greatest of them, a kind of Old Testament in modern dress, a blood-soaked Calvinistic horror comic, and of course the undoubted hero who fascinated him most was David, master of word and deed, of daring and subterfuge, the man of power and propaganda, the gangster-politician. And David, be it noted again, could sing and talk as well as act.

Apart from his own prodigious reading in the first years of his arrival in Britain, it was Arnold Bennett who guided or kept pace with his enthusiasms either in person or in the *Evening Standard* 'Books & Persons' column. Always thereafter Beaverbrook wanted to recapture the exhilaration of that book column, the best that ever was, and always he would be berating his barbarian editors who failed to comprehend that all wisdom could be found in books and that at that precise moment all over the planet authors in their solitude were producing the stories which each intelligent editor should seek to purvey first to his readers. Arnold Bennett said that his own curiosity about new books was unappeasable and divine; Beaverbrook's was not quite in that class, but almost. His own library, like that of other rich men, had been partly bought for show; but some authors, apart from the Psalmist, he knew intimately and could summon to his aid at will. The interaction between his mind and Arnold Bennett's offers sidelights into both. His first interest had been excited by the author, before he ever met him, not by any Five Towns' saga, but by the much slighter and lesser-known *The Pretty Lady* which no doubt started with the advantage, with Beaverbrook, of its semi-salacious appeal. But no doubt is possible also about their shared instincts and cast of mind. They had the same down-to-earthiness, the same idolatry of commonsense, the same streak of radicalism, the same taste for champagne and the sybaritic life, and the same lack of cant in avowing it; above all, the same faith in life itself sometimes and in books *always*, the same sacred gift of enthusiasm, Hazlitt's gusto. It was Beaverbrook who prompted, cajoled, bribed Arnold Bennett into writing that famous book column in the *Evening Standard*—just another proof of his inspiration as an editor. The whole collection (not republished, amazingly, until 1974) shows what a bursting storehouse of literary intelligence, knowledge, generosity and discrimination Arnold Bennett's mind truly was. Without Beaverbrook, this last particular display of Bennett's genius would never have happened; without Beaverbrook, the forthcoming Bennett revival would have to wait a few more decades. Once Rebecca West wrote a piece in which she referred to the four 'uncles' of her youth, Shaw, Bennett, Galsworthy and Wells; the iconoclastic Rebecca being capable of worshipping four literary uncles in place of gods. Three of those four were my uncles too, as they were for the whole of our Socialist generation, and here, lo and behold, before my eyes, was a fellow who certainly knew Arnold Bennett, knew him indeed as few others ever knew him.

So I soon discovered that, along with the political-cum-journalistic obsession, I shared with Beaverbrook other oddities or interests: a firm Biblical grounding, if a lapsed Methodist may make the generous concession to a lapsed Presbyterian; a taste for films and pop music perpetually on tap; an asthma affliction, both real and exploitable; and an eye for the same girl—but more of that in a moment. When I had a bout of asthma, Dan Davies (not yet Sir Daniel and physician to the Queen, but already Aneurin Bevan's friend) was despatched to my bedside. He brought no cure but all the mitigating potions without which asthma can be hellish and to which Beaverbrook was perpetually resorting. My brand, I believed, was at that time considerably more chronic than his but the claim was not pressed too hard. As for the pop music, the place shunted when I first went there, to the rhythm of 'A tisket, A tasket, my little yellow basket', and since that was my current favourite too, I took it as an augury. His favourite of all time was, 'See what the boys in the backroom will have, and tell 'em I'm having the same', sung by Marlene Dietrich as she danced along the bar counter in *Destry Rides Again*. A topic never to be mentioned was Orson Welles's *Citizen Kane*. No one could deny it: there was just an element of Citizen Kane in him, and he could be furious with any reference which exposed it; for instance, the speech in the classic film did give a flash of Beaverbrook on the hustings, and there are other glimpses too. It was deeply sad that he never appreciated Orson Welles who could worthily have taken a place alongside his Edward G. Robinson. However, there was never any danger, as enemies suggested, that Beaverbrook might lapse into the paranoiac condition of a Hearst or a Northcliffe. His sense of humour remained his life-line to sanity.

He was saved, moreover, by the war which he had said would not or should not come. Deeply shaken as doubtless he should have been by the collapse of the appeasement policy, he scarcely emerged, in the first few months of the so-called phoney war, from the worst bout of surliness which he—and we—ever experienced. But the release and rejuvenation when they came were all the more spectacular. Long before the Norway fiasco, he and we and most of the nation besides (there was nothing perspicacious in the observation) had been coming to recognise that a dramatic change in the constitution of the British Government would have to be engineered. Who better to conduct the conspiracy than the arch-conspirator of 1916? As it happened, his hand was not required for that purpose, but he was emotionally prepared to play his decisive role in the greatest crisis in British history, the moment when we could have become the victims of a Nazi conquest and when we saved ourselves by our exertions, with Beaverbrook's among them.

Nothing can ever take from him what he accomplished then, and indeed the achievement grows in retrospect. He had an original grasp of the necessities of the Battle of Britain four precious months before it happened, and his essential conclusions were not the result of inspiration alone. Nor were they due only to his obvious qualities of energy and daring. They were the fruit also of that extraordinary faculty for *listening*, for extracting the facts of a novel situation, for making himself the best informed person in the land—or the War Cabinet—on the immediate matter in hand. In those hectic months of 1940 he picked the Hennesseys and the Westbrooks who came from the factories and were capable of withstanding his deadly verbal scrutinies, and discarded the Nuffields who could not. He listened to Sir Hugh Dowding and preferred his still small voice to the massed chorus of all the other assembled Air Marshals. And he listened too, while pretending that his ministerial position forbade him to do anything of the kind, to the first-hand reports which Max Aitken brought back from the skies. 'Tell an old man what young men are thinking', he said to his secretary, David Farrer. Night and day that ceaseless curiosity never deserted him, and it helped him to ride the whirlwind when the men of the old Treasury Establishment held up their hands in defeatist horror at Ministers determined to command events.

Yes, he truly played his part in our finest hour, preparing for it and at the moment itself, and in the *Evening Standard* office we naturally watched the performance with some pride. In those first weeks we had another interest too. Right up till the moment when Hitler's tanks smashed through the Ardennes, Beaverbrook had continued to exercise his perpetual, erratic, inescapable surveillance over the newspaper; he was the editor-in-chief and everyone inside the office knew it. Then, one fine memorable morning, peace descended. The blitz was just about to burst upon us in all its fury. All Beaverbrook's improvising energies were devoted to the task, night after night, for weeks on end. So, led by Frank Owen, we on the *Evening Standard* went about our task all the more zestfully, producing the best paper sold on the streets of our beleaguered city. Day after day, I dare say, our tone become more exhilarated and revolutionary—that was the mood of the time. And one fine morning I embroidered a leading article with a quotation from Cromwell on the eve of the battle of Dunbar: 'We are upon an Engagement very difficult . . . But the

only wise God knows what is best. All shall work for Good . . .'
that and more. Within a few hours, it seemed more like minutes,
of that paper reaching our street-sellers, the blitz-laden peace of
the previous weeks was broken by a thunder-clap. It was
Beaverbrook back on the telephone:

> How dare you, Mr. Foot, how dare you use the columns of the
> *Evening Standard* to attack the Presbyterians. The tale is spread in
> Westminster and Whitehall that Beaverbrook no longer takes an
> interest in his newspapers. I would have you understand, Mr. Foot,
> that his newly-developed good nature does not extend to some
> damned dispensation permitting attacks on Presbyterians. And
> Cromwell at Dunbar, I would have you know, had no title to pray to
> the god of battles to destroy his Presbyterians.

So the tirade continued, and I had no courage left at the end to
remark that Cromwell's prayers at Dunbar were in fact answered.
Still, it was good to know that our most regular reader was still
reading the newspaper.

Most close observers of the spectacle, even those at the
Treasury, were willing to admit, once the assault course was over,
that Beaverbrook was an inspired improviser. As Carlyle replied
to the philosopher who said he'd accept the universe, they'd
better: without him the famous few would have had even fewer
aeroplanes with which to fight the battle. But the admission,
ready or grudging, was also used to imply that he was not much
good at anything else. He was the great disorganiser, the
untrained, disorderly mind, the inveterate intriguer, the evil
spirit with circuitous access to Churchill's ear. Whitehall and
Westminster overflowed with interested individuals and groups
who would join in this denigration: Sir Archibald Sinclair and the
outraged Air Marshals, Labour Cabinet Ministers who could not
see what right the buccaneer Beaverbrook had to be in the War
Cabinet at all, civil servants who might still imagine that wars
could be conducted according to rules, fellow newspaper proprietors who felt towards him no spirit of fellowship, above all,
the old Conservative Establishment in the House of Commons
and the Carlton Club which had still commanded a considerable
numerical majority in the House of Commons at the end of the

fatal Norway debate and which indeed still retained a large number of plum places in the Churchill Cabinet. Beaverbrook, for all his pro-Chamberlainism, had never been a favourite even with the Chamberlainites, and their sensitivities were ruffled when a few weeks after the retreat from Dunkirk a book was published called *Guilty Men* in which the leading figures of the Chamberlain set figured prominently and specifically in the cast. The pamphlet touched the temper of the times, epitomised in the two quotations which appeared as the preface, one from the Winston Churchill of 1936, now Prime Minister—'the use of recriminations about the past is to enforce effective action at the present'—and the other recalling the far-off spring day in 1793 when an angry crowd had burst their way into the assembly room of the French Convention and demanded 'not a lot of phrases', but 'a dozen guilty men'. What had that to do with Beaverbrook? Nothing which could be proved but much to be suspected. Occasionally the pseudonymous author 'Cato' seemed to lapse into a pseudo-Beaverbrook jargon, and at the end, when a sharp revolutionary distinction was drawn between sheep and goats, between those led to the slaughter and those who did the leading, between the new potential saviours of the nation and the guilty men, Beaverbrook was safely shielded in the first category. Enticing rumours spread about the identity of Cato. Who could it be: Duff Cooper? Randolph Churchill? Beaverbrook himself? The man would stoop to any gutter.

The idea of *Guilty Men* was in fact concocted on the roof of Beaverbrook's *Evening Standard* where Frank Owen and I and a few others might assemble, after the last edition had gone and before The Two Brewers opened across the road. Peter Howard, then the political columnist on the *Sunday Express* and not yet a convert to Buchmanism, was a frequent fellow-conspirator and imbiber. One Thursday or Friday night in that summer of 1940, as the reporters were returning to Fleet Street with their first batches of first-hand interviews with those saved from the beaches of Dunkirk, we had the idea. I suggested the title, taken from a story in J. B. Morton's *Saint-Just*. What we needed was a publisher and speedy action, and next day Frank had summoned one, Pinker, from the famous firm of literary agents, to our secret roof top. He swiftly made arrangements with a slightly hesitant Victor Gollancz; after all, the book at first hearing might sound like a seditious attack on the new Government, and who wanted or would tolerate that? However, we divided up the work between the three of us and literally produced it over that weekend. Three weeks later it was published. Victor Gollancz had insisted, with good reason, on a softening of the final pages; even so some thought it too hot to handle. An early ban by W. H. Smith proved marvellously counter-productive and we made arrangements to sell copies from barrows round Ludgate Circus and Charing Cross. That enticing title also had a special appeal for the bookshops in Leicester Square.

However, the bashful, breathless authors were not concerned with the mass sales which might come later; we were more interested in the reactions of one particular critic. He was puzzled and gratified and circumspect. Maybe some of his Cabinet colleagues were aggrieved, but since he could sincerely disown any knowledge of the authorship, must he share their grief? He himself emerged from the whole story better than he might have dreamed and deserved; how much more deadly the indictment could have been? And Churchill was lauded to the heavens; he might growl a momentary resentment, but had other matters on his mind. Beaverbrook hated not to be the best-informed man in London on matters of disputed gossip, and the more so, naturally enough, if he was alleged to be personally implicated. During the early weeks when he might have reached an adverse verdict on the whole affair, it was the three-way split in the authorship which put him off the scent, assisted by a justly critical review of the book under my name in the *Standard* itself. Anyhow, and for whatever reason, he never put to me the direct question. Within a couple of months, *Guilty Men* was a roaring success, and one by one, by one route or another, the guilty men did disappear from the central stage. Later still, the story circulated that Lord Halifax (one of the guilty men, for sure) had condescendingly remarked to his fellow-Cabinet Minister, Beaverbrook: 'You must find it hard to live on your Cabinet salary of £5,000 a year', to which Beaverbrook allegedly replied: 'Ah, but I've always got my royalties from *Guilty Men*.' Whether he actually said it, to Halifax's face, I know not; even if he fabricated the whole exchange, it is hardly less endearing. What could be done with a boss like that?

However, before they were finally removed, the guilty men were among the most prominent who joined others with better credentials to deny to Beaverbrook his true worth amid the tests of the greatest war in history. For allied with his virtue as an improviser went another quality scarcely less precious at such a time. His thought-process was entirely different from that of most English politicians; he understood the Americans better than many who sat round the Cabinet table. He had few of the prejudices of English Conservatism; so he could conceivably understand the Russians better too, and this last advantage applied in comparison with some of the Labour Ministers hardly less than the Tories; with Ernest Bevin, for example, of whom, according to the old instructive joke, it was said that he never ceased to regard the Soviet Union as a breakaway organisation from the Transport & General Workers' Union. Beaverbrook, the splendid isolationist, had never favoured the Polish alliance which had helped, at a fatal moment, to block any chance of establishing an Anglo-Soviet alliance. He had been implacably opposed, at the time of the Russo-Finnish war, to those who were ready to invite conflict with the Soviet Union as well as Nazi Germany. And all through the period of the phoney war and the period of Hitler's conquest of France, he had kept alive his link with another in the company of his incongruous friends, Ivan Maisky, the Soviet Ambassador in London, an old Bolshevik and an old Anglophile. Beaverbrook's *Evening Standard* was the one paper in London which, along with Aneurin Bevan's *Tribune*, all through 1939 and 1940 and the early months of 1941, returned persistently to the theme of how the world-shaking catastrophe of a full-scale Nazi-Soviet military alliance might be avoided, might at the very least not be encouraged. Maisky sent back reports to Moscow that the Britain of 1940 would survive; they may have had some minute marginal influence on events, and certainly they owed something to Beaverbrook's association with Maisky. He tried, and alas failed, through those same months, in our finest hour, to exorcise any tendency toward defeatism at the

United States Embassy—then conducted by Joseph Kennedy—in London.

So, with no thanks whatever from orthodox or Establishment opinion, Beaverbrook had equipped himself to exploit, when it came, a new emergency and the new magnificent hope of national deliverance. The news arrived on the morning of 22 June 1941. Of course there had been rumours before then, even reports brought back by Stafford Cripps from Moscow and re-despatched by Churchill to an incredulous Stalin. But when the Cherkley house party retired late on the night of Saturday 21st, the talk was on quite other themes. I heard the news first on the early morning radio, and then I heard it again, and then I ran down the stairs and ransacked from the gramophone cupboard the record I knew was there of the *Internationale*, and turned it on full blast. The whole place was awakened, and as they poured downstairs, I was happy to inform Beaverbrook's bleary-eyed household, guests and butlers alike, that they were now allies of the Soviet Union. No one seized the moment more exuberantly and imaginatively than Beaverbrook. That morning he went to Chequers; all day he assisted in preparation of Churchill's famous broadcast, and a reception committee awaited at Cherkley for his return.

Our chance of survival was fortified; a hope of victory was reborn; the whole world-prospect was revolutionised if, and *only* if, the new great ally could be sustained. So much was obvious to us, obvious to Beaverbrook, obvious to the mass of the British people, obvious to babes and sucklings, and, so it must appear to the historians, obvious to all. But, incredibly, it was not so at the time. The military vision of Churchill and his chief advisers was still fixed on other and lesser objectives, and it was Beaverbrook who, within the Cabinet, within the Government machine, seized and sustained the initiative to turn the national energies along the road of commonsense. He feared with much justice that the orthodox military mind, granted plenary command, could lose the Second World War as it had come so near to losing the First. But thanks to those old memories too, he knew perhaps that he was the only man who could argue with Churchill as an equal. Since he had sustained his leader at one desperate hour, he was the better entitled to debate with him about the next necessities, and in public, if need be. The scurryings of the guilty men contrast somewhat sharply at such a moment with the independence of Beaverbrook's mind and action. When the test came, how different a creature from them he truly was.

Yet a qualifying judgement must even now be added, since any portrait of Beaverbrook, even in the war, which stressed too insistently his assiduity, his consistency, his fiendish powers of application for himself or others, would be a travesty. He could also be wayward, quickly bored, moved by whims, and for all his dogmatic manner of expression, he often lacked an inner confidence. This facet of his character, about which everyone who knew him best could testify, made his periods of resolution —as on the aid to Russia issue—the more remarkable and honourable, but it is the clue to his comparative failures in politics. He was regarded, and often regarded himself, as the master of backstairs manoeuvre, and yet I have often imagined that he printed the verse at the beginning of his book, *Men and Power*, with a touch of envy, as a rebuke to himself. Churchill and Lloyd George might possess the unfaltering diligence which high politics demanded, but not, alas, he.

> *The heights by great men reached and kept*
> *Were not attained by sudden flight,*
> *But they, while their companions slept,*
> *Were toiling upward in the night.*

Beaverbrook did not pass that test. He revelled in the excitement and crises of politics but had no taste for the slow grind, without scorning those who had. He could feed the resolution of others so much better than his own. Besides, he had other nocturnal preoccupations.

Apart from that most memorable feast of celebration on 22 June 1941, Cherkley at the weekends in wartime offers such crowded recollections of Beaverbrook in action and Beaverbrook in manoeuvre that it is hard to disentangle one from another. The most regular attendants were no longer the journalists, apart from a very few, but the aircraft factory managers, the civil servants and visiting firemen from across the Atlantic and the world. Cabinet Ministers, Ministers, ex-Ministers and would-be

Ministers jostled one another, and it was pleasant to watch the various means they might employ to parry the Beaverbrook seduction or persiflage: Herbert Morrison, chirpy, well-informed, eager for good publicity and often getting it; A. V. Alexander, handy to have for strumming at the piano, and handy to have at the Admiralty too; Ernest Bevin, dignified, opinionated, utterly unseducible by Beaverbrook, monologuist and not invited a third time. I recall too Leslie Hore-Belisha, out-of-office and out-of-temper, sitting up in bed one Sunday morning with all the newspapers scattered around him on the day after Stafford Cripps had just returned from Moscow, trailing stolen clouds of glory as the man who had shaped the Anglo-Soviet alliance and who could even very soon step into Churchill's shoes. 'How does he do it!' I pretend I can still hear poor Leslie's baffled lament. Or one night, bursting into what was called the saloon where visitors might be offered a fortifying but watery whisky before moving to their appointment with Beaverbrook in the library, I saw, sitting bolt upright in his chair, a Wodehousian figure, at least on the evidence of his accent and moustachios, who at once launched into a fulsome tribute to the varied and matchless talents of the Max Beaverbrook to whose office at the Ministry of Supply he had just been appointed as Parliamentary Secretary. The point of the over-rehearsed oration, I supposed, was that he wanted his perceptive verdict on England's man of destiny, second only to Churchill, passed on, quite casually of course, to the proper quarter which I faithfully, but not quite so casually, did. Beaverbrook adored praise but he could, usually, detect syco-phancy. It was Harold Macmillan; I could never quite take him seriously thereafter; an error no doubt.

However, colliding and colluding with one another in that saloon were the press lords and ladies of the Western World: Clare Boothe Luce who wrote *The Women* and was reputed next day to have said that hers was kindergarten stuff compared with what she had heard round the Cherkley dinner table, or her husband, Henry Luce, creator of *Time, Life* and *Fortune* who saw Fleet Street surrendered, hook-line-sinker, to a bunch of Russian-loving Reds, or our own domestic breed, headed by Esmond Harmsworth, treated most politely while the later Mrs. Fleming was in tow but whipped unconscionably when she was out of the room. One of these, Lord Kemsley, was never, so far as I recall, seen on the premises, yet he was raised from Baron to Viscount in one of Churchill's first Honours Lists. Lloyd George could not resist telephoning that Sunday morning to ask what had happened and offer commiserations, but Beaverbrook was not so easily nettled, and his reply came pat: 'Better a Lloyd George Baron than a Churchill Viscount.' It was one of his last tributes to his old master.

A little earlier Frank Owen and I had been despatched by Beaverbrook on a private mission to see Lloyd George at Churt to feel out the ground and discover how much he might be interested in joining the Churchill Government. Whether we were sent with Churchill's connivance, who knows? More conceivably, Beaverbrook saw Lloyd George as a potential ally in a War Cabinet where he so often acted in isolation and one like himself who had kept open the line of friendly communication with Maisky and the Russians. Anyhow, naturally enough, Frank and I leapt at the suggestion. Frank, as the one surviving member of the rank-and-file of the old 1931 Lloyd George Liberal Party rump, was always welcomed there as a brilliant disciple, and I had written a recent editorial in the *Standard* comparing a Lloyd George return to the House of Commons with that of Chatham in 1761. I had heard Ll. G. many times on the platform and most memorably of all from the House of Commons press gallery in the Norway debate when it was his speech which stabbed Neville Chamberlain to death in the open forum. By the time Frank and I went to Churt, Lloyd George was still in full control of his incomparable faculties but he was also, in his heart of hearts, defeatist. He did not see how we could win the war, and he did not see, in particular, how Churchill could lead us to the victory. He was deeply offended by a remark Churchill had made in a debate a few weeks earlier comparing one of his own sombre wartime speeches to the kind of speech with which Marshal Petain might have sought to enliven one of the last French Cabinet meetings, before his surrender to Hitler. So when we talked of our mission, he brushed the suggestion aside with the inquiry: 'What me? Old Papa Petain?' And as he talked, he resorted to mimicry, and soon cheered himself and the company by the malicious impersonation of one political character after another. He professed to be shocked by the subservience shown by members of Churchill's War Cabinet and the high-handed manner which Churchill displayed towards them. 'Now my War Cabinet was different', he insisted. 'They were all big men. I was never able to treat *any* of my colleagues the way Churchill treats *all* of his.' Then the old man paused, and his eye twinkled. 'Oh yes, there was one I treated that way—Curzon.' Beaverbrook at least could never be treated by Churchill the way Lloyd George treated Curzon.

Like Beaverbrook himself, I could not live by politics alone, and Cherkley for me in those years had one special irrepressible attraction. Making a pass, however shyly or ineffectually, at the boss's girl may not normally be recommended as the road to fortune, but I never lived to repent it and I never quite knew how he viewed the matter. I had had my first glimpse of Lili Ernst on the very first night I had arrived at Cherkley in the autumn of 1938; it was a stunning glimpse too, but then she vanished before I knew who or what she was. She was the Hungarian countess who in reality was neither Hungarian nor a countess but a much more exciting combination. Many months later, after the war had started, I wrote an article about the civilised treatment which should be offered to refugees from Hitler's Europe, and she wrote to me. I met her again, and she told me part of her story, and no one in his senses could fail to be captivated. She was a Yugoslav Jewess, a ballet dancer attached to a famous Viennese opera company, beautiful and delicate and fragile, and Beaverbrook had met her when she was dancing in Cannes, and had told her to communicate with him if she was ever in trouble. Thanks to his intervention, she was smuggled out of Vienna a few weeks after Hitler's troops had occupied the city; thanks to his assistance, she had what proved to be a last, fleeting glimpse of her parents on a holiday in Switzerland. Beaverbrook had fallen for her; no possible doubt about that, and one day, just about the time when I was having troubles with Captain Wardell, I wrote, on Beaverbrook's incitement, a full length leading article in the *Daily Express*, not the *Evening Standard*, on the Jewish Feast of Purim, on how Haman was hanged in place of Mordecai, on how the

Nazis would never be able to execute their monstrous programme for the final extermination of the Jews. Readers of the
Express must have rubbed their eyes in some amazement; never
before had the paper shown itself so passionately pro-Jewish.
Readers of the Bible must have rubbed their eyes too, for
although the story was retold, I trust, well-enough and reverently
in the space available, it was the story of Haman and Mordecai
without Esther, a serious, a most unconscionable omission. When
Beaverbrook had recited to each of us, Lili and myself, that Bible
story, Esther had certainly not been overlooked; she is, and was,
and always will be, the heroine. However, the leading article did
serve its purpose. Lili was pleased, and he was pleased, and the
readers of the *Express* could lump it. Thereafter, I took leaves,
whole chapters, from his book, and wrote in the *Evening
Standard* on Jewish themes and Yugoslav themes and sometimes
the two together (we became, at a somewhat later date, enthusiastic supporters of Tito) at every available opportunity and
thereby helped to win her friendship but not her heart. Then
came graver, terrible complications. What happened to Lili's
family and friends in Yugoslavia when it was overrun by the Nazis,
no one could know; the assumption was that they had been
hauled off to Auschwitz. Her home in Yugoslavia was gone;
never to be revisited. She loved Beaverbrook, and he loved her,
but doubtless he could be hard and demanding as well as sensitive,
possessive and wayward by turns, as he was in politics. Her health
broke and the doctors, including the expert Dan Davies,
diagnosed the disease as incurable. She moved from hospital to
hospital, from doctor to doctor, and then finally devised her own
cure. She made her escape from him and lived (and still lives)
happily ever after. She was lovely, zestful, affectionate, independent, inquisitive, a passionate Maccabean upholder of the rights of
the Jewish people, just like Esther. And the best thing I ever knew
about Max Beaverbrook was that Lili Ernst had truly loved him.

   To set the chronology straight, I left him about three years
before she did, and I took what I thought was the proper course of
doing it without a row. For two years, since the departure of
Frank Owen for the forces, I had had the enthralling job of
editing the paper which he above all others had created, the war-

time *Evening Standard*, the *Standard* in its very greatest days I naturally contend, although it has had some other great ones since.

The war, as one of its minor by-products, raised the quality of British journalism as a whole and especially London journalism in a manner which has never been properly and collectively acclaimed. For one thing, the profit test, advertising pressures, were overnight tossed out of Fleet Street's bomb-threatened windows, and there prevailed instead a genuine competition of merit to use the precious supplies of newsprint to serve the supreme common interest of the hour. We believed on the *Standard* that we changed to meet the new conditions and caught the new atmosphere better than any rival. For a start, we reported the new kind of war itself more freshly, analysed strategy more contentiously. For this, Frank Owen, an inspired military reporter himself, was chiefly responsible, but he hired a remarkable and strange company to help him. During the pitiful period of the phoney war, Liddell Hart had been the principal military writer on the paper, but his reputation, somewhat unjustly and only temporarily, was knocked through the ropes by the same Nazi tanks which smashed through the Ardennes. By a similar reckoning, Major-General J. F. C. Fuller, the so-called father of the tank, disinherited by the British War Office, saw his reputation suddenly restored. In his bitter frustration, he had even dabbled with Fascism itself, and it would have been easy to outlaw him from our democrat columns on that ground alone. But Frank would tolerate no such nonsense; he knew, and the *Evening Standard* readers came to know, that Fuller was the best professional military writer in the business. Yet Fuller was never '*the* military correspondent of the *Evening Standard*'; *his* identity, much to the fury of the War Office, was itself preserved as a military secret. Either it was Frank himself or it was our new-found independent monitor of the Western war. Down towards Ludgate Circus was a little I. L. P. bookshop where Frank and I made purchases of such essential topical documents as the writings of Leon Trotsky or Tom Wintringham and which was run by a Swiss Socialist called Jon Kimche. He listened to the babel of Europe's battling radio stations in God-knows how many languages, and out of it distilled another original approach to the new kind of war, and a new profession for himself. Another independent voice which caught Frank's ear was Polish. He could not speak much English as yet—although, as Lenin said of Rosa Luxemburg, he already spoke excellent Marxism: his name was Isaac Deutscher, and he lived to write, in English, the best biography of the century. All kinds of degrees of independent persons were drawn to Shoe Lane or to the surrounding consulting rooms. Wilfrid Macartney, author of the prison best seller, *Walls Have Mouths*, having served a sentence in Dartmoor for giving secrets to the Russians, was now happy to discover that he had been assisting our allies all along; he came to propose a series of Second-Front-Aid-to-Russia meetings, to be organised by the front organisation, the Russia Today Society. We agreed, and at the Stoll Theatre the first of the great mass meetings of wartime was held with the following speakers: Aneurin Bevan, Frank Owen, Harry Pollitt, and myself. Harry Pollitt, leader of the Communist Party, removed from that post for his patriotic defection in September 1939, had indeed been a frequent, frustrated, drinking companion of those wretched months; he deeply believed that another kind of opportunity would develop, and so did we. So did a young soldier called Orde Wingate, as frustrated as Harry Pollitt, who much to my amazement sat up through one whole night at Frank's flat in Lincoln's Inn and drank even Frank under the table. He told us how he had trained Jewish boys in Palestine to fight the Arabs at their own guerilla game; how the War Office had never quite favoured his politics or his new notions of partisan war; how he was exiled at that precise moment to some training backwater on Salisbury plain; how he saw the war as one directed by Jehovah-Nemesis and designed to expunge all the wickedness of the appeasement years. The Jews, the Czechs, the Spaniards, the Ethiopians, all would be avenged. He himself intended to walk through the streets of Addis Ababa by the side of Haile Selassie. At five o'clock in the morning, with Frank's last bottle of sparkling Burgundy deflated and dead, all seemed possible—and two years later he did it.

Not everyone attracted by our *Evening Standard* magnet could quite equal that. Seaman Frank came to see us or rather we went in search of him, having heard the ever-memorable broadcast in which he described how he had lost his leg in the world-famous wreck of the *San Demetrio*; how when the torpedo had hit the ship it had made a noise like the opening of the gates of hell; how he had run across 'a gruel of men's bodies', to the life boats; how the shark had taken his leg; how he had made the miraculous return-journey to his native Liverpool. Seaman Frank could talk like that at will; he was soaked in Joseph Conrad, if not the *San Demetrio* waters. I wrote a leading article called 'English Seaman' with many overtones of Froude. For a few weeks we placarded his name all over our delivery vans and even started to remind him how splendid it would be for our sales when he went to sea again. However, a few had had doubts from the beginning, and when we heard that a reporter from the *Evening News* was allegedly being despatched to make some first-hand inquiries in Liverpool, we sent our best reporter, Leslie Randall, on the same trail and to get there first. Seaman Frank had never been nearer to the sea than Birkenhead ferry; he had lost his leg in a tram accident. He *was* an admirer of Conrad, long before Professor Leavis. But we hardly believed that Beaverbrook, for all his special interest, would be concerned with these distinctions, and Seaman Frank was allowed to withdraw quietly from the literary scene.

With or without Seaman Frank's inspiration, we did transform the political tone of the *Evening Standard*. (We also just about overhauled the *Star* in circulation figures for the first time in history.) Some long-standing readers were naturally offended. I had written some editorial which concluded with the claim that 'we are fighting this war to uphold the principles of the French Revolution', whereupon I received the most treasured protest ever to come my way. The writer was Lord Alfred Douglas, the same whose sonnets my father had so justly taught me to revere. Whatever his other delinquencies, Lord Alfred had mastered the form of the sonnet to place him among the masters. This is what he sent in reply to my editorial:

Not by Beelzebub is Satan cast
Out of the mind possessed; darkness abides
Unexorcised by darkness. Who that rides

In Error's dismal train can face the blast
Which Error's self engenders and stand fast?
You challenge Hitler, but your dullness sides
With Hitler's blackness, and plain sense derides
An idol-worshipping iconoclast.
Sinistral sheep, poor mass-suggestioned dupe
Parrot your catchwords, crook your governed knee
Before your goatish god; your little span
Will not endure, and we will never stoop
To make a fetish of Democracy
Or worship at the shrine of Caliban.

Of course, the protest was prominently printed; indeed it supplied the distinction for a regular page of protest on which we encouraged old or new readers to try their hand at invective. Once I had expressed my admiration for his poetry, Lord Alfred and I became pen pals. Another of the sonnets he wrote at this time was dedicated to Winston Churchill, a magnanimous gesture since it was Churchill who had once despatched Lord Alfred to serve a prison sentence for criminal libel. However, we, the sinistral sheep, could not quite follow him there, and, to say all we wished, we looked for other pastures to combine with those which the *Standard* offered.

Another pseudonym provoked a real stir. On 1 May, 1942, *Tribune* started publishing under the title 'Why Churchill?' a series of articles written, so they claimed, by a brilliant and unusually well-informed writer who had adopted the name of Thomas Rainsboro', the Leveller captain in Cromwell's army. No such attack on Churchill himself, no comparable and comprehensive critique of the general war strategy, had been published anywhere in any wartime newspaper before, and quite a number of well-informed readers did accept the general critique. The disguise was successful; Aneurin Bevan or Jon Kimche who was now working full-time for *Tribune* had to carry and share the blame or glory. But, of course, the real author was Frank Owen, then established for his tank training in a barracks near Andover. Once War Office or MI5 agents had accompanied us over most of the country, at our Second Front Campaign meetings, vainly in pursuit of treasonable utterances; but everything said from those platforms was patriotic to the finger tips, as royal and loyal as the Russians themselves. But highly well-informed articles on issues of military strategy, all too redolent of the very criticisms which were now being uttered in army messes, were another matter. It was Beaverbrook who gave me the tip. 'When's the next article due from Frank?' he asked without any preliminary discussion on the point. 'This week,' I replied. 'You'd better stop it—tonight'. So I raced off to Andover, scoured the pubs, found Frank, took the copy off him, started to race back to London, crashed the car on the humped bridge on the London road outside Andover, and was taken off for repairs to the nearby Army camp who put me on the road next morning. It was one of the few occasions when Frank, the professional journalist, was ever late with his copy, and one of the few occasions when Beaverbrook probed a little more closely than he himself, a member of the War Cabinet, might have thought prudent into those tender relationships between the *Evening Standard* and *Tribune*.

However, the wartime *Evening Standard* was concerned also with more than these mere military matters. I think we did capture something of the special flavour of what London was like amid the greatest war for freedom ever fought. The people of London did truly play an heroic role, and the *Standard* reported their daily and nightly ardours, gave voice to their protests against blind or tardy bureaucracy, and endlessly argued about the way in which the supreme common objective could be achieved. For London was also the nerve-centre of the whole world-wide struggle against Nazism, and, for all our love of our precious city and our precious island, no insular imagination could express fully the spirit of the age. When officialdom started the momentary madness of locking up all aliens, many of them to be counted amongst our most devoted allies, we helped to put a stop to it with an article: *Why Not Lock Up General de Gaulle?* When a handful of twentieth-century French revolutionaries aided our cause by blowing up French battleships in Toulon harbour, we printed several verses of the *Marseillaise* on the front page. And when we got the news late one evening that Mussolini had been overthrown by a handful of brave Italians, we sat up all night to produce a souvenir edition, telling his whole life story from the march on Rome to Abyssinia and to Spain, embellished with Low cartoons, and all designed together, to carve him at last as 'a carcase fit for hounds'. I had always had what I presumed to regard as a proprietary interest in the overthrow of Mussolini ever since I had been instructed in the matter by Ignazio Silone in his *School for Dictators*. So I wrote a swift sequel to *Guilty Men* called *The Trial of Mussolini* by Cassius, in which I hoped that the truly Socialist and internationalist issues at stake were properly celebrated. This time any mystery of authorship lasted little more than a few hours, and Beaverbrook with whom I'd been arguing on other political topics made the legitimate point that I could be an editor or a pamphleteer but not both at the same time. And, incidentally, what had happened to the form, circulated in the *Guilty Men* aftermath, requiring all Beaverbrook employees to inform the management about prospective books they had in mind? No I had not signed it; I had put it in the wastepaper basket where indeed, after a suitable interval, we would assign all the awkward messages from the Beaverbrook dictaphone which we hoped would not stir future animosities. There had been trouble, too, about the Beveridge Report about which the *Evening Standard* had secured an excellent scoop and we had stepped in to welcome the document itself. For a while, having left the *Standard* editorship, I was in a ridiculous limbo on the *Daily Express*, and then in June I wrote him a long letter. 'Your views and mine are bound to become more and more irreconcilable. As far as this Socialist business is concerned my views are unshakable. For me it is the Klondyke or bust, and at the moment I am not sure I am going the right way to Klondyke . . .' and much more to the same effect. So I took the offer from an old friend and fellow-Beaverbrook spotter, Percy Cudlipp, to join the *Daily Herald*— whether that Long Acre route was the right way to Klondyke is another matter.

But back to Beaverbrook: during the next few years my association with the old man became bruised almost beyond recognition or repair. Beaverbrook in the distance looked a very much less enchanting figure than he had done at close quarters. All through the period towards the ending of the war, the election of 1945, the overthrow of Churchill, the instalment of the Labour

Government, my own election in Devonport, every public issue seemed likely to inflict fresh wounds on any private feeling which remained. Perhaps also there were jangled jealousies left over from the Lili Ernst days. Many who had worked for Beaverbrook would devote a considerable part of the rest of their days to his vilification, and perhaps I had started down that same path when I said in a Commons debate on the Royal Commission on the Press, instituted by the Labour Government, that the occupational disease among newspaper proprietors was megalomania. Many a true word is spoken in venom; and yet for me to have wasted much time on that theme in dealing with Beaverbrook would have been dust and ashes.

Providentially, an occasion occurred which set matters aright. Someone invited me to a dinner to celebrate Beaverbrook's seventieth birthday at the Savoy Hotel on 28 April 1948; and the chairman asked me to speak. It was natural to recall the finest hour when he had waited each night for Max's return from the skies where London was saved and when he himself had seemed to be translated into another being. I quoted Milton:

> . . . *with grave*
> *Aspect he rose, and in his rising seemed*
> *A pillar of state; deep on his front engraven*
> *Deliberation sat, and public care;*
> *And princely counsel in his face yet shone,*
> *Majestic, though in ruin: sage he stood,*
> *With Atlantean shoulders, fit to bear*
> *The weight of mightiest monarchies; his look*
> *Drew audience and attention still as night*
> *Or summer's noontide air.*

The diners were properly hushed and impressed, and then I had to remind the ignorant bunch that they were that, of course, those famous lines had been written about Beelzebub. It was a trick purloined straight from my father but I doubt whether he had ever had a more apposite occasion for working it. Beaverbrook was overcome; he sent me next day a touched and touching letter, scrawled in his barely legible hand. Our friendship was renewed, and never collapsed thereafter. Destry rode again.

I think I was as well placed as anyone to see what Beaverbrook did for all of us in those supreme years, and I am prepared to repeat the testimony anywhere and at any time, including the Day of Judgement, where possibly, now the thought occurs, I may have a chance of giving evidence before he does. But at that higher tribunal, I suppose, one would have to be careful about quoting Milton with effect: there it may not so readily be appreciated that Beelzebub had a better side to his nature.

Two other improbable friendships contributed to mine with Beaverbrook. First and foremost, Jill, my wife, knew how to deal with him from the very first meeting, how to awaken and sustain his curiosity, how to keep his eyes on today and tomorrow and not the past, how to appreciate all those human sides of him which the outside world believed not to exist. Mostly Beaverbrook was on uneasy terms with the wives of the journalists who worked for him; he wanted exclusive rights. Many quarrelled with him because of their wives, and some of the wives he preferred were already on bad terms with their husbands. But Jill was one of the very few who knew best how to deal with him in every mood and extremity. And it was with her blessing that I went off one hazardous morning to get £3,000 from him when *Tribune* was faced with extinction in 1951. Without it, we would not have survived and I felt I could argue that the *Express* newspapers had not paid me a penny when I left in June 1944. However, that was really beside the point. At the time no one except Jill knew where the money had come from, but when Alan Taylor was writing Beaverbrook's biography, he wrote me a personal letter as follows, on 6 May 1970:

Here is a little query to take your mind off greater things. You told me that Max gave *Tribune* £3,000 in 1951. I decided to forget it. Now I find from the letters that Max told Robertson to charge this to the *Daily Express* and added: 'What would we do for recruits without *Tribune*?' My rule is everything about Max good or bad. Like all rules it has an exception which I know Max would have approved of: nothing to hurt Mike. So if you ask me to forget it again, I will do. Otherwise I'll put it in. It is for you to decide. A Yes or a No on a postcard is all I want.

I said, and Jill said: 'Put it in', and quite right too.

How deeply corrupted *Tribune* was by Beaverbrook gold is a research-subject not yet completed by the Nuffield School, but one affair, awkward perhaps for their verdict of damnation, ran concurrently with my rapprochement with the old friend and new benefactor. On 2 March 1950, the *Evening Standard* produced a scandalous front page under the headlines 'FUCHS AND STRACHEY: A GREAT NEW CRISIS. War Minister has never disavowed Communism. Now involved in MI5 efficiency probe.' *Tribune* hit back harder than anyone else in Strachey's defence. When I'd written the article, someone in the office suggested the title: 'Prostitutes of the Press.' I thought that too banal and too defamatory, and we therefore substituted what I thought to be the more anodyne, but equally accurate and insulting: 'Lower than Kemsley'—Lord Kemsley, proprietor at that time of the *Daily Sketch* and the *Sunday Times* and held to be in our estimation the criterion of low Tory journalism. Kemsley instituted libel proceedings against us, and the case which dragged on for the next three years, and which could have landed *Tribune* and myself and all my fellow directors in the bankruptcy court, had many legal and political aspects of lasting fascination. Eventually the cause of Right prevailed—and in the House of Lords of all places. There for five long days our fate was in the balance while lawyers argued, the costs mounted and the Lord Chief Justice, Lord Goddard (who happened to be the victim of another of *Tribune's* onslaughts in the very same issue of the paper where the alleged defamation had occurred), probed and ransacked the mysteries of libel precedent. But there were no precedents; so the point had much significance for others besides ourselves. To plead 'fair comment' in a libel action it is necessary that the facts on which the comment is based should be 'truly stated'. In the offending *Tribune* article, *Tribune* with its customary respect for the quick awareness of its readers, had stated none of the facts on which the comment was based. Was the defence of 'fair comment' still available to us? The Master in Chambers said 'No'. The court of Appeal said 'Yes'. Eventually, the House of Lords agreed with the learned legal interpretation reached without all that expense in *Tribune's* office three years before.

Beaverbrook followed each twist and turn in the affair with his customary solicitude. He was not at all eager to see his secret £3,000 finish up in Lord Kemsley's clutches. As a journalist, he was on *Tribune*'s side in the fight to prevent any tightening of the libel laws. And behind the scenes too, although in deference to his existing editors he would not admit as much to me, he believed the original *Evening Standard* headline was an outrage and a blunder. The editor concerned did not last long thereafter.

Thus, absurdly in a sense, the 'Lower than Kemsley' episode proved more of a new bond between us than anything else. However, that the *Standard* of all papers should have indulged in such scurrility-cum-hysteria gives a forgotten hint about the political climate of the time. It was the age of the spy scares, of Burgess and Maclean, of the renewed cold war, of the sudden mounting fear, on both sides of the Atlantic, that it might break out into a hot one. Beaverbrook, whatever his paper might say in public, never surrendered to the hysteria in private. One evening he was somehow stirred into describing to the astonished company how the cold war had started, or rather how the Russians might reasonably imagine it had started, and he went back to the fateful months of 1945 and 1946, and recited the individual events of the time in a novel sequence. It was not his verdict on the whole business; it was his imaginative flight, assisted by a considerable quantity of hard fact, to see how his old wartime associate Stalin and the others in the Kremlin might intelligently view the scene. The dinner party was overwhelmed. Some Canadian banker or American newspaper proprietor, sitting next to Jill, muttered under his breath 'He's a Commie!' It was the first time Jill had seen his imaginative side in action; and that formed one part of the quality which had made Arnold Bennett say he was the best dramatic raconteur he ever heard.

One other scene of corruption at the hands of the old man cannot be omitted from the record. Round about the year 1954 we had to leave our house in Rosslyn Hill, Hampstead, in a hurry since the ecclesiastical Commissioners who owned the place would not renew the lease on acceptable terms. For about six months on end, we were gipsies, driving around in two cars, one which took Jill to her work and the other which took me. We cadged odd nights off friends while we looked for a new house, and one day Beaverbrook, hearing of our plight, rang up to say that he could offer us a roof for our heads; he had especial sympathy for refugees from the English Church. So we turned up at Cherkley in the late afternoon, supposing we had been offered a bed for the night. Instead we were taken on a tour of four dere- lict cottages on his estate, each more dilapidated than the other and none of them conceivably habitable on the spot. His eye normally so observant, was averted from our car-cum-caravan; the procession plunged deeper across the fields and darkness descended. 'Well, choose which you like', he said, and 'let me know', and he waved us goodbye. We hastened off that night to find a bed at the house of Curly and Rita Mallalieu where we asked to stay for one night and in fact stayed for six months. But the picture of Paddock Cottage, stuck in the middle of one of the Cherkley fields, stuck in our minds too and, more especially, in Jill's imagination. She could see what it could be and what she could make of it. But there was also the moral question, if indeed, as it seemed, he was offering us it on a peppercorn rent? We consulted Aneurin Bevan and he replied: 'It isn't what you take, it's what you give.' And Jill consulted my father whom she justly regarded as an expert on such questions. Anyhow, with his blessing, she took the whole project in hand, painted the cottage white, introduced calor gas, and made it into a marvellously convenient hide-out for a writer. Both the old man and young Max to whom great stretches of the estate had been handed over marvelled at the transformation. Max promptly decided to follow Jill's example with the other cottages, and when the old man died, told us we could keep it as long as we wanted, but Jill was already working a similar miracle with an old miners' cottage in Tredegar; so Paddock Cottage was handed back to the Cherkley estate. It had only had one snag. Remote from the road and most other signs of human association, there was however a path nearby which led soon to the neighbouring Rowton House. When we were absent, the temptation for the Rowton House population to have a night out in the cottage was overpowering. The police could never track them. The visits became so frequent that we almost had a sense of communal living. And the real risk was fire; not all our visitors had made themselves experts in dealing with the calor gas apparatus. On a winter's night they were inclined to use the furniture for firewood. Jill feared she might have to confront Max one morning with the old greeting from the P. G. Wodehouse story: 'I fear you're a cottage short, old boy.'

Alan Taylor's friendship was the other unlikely one which shaped and enlivened Beaverbrook's life in the last decade, and it all started because Alan read Beaverbrook's books with fresh eyes. His style, in any case, had a kinship with Alan Taylor's own; the taste of the two men for brevity, clarity and mischief was similar. But Alan also set aside the preconceived assumption that Beaverbrook must be a second-rate journalist writing for the hour or the day or for the immediate sensation. He wrote a review in the *Observer* in which, incredibly in the light of all previous academic judgements, he compared Beaverbrook with Tacitus.

I was present in the room when he read that review, and his life took on a new exhilaration. He had truly always been most modest about his own writings, never expecting to be regarded as anything more than a chronicler, the good teller of a tale which he knew himself to be and had every right to accept as a fair assessment. As for the comparison with Tacitus, utterly flattering as he believed it was, it meant that a new world and a new friendship had opened before him. Alan Taylor became his intimate confidante on all these questions, his biographer and his friend indeed. Certainly the public judgement on Beaverbrook as a writer was revolutionised by that single verdict. Not all his writings, of course, are in any sense in the same class. Most of them were sheer journalism, good or bad. But the three or four main books on politics *are* masterpieces of political writing, and it took Alan Taylor's discernment to make the discovery in full measure. Moreover, as with Taylor's own style, there are no adventitious aids to conceal the quality. Dubieties are made as hard as diamonds. The high, bold, bald claims can be put to the test; he is never seeking to dodge or prevaricate. Beaverbrook, the historian, is always giving the evidence, if it is there, against his own pre-conception, against his own Party, even against his own heroes. Who could ever have believed that he of all people would have assumed the mantle of historian? Yet, it is true, and, in the case of his Conservative Party, he plays the part with a special relish and glee.

It is there, to his humour, we must always return. 'If Max gets to heaven', wrote H. G. Wells, 'he won't last long. He'll be chucked out for trying to pull off a merger between Heaven and Hell . . . after having secured a controlling interest in key subsidiary companies in both places, of course.' But the merger had already taken place under his roof; a mixture of Heaven and Hell was what it could be like but, after some moments of Miltonic doubt about the outcome, it was usually heaven which triumphed in that combat, and a heaven too which no Calvinist could recognise, one which was always liable to dissolve in laughter. Even at the gravest moment the chance of such a beneficent explosion would reappear, and the House of Rimmon might resound to the healing strains of *The Red Flag*, led, say, by another companion treasured for his company alone, Stanley Morison of *The Times*, ex-jailbird, ex-pacifist, militant Catholic, and, as far as I can recall, a light baritone. 'Stanley,' said Beaverbrook, 'does not make the mistake of pouring old wine into new bottles. If the wine is old and really good, he has another use for it.' Truly, it was his humour which had a special all-encompassing dimension. This was more part of him, I believe, even than the ceaseless energy with which he could whip everyone in sight, the furious yet fitful zeal for the great causes and the others, strange and terrible, in which he believed. Not all the paroxysms of anger, of urgency, of frustration could shake those walls as the laughter did, and there was in it no vein of pretence or hysteria but rather a rich comic view of the human species. It could be called Dickensian or Chaplinesque were it not for the fact that Dickens and Chaplin, along with the Co-op or Covent Garden or the British Council, were listed among his absurd *bêtes noires*, and were it not that he lacked the last full measure of compassion which only the greatest comedians have. Anyhow, Beaverbrook's was a volcano of laughter which went on erupting till the end. No one who ever lodged for a while beneath that Vesuvius will ever forget.

FIVE

Hyde Park Sceptic

England must remember that the Keltic fringe has been a
bulwark of gay and lively steel around these islands.

SEAN O'CASEY

OF ALL THE SIGHTS and sounds which attracted me on my first
arrival to live in London in the mid-thirties, one combined
operation left a lingering, individual spell. I naturally went to
Hyde Park to hear the orators, the best of the many free
entertainments on offer in the capital. I heard the purest milk of
the word flowing, then as now, from the platform of the Socialist
Party of Great Britain. I heard at the May Day meetings some of
the old masters, not at their greatest but still magical in their
presence and presentation—Ben Tillett, Tom Mann, George
Lansbury, Jimmy Maxton. I heard a striking and handsome
young Methodist preacher who insisted on dressing in a strange
costume which my father would have doubtless described as
Popish but who advocated Socialism and pacifism in ever-fluent
classical English; my mother was the one who urged that I should
hear Donald Soper, hoping, and I'm sure praying, that he might
be the divine agent to reconvert me, via Socialism, to the family
creed. I heard the whole range of religious crusaders, including
the unsuccessful pugilist who had taken to evangelism; pug-
nosed, black-eyed and cauliflower-eared, he was still singing:
'Jesus wants me for a sunbeam'. However, in defiance of all my
mother's prayers, I heard, most potent and perilous of all, Bonar
Thompson, the one-man satirist of the universe, this world and
the next.

I quickly became an addict. Twice or thrice every Sunday,
weather permitting, he gave his review of what had happened the

week before. He knew what had passed or been perpetrated in Buckingham Palace, the Cabinet, the Kremlin, the Vatican, and the Stock Exchange, and he didn't think much of it. All the stridencies of the thirties were at their highest pitch, and all the religious wars, for a start, were being refought across the same ground in Hyde Park. Bonar Thompson's scepticism was, I suppose, the sanest thing in the land. Certainly he was the most innocent citizen of the whole metropolis; he never did anybody any harm and did nameless, countless multitudes plenty of good.

I learnt from him much useful or, better still, useless knowledge which, as they say, stood me in good stead ever after. I learnt, for example, the secret of Anthony Eden; it was not so easy to spot then. He was, said Bonar Thompson, 'the best advertisement the Fifty Shilling Tailors ever had'. I learnt an elementary suspicion of policemen, particularly the plain clothes type. 'By their boots ye shall know them', Bonar would gravely announce from the platform, and the whole audience would automatically look down at their feet and at their neighbour's feet too, much to the embarrassment of the few plain clothes spectators who naturally preferred his platform to all others. I learnt some other knowledge quite unavailable elsewhere: 'On the London buses a notice says *Spitting Prohibited: Penalty 40/-*. In the British Museum a notice says *Spitting Prohibited: penalty 20/-*. What's the moral? If you must spit, spit in the British Museum.'

Bonar Thompson was, of course, an anarchist, although even this most honourable title gives too feeble an indication of his comprehensive iconoclasm. Freedom meant more to him than to anyone else I ever met; a kind of added dimension. He had talents enough to have gained an agreeable income as an actor or a writer; but the very idea of any form of regular employment offended his heart and soul. He would not soil his hands or his faith with actual work. He had had nothing whatever to do with authority ever since, as he told us, he had refused to join the Army in the First World War because he wasn't approached in the right manner. Yet his attitude, his whole life-story, had a quality more all-embracing than anything suggested by the customary revolt of the young against authority, military or civil. He loved the good things of life: food, drink, love-making, the countryside, waywardness, ease; above all, the theatre, literature, the English language. Yet he would sacrifice any and all of these delights in the last extremity, to preserve his precious independence, or, perhaps it might be truer to say, to preserve his right to make the enjoyment of literature literally a full-time occupation. He knew Shakespeare and Dickens and Yeats and Sean O'Casey and a few others besides, as well as any man ever knew them. It was from him that I learnt that the fellow called Yeats, of whom I'd never heard, was destined to be the poet of the century. He could extract from all these favourites a pleasure which was sensual as much as artistic; he could not waste time on trivialities or diversions, or so he appeared, at the height of his powers, in the thirties and the early forties. His immaculate independence and all its outward manifestations were glories to behold. Yet the means by which it was established and sustained surely make the achievement the more remarkable.

He wrote an autobiography, *Hyde Park Orator*, which unfortunately did injury to his reputation, since running through it was a strand of sourness quite uncharacteristic of the public or, indeed, the private man. Sean O'Casey, the most generous of comrades, felt obliged to remark upon these political and other delinquencies in his preface; rarely has a book been presented to the world under such damning auspices, and Sean O'Casey had an excuse; repeatedly in those pages the author reveals a spleen, especially against political enemies in the mass, which he rarely showed in real life and never against individuals. Yet the book's inherent virtues should surely have been sufficient to subdue all such criticisms from O'Casey or anyone else. The bareness of the combined effect of poverty and Puritanism in the Ulster where he was born is there for all to see and feel; the road from the glens of Antrim is more sharply marked than Orwell's road to Wigan Pier. Indeed, the poverty of Edwardian Ireland and Edwardian England, Edwardian Manchester and Edwardian London, was, as Bonar Thompson knew, in his own aching bones and bleeding feet, a physical pain for multitudes of our people which by comparison even the thirties never experienced.

Bonar's humour was a triumph of the human spirit over all these conditions. It was not part of some indictment against him, as several of his humourless ex-comrades alleged; it was rather part of the counter-attack against the capitalist system. Bonar Thompson could at least boast—how many other Socialist propagandists could say the same?—that he had never helped to sustain that system with so much as a single movement of his hand or finger. To that particular article of his faith he never found it too difficult to remain true. But he had other tests and trials, and some of them were traceable to the overflowing appearance of good nature which he brought along with all the horrific memories of Ulster and of the north and industrial England.

'Good God!' he once wrote to me when quite unconsciously I had apologised for not having replied to some earlier letter. 'Good God! The most exemplary heaping of coals of fire on an offender's head I have ever known in the course of a long-suffering career of default and procrastination by land, sea and air! It is an open secret that I am not only an habitual and inveterate procrastinator but a confirmed and case-hardened prognosticator as well.' But how he suffered:

My appearance and manner are deceptive in every way. I generally look in good health and the truth is I'm nearly always very far from well. I look fairly prosperous and am almost always on the verge of destitution, and often over the precipice into the deep abysses of penury. I look stout and even plump as a rule and am a walking skeleton. . . As to age, I looked about thirty-five until recently, while actually I have been an old man tottering towards senility for over five years . . . And then I appear to be a merry fellow when in reality I'm a melancholy brooder on death and the meaningless futility of life. I could furnish a fuller list of ironical contradictions, tending to prove me the most deceptive entity now extant upon the surface of this strange and tragic planet. Arrogant and bombastic on the platform and in private the most hopeless embodiment of diffidence, timidity and self-obliterating nullity it has ever been my misfortune to meet. A robust invalid who has been masquerading for years as a living being when actually a member of that grey company of human simulacra that I've made fun of so often in days gone by—the Unburied Dead . . . In justice to myself it is only fair to say that all this is no more than 20 per cent my fault. My birth was a *faux-pas*, the tragedy, not of being born *out of wedlock* but being born *out of pocket*. My continued stay in the world has been a lamentable solecism and the whole affair a regrettable lapse on the part of Fortuity.

(You may not know that word existed, but he knew) . . . And then, after much more he added, a typical postscript:

If you see Frank Horrabin, please give him my kind regards. He flabbergasted me when he spoke at the Conway Hall last winter. I had dropped in to hear him speaking on Socialism and Art. Suddenly and without having given me notice of the question he launched into a glowing tribute to my acting in *St. Joan*. He had seen me in the play at Brighton in the summer. Naturally I demanded an apology for his daring to find merit in a performance where I had never been able to detect any myself. A good chap—and speaking more seriously—a penetrating and illuminating critic of the art of acting, for I can say in all humility that my performance in *St. Joan* was a *tour-de-force*, worthy of Edmund Kean at his very best. *Bon Voyage*, as Sam Goldwyn would say.

How many times did he pick himself up from the dust so bravely, and stagger to his feet and to his own independent pulpit in Hyde Park. There, for most of his years, instead of genuinely seeking work, he made collections from his fans and cheerfully condemned those who listened without paying to an endless, excruciating inferno of his own making. He did not believe in an after-life, but for those who habitually offended in respect of the collection he was prepared to make an exception. Then, at one stage in his career, bumbledum contrived the by-law—no collections within the Hyde Park gates, a piece of gratuitous tyranny if ever there was one. Bonar Thompson bore it all with the sweetest of smiles, and he managed to convert this blow to his fortunes into the most admired of all his perorations. Though he preached no cause, though he offered no remedy, though he would countenance no hint of a conceivable improvement in the human condition here or, more especially, hereafter, yet he was still persuaded that his vast heaving audience, the most upright and farseeing which he had ever seen assembled in his long memory of the Park's history, would march, shoulder to shoulder, twenty abreast if need be, in one mighty all-conquering phalanx, TO THE GATES—in such accents had the people of Paris been roused by the *ça ira* and sent to storm the Bastille. There, outside the gates, beyond the eye of any prying policeman and beyond the range of their thumping boots, where authority could still be successfully defied, he would be prepared to discuss in the strictest confidence with any curious client either the Swedish banking system or the likely fall in the value of the rupee or any other convenient financial topic 'under the blue canopy of heaven'. All the accumulated knowledge of the House of Rothschild would be at the disposal of the favoured few, the tramping masses, who would march with him, 'to the great rosy dawn', TO THE GATES, to death or glory.

As it happened, he lived, rickety and rosy to the end, to the age of seventy-five and died, as he was born, out of pocket. He himself once wrote: 'Most people, says a brilliant writer, are other people. I have never had any difficulty in remaining myself.' It had not been quite as easy as that; all manner of circumstances combined to prevent him from succeeding. But he did seem to create himself more than any other human specimen, and in the process he became the best one-man act London ever saw in his own time at least, a priceless piece of England's endless loot from across the Irish sea.

SIX

Philosopher-Englishman

'He was a warm friend, not to liberty merely, but to English liberty.'

> LORD JOHN RUSSELL, grandfather of Bertrand Russell, writing of his ancestor, William Lord Russell, executed by Charles II on 21, July 1683.

MY FIRST INTRODUCTION TO Bertrand Russell occurred when someone at Oxford gave me a copy of his book, *The Conquest of Happiness*. Then, a few weeks later, he turned up in person for a University meeting of some sort, spreading his own special blend of wit and wisdom and beaming with happiness. Who could resist so radiant a practitioner of his own theories?

I reread that volume recently, exactly fifty years after its first publication, and, amid the modern Muggeridgean gloom, it is a light from another world. Bertrand Russell himself acknowledged that the light of nature shone more brightly in a past age, and in almost everything he ever wrote he strove to recover that particular translucent quality. It is the liberal glow of the eighteenth-century enlightenment which he transmuted into twentieth-century terms more intrepidly than anyone else: the spirit which Thomas Jefferson, with the assistance of Thomas Paine, instilled into the American Declaration of Independence, and which provoked Saint-Just, the twenty-four year old French revolutionary, to declare: 'Happiness is a new idea in Europe.' But it is Bertrand Russell who gave, and can still give, to the word its special English accent. *The Conquest of Happiness* itself was little more than a footnote to his larger philosophical theses, a practical manual not merely worth reading but ready for immediate application in everyday life. It works; contrary to Shakespeare's verdict, here at last a philosopher had appeared who could cure the toothache or at least the slightly less formidable ailments with which psychoanalysts claim to contend.

However, both before and after that little textbook was published, the conquest was carried into many other territories, by taunts, witticisms, light-hearted forays and full-scale philosophical assaults. 'Really high-minded people', he said, 'are indifferent to happiness, especially other people's.' Or again, 'If you wish to be happy yourself, you must resign yourself to seeing others also happy.' Or more aggressively:

> There have been morbid miseries fostered by gloomy creeds, which have led men into profound inner discords that made all outward prosperity of no avail. All these are unnecessary. In regard to all of them, means are known by which they can be overcome. In the modern world, if communities are unhappy, it is because they choose to be so. Or, to speak more precisely, because they have ignorances, habits, beliefs, and passions, which are dearer to them than happiness or even life. I find many men in our dangerous age who seem to be in love with misery and death, and who grow angry when hopes are suggested to them.

That is an extract from *Portraits from Memory*, published nearly thirty years after *The Conquest of Happiness*. It was not, heaven forgive us for even mentioning the term in such a connection, the consistency of a feeble mind. It was all part of the spacious liberating doctrine of one who—more than any great man of his century, as I shall try to hint later—never sought to dodge the realities, bitter, tragic or whatever else they might be, which most directly challenged his creed. He could after all put Malcolm Muggeridgism or Christopher Bookerism or Bernard Levinism or whatever label may be attached to the latest outbursts of mystical reaction in some perspective. He wrote in that same *Portraits from Memory*:

> For over two thousand years it has been the custom among earnest moralists to decry happiness as something degraded and unworthy. The Stoics, for centuries, attacked Epicurus who preached happiness;

they said that his was a pig's philosophy, and showed their superior virtue by inventing scandalous lies about him. One of them, Cleanthes, wanted Aristarchus persecuted for advocating the Copernican system of astronomy; another, Marcus Aurelius, persecuted the Christians; one of the most famous of them, Seneca, abetted Nero's abominations, amassed a vast fortune, and lent money to Boadicea at such an exorbitant rate of interest that she was driven into rebellion.

Our English Epicurus was the target, throughout most of his life, of lies hardly less scandalous, but fortunately he devised for himself a shield which will never be penetrated. He translated the word freedom from Greek and Roman and any other language into the purest English, or rather he saw how the English people and so many English writers had been engaged in this work before him, and not merely those directly in the liberal or revolutionary tradition but, hardly less, men like Francis Bacon, Thomas Hobbes, David Hume; all these too are enfolded into the great Bertrand Russell synthesis and help to make that shield irrefragable.

One part of the debt, his and ours, must be accorded to an English phenomenon, the Whig aristocracy which somehow made a most appealing virtue of not caring a damn for anybody. Hard, self-centred, materialist, pleasure-loving, it still offered, against all the odds, and in contra-distinction to what was happening in almost every other country at the time, the essential protection for scepticism and the thought of the future. Bertrand Russell was born into the bosom of it and never wanted to disown his heritage although he came to appreciate its insufficiency. Daring and eccentric thought was encouraged at his fearless old grandmother's knee. 'Thou shalt not follow a multitude to do evil' was her favourite text. At the age of two, young Bertie rebuked a garrulous Robert Browning: 'I do wish that man would stop talking.' And the famous poet did. He could remember his grandfather recalling a visit to Napoleon in exile on Elba and a niece of Talleyrand giving him chocolates. He went to church with Sir Charles Dilke and often wondered what the Liberal statesman's thought must have been when he heard the Seventh Commandment. He shook hands with Parnell and Michael

Davitt, and recollected, still with a tremor, how the hawk's eye of Mr. Gladstone had quelled even his formidable grandparents. He wrote a loving essay on that grandfather, one which can help us to understand better than the historians why Lord John Russell had such a hold on the affections of his countrymen, yet the essay too, has its hints of criticism.

> My grandfather belonged to a type which is now extinct, the type of the aristocratic reformer whose zeal is derived from the classics, from Demosthenes and Tacitus, rather than from any more recent source. They worshipped a goddess called Liberty, but her lineaments were rather vague.

But was that quite fair to one who, after the true English style, battled for so many particular liberties? Moreover, Lord John Russell was more fascinated by the name and superscription of his ancestor Lord William Russell than by any Roman—the same of whom Bertrand Russell wrote: 'Of remote ancestors I can only discover one who did not live to a great age, and he died of a disease which is now rare, namely, having his head cut off.' No other family in English history can claim to have worshipped the Whig goddess so long and so nobly, and in the process they reshaped her limbs to match the modern age.

But it was not achieved, in Bertie's own case, without much pain and trial. Due perhaps to the death of his mother and father in his infancy, he was inexpressibly lonely and shy and awkward. He was blessed or cursed by a Puritan soul, weighed down by a sense of sin and the wickedness of sex. To achieve his own liberation from this encircling darkness was a Herculean labour, and doubtless this is the reason why in his books he could so well strike off the chains of others. But the feat in his own case was accomplished by the most original means. His introduction to Euclid—at the age of eleven—was 'one of the great events in my life, as dazzling as first love'. He rejected suicide 'because I wished to know more of mathematics'. And scarcely less excruciating was the story of the young man who fell disastrously in love with the Quaker girl, who thought sex was not merely wicked but beastly: the two condemned by the general ignorance of the time to endure the most haunting Victorian terrors. Poor Bertie had indeed to find his own way to the conquest of each particular happiness—even drink:

> I did not take to drink until the king took the pledge during the first war. His motive was to facilitate the killing of Germans, and it therefore seemed as if there must be some connection between pacifism and alcohol.

As usual, he saw the comedy of his situation, but he could, without histrionics, be truly noble too.

The picture of what Bertrand Russell meant to those, young and old, who refused to fight in the 1914–1918 war is presented best of all by Lytton Strachey. Lord Russell, on the scaffold in 1683, could not offer a braver example:

> Bertie's lectures help one. They are a wonderful solace and refreshment. One hangs upon his words, and looks forward to them from week to week, and I can't bear the idea of missing one. I dragged myself to that ghastly Caxton Hall yesterday . . . It is splendid the way he sticks at nothing—governments, religions, laws, property, even Good Form itself—down they go like ninepins—it is a charming sight! And then his constructive ideas are very grand; one feels one has always thought something like that—but vaguely and inconclusively; and he puts it all together and builds it up, and plants it down solid and shining before one's mind. I don't believe there's anyone quite so formidable to be found just now upon this earth.

That was in February 1916. Throughout that war, he hurled his whole fragile frame against established institutions until, happily, they put him safely behind bars and lifted the anxiety that he might not be resisting ardently enough. ('Prison has some of the advantages of the Catholic Church.')

Yet if any might consider that his finest hour, a finer one quickly followed. The months which marked the ending of that war and the year or two which followed were among the most tumultuous and seminal in the history of modern Socialism. They

were the years of the Russian revolution, of a moment of
European opportunity which was lost, of a moment for England
too. Bertrand Russell wrote in March 1918, while the tumult was
all around him, a book, *Roads to Freedom*, which showed how
deep were the sources of his democratic Socialism, how much he
respected the Marxist tradition but how much he feared and
hated its totalitarian potentialities. What other Socialist, writing
at that hour, could so readily and appositely see his books republished today? And it was not merely his deliberate, published
works. 'I am troubled at every moment by fundamental questions,
the terrible, insoluble questions that wise men never ask'—so he
wrote from Petrograd in May 1920, but the place and time could
be endlessly multiplied. He was always ready to pose the truly
awkward dilemmas, and time and again he swam against the
stream, risked reputation and livelihood to state and act upon his
arduously-discovered opinions. Few figures in history can match
his persistent intellectual courage. He was the twentieth-century
Voltaire, and one, moreover, who never bowed to any power and
principality whatever. Here again, just to select one glance from a
hundred equally penetrating, is his 1920 view of the world, on the
eve of his departure for revolutionary Russia. How freshly the
words still read; how closely interwoven his story appears to be
with that of the human race itself:

Reason and emotion fight a deadly war within me, and leave me no
energy for outward action. I know that no good thing is achieved
without fighting, without ruthlessness and organisation and disci-
pline. I know that for collective action the individual must be turned
into a machine. But in these things, though my reason may force me
to believe them, I can find no inspiration. It is the individual human
soul that I love—in its loneliness, its hopes and fears, its quick
impulses and sudden devotions. It is such a long journey from this to
armies and states and officials, and yet it is only by making this long
journey that one can avoid a useless sentimentalism.

That was Bertrand Russell in 1920; he kept his balance, amid all
the storms that blew. Thanks to his scepticism about the Soviet
revolution, thanks to his boldness in declaring his doubts, it

might have been expected that the Establishment would rush to embrace him. But no; he was more untouchable than ever. For it was during the twenties and early thirties that he expounded his views on marriage and morals in a manner which outraged Christian and kindred orthodoxies. He did it with a ferocious deliberation. Nothing angered him more than the way the English law or legal system seemed to operate. Books about sex which could be understood only by the middle or upper classes were not prosecuted; books about sex, which could be understood by working people and which might spare them endless, needless misery, were to be tracked down and suppressed by policemen who did not know what they were doing and magistrates and legislators who presumably did. *Marriage and Morals*, published in 1929, contained pages of divine, or rather, I suppose we should better call it, human, fury. It was written in a language every single word of which could be understood by everybody; it is, I suppose, the book which more than any other opened the gates to the truly liberating aspects of the permissive age which came two or three generations later. He said what others said, but he said it more gaily, more mercilessly, as well as more clearly. I once wrote to him, as editor of *Tribune*, asking him to review a book on the subject and received in reply this treasure:

> Dear Michael Foot,
> I have read the document on Sexual Offenders and Social Punish-ment with great interest and surprised approval. I should be very glad if homosexuality between adults ceased to be a crime, and if I thought that I could hasten reform in this matter by expressing approval of the report, I would certainly do so. But, in view of the fact that I have been judicially pronounced 'lewd, lecherous, lascivious and obscene', I fear that my support might do more harm than good. The comment on my book *Marriage and Morals* which is made in the report concerns only sacred prostitution in antiquity, and does not seem to me sufficiently important to need a reply.
> Yours sincerely,
> Russell.

But let me set beside that masterpiece another burst of astrin-gency. Just after that visit to Oxford recorded earlier I was engaged in organising an all-party anti-Nazi demonstration, and received the following from the Deudraeth Castle Hotel, in North Wales, on 14 November 1933:

> I am sorry to inconvenience you in arranging your meeting, but I can't speak with Pollitt. I was at an anti-Fascist meeting in London when, after Ellen Wilkinson had shown implements of torture used by the Nazis, Pollitt made a speech saying 'we' would do all the same things to them when 'our' turn came. One was forced to consider that if he had his way he would be just as bad as they are. I know and admire Toller, and I know Pollitt.
> Yours very truly.

The reference to judicial proceedings was to the New York Court where the pronouncement of prosecuting counsel was indeed even more elaborate than this letter records. He called Russell's writings as a whole 'lecherous, libidinous, lustful, venereous, erotomaniac, aphrodisiac, irreverent, narrowminded, untruthful, and bereft of moral fibre', to which Russell modestly retorted that the point was somewhat simpler. 'It is', he said, 'the principle of free speech. It appears to be little known. If therefore anyone should require any further information about it I refer him to the United States Constitution and to the works of the founders thereof.' No one was better qualified than himself to make that reference, and especially to Thomas Jefferson, the nearest thing to an English Whig who had ever held high office beyond our English shores, one qualified to take his place at the side of the Russells and one of whom Bertrand Russell had taken the precaution of writing a suitable encomium.

Sometimes friends would plead with the philosopher-Englishman to return to the academic studies from which he had been expelled by universities on both sides of the Atlantic. 'The fact is', he replied once, 'I am too busy to have any ideas worth having, like Mrs. Eddy who told a friend of mine that she was too busy to become the second incarnation.' Or he would offer his view on philosophers generally and their chronic timidity, or their particular vices—'I disapprove of Plato because he wanted to prohibit all music except Rule Britannia and The British

Grenadiers. Moreover, he invented the Pecksniffian style of *The Times* leading articles.' At that, one can perhaps hear from many quarters the rising mutter of protest against the 1914 pacifist, the 1940 emigré, the father of our permissive, decadent society, the friend of every country but his own, the scoffer at every British institution, not to mention still more heavenly bodies. How swiftly the features can be twisted to fit the caricature which made him so often the butt of respectable, diehard xenophobic fury. But how sure, if unexpected, was his own answer to all such slanders. 'Love of England is very nearly the strongest emotion I possess . . . the history of England for the last four hundred years is in my blood . . . I simply cannot bear to think that England is entering on its autumn of life—it is too much anguish . . .' It was in such a mood that he returned to England having barely survived years of suffocating exile in the United States. Not merely did he rejoice in the feeling of home; not merely was it agreeable no longer to be treated as a malefactor. Not so long afterwards, honours were on the way, and the only one worth having and probably the only one he would ever have accepted. Thanks to his opposition to communism, maybe, or thanks to some ill-advised but much-misinterpreted words about dropping the atom-bomb on Russia, the English Establishment felt the time had come to fold this eighty-year old rebel to its bosom. Anyhow, a scene of matchless combined irony and comedy followed. Bertrand Russell went to Buckingham Palace to receive the Order of Merit from an affable but somewhat embarrassed George VI. How could the King behave towards 'so queer a fellow, a convict to boot'? In fact, he remarked: 'You have sometimes behaved in a way which would not do if generally adopted.' The instant reply which sprang to Russell's mind was: 'Like your brother.' But he refrained from uttering the words and was always glad that he did so. Instead, knowing that the King must be referring to such matters as his record as a conscientious objector and feeling that the remark could not be left to pass in silence, he said: 'How a man should behave depends upon his profession. A postman, for instance, should knock at all the doors in a street at which he has letters to deliver, but if anyone else knocked on all doors, he would be considered a public nuisance.' It is not clear whether the point was appreciated and, in any case, everyone probably thought that Bertrand Russell's 'public nuisance' days were over. Receiving a Nobel Prize to set alongside his OM, he himself felt the onset of an incipient mellow orthodoxy. 'I have always held that no one can be respectable without being wicked, but so blunted was my moral sense that I could not see in what way I had sinned.'

But in fact he was just stopping to get his iconoclastic breath back in the exhilarating English air. Ahead of him was another lifetime, another marriage, nearly two more decades of campaigning in which he would become the great prophet of the nuclear age, with his gospel that life and joy are better than dusty death. I had the good luck to be present at the meeting in Canon Collins' home in 2 Amen Court when the effective decision which launched the Campaign for Nuclear Disarmament was taken. Bertrand Russell and J. B. Priestley were the two men who above all others gave to the movement its imaginative appeal, its passionate impetus, its intellectual distinction and force. Russell himself had not come to the meeting prepared to advocate a British *unilateral* repudiation of nuclear weapons. He had just written a most powerful declaration—*Commonsense about Nuclear Weapons*—which advocated multi-national nuclear disarmament as the only safe and proper course for mankind as a whole, but he had also just written a scarcely less powerful article which condemned the British bomb as 'a frivolous exercise in national prestige'. It was the decision to demand *unilateral* action by Britain which gave to the Campaign its originality, its fire, its inspiration. Gradually at that meeting, he concurred with the majority opinion, and became the most passionate advocate of the lot. In that very same year when he staked the prestige of his life afresh in such a cause, the Bishop of Rochester was telling him how, in his book *Marriage and Morals*, 'the cloven hoof of the lecher cannot be disguised; it is lechery that has been your Achilles heel'. Things were back to normal.

Of course the old man was not deterred. He was not cowed by the epoch of the cold war when freedom came to be thought of as weakness, and tolerance was compelled to wear the garb of treachery. He continued to rephrase his old liberal creed in a new idiom:

> There are certain things that an age needs, and certain things that it should avoid. It needs compassion and a wish that mankind should be happy; it needs the desire for knowledge and the determination to eschew pleasant myths; it needs, above all, courageous hope and the impulse to creativeness. The things that it must avoid and that have brought it to the brink of catastrophe are cruelty, envy, greed, competitiveness, search for irrational subjective certainty, and what Freudians call the death wish.

Occasionally he did despair and would announce his shame at belonging to the species *Homo Sapiens*, and yet it was at those moments in particular, surely, that his English pride, his love of England's literature, history, language and beauty helped him to recover; helped him to proclaim at the end of his autobiography, one of the truly great autobiographies of all time: 'These things I believe, and the world, for all its terrors, has left me unshaken.'

He became one of the chief glories of our nation and people, and I defy anyone who loves the English language and the English heritage to think of him without a glow of patriotism. The world-famous philosopher, the international publicist, the critic of all principalities and powers, the incorrigible dissenter, the foremost sceptic and exponent of free thought throughout the last half-dozen decades was English to the core, as uniquely English as the free-thinking Whiggery in which he was reared and against whose complacencies and limitations he revolted.

Yet the old Whig or the young Whig, whichever he was, should not quite have the last word. One of his last writings was an article which appeared in *The Times* a few days before men landed on the moon. He argued the issue of whether it was right and intelligent for us to seek to do so with his usual fairness and readiness to see both sides of the question. But there could be little doubt about his verdict, and in the course of the article, which bears the stamp of Bertrand Russell at his greatest, comes the sentence which nobody else could have written: 'It is not by bustle that men become enlightened. Spinoza was content with The Hague, Kant, who is generally regarded as the wisest of

Germans, never travelled more than ten miles from Konigsberg.'
Our philosopher loved his home and his country too. He was a
passionate patriot. In his nineties, he had caught the ear of the
whole wide world as well as his countrymen, and my guess is that
his last, almost his everlasting, service to the British people will be
that, now and hereafter, countless millions of the world's
inhabitants will learn to speak the international language in the
pure English of Bertrand Russell.

SEVEN

Knight Errant of Socialism

Brave to the point of folly, and as humane as he was brave, no man in his generation preached republican virtue in better English, nor lived it with a finer disregard of self.

H. N. BRAILSFORD, in his
essay on Thomas Paine.

HIGH UP ON ANY LIST of classics in Socialist literature, I would include a modest little volume in the Home University Library, first published in 1913, called *Shelley, Godwin and Their Circle* by H. N. Brailsford. Brailsford himself once told me that it was Shelley who made him a Socialist, and here is the proof. Here in this volume is fittingly portrayed the ferment which the French Revolution produced in the English mind, and which later found expression in Chartism and in the revolt against the savageries of nineteenth-century industrialism and modern imperialism, and in the ideals of twentieth-century democratic Socialism.

The book is well-nigh perfect. Every sentence rings true. Every page glows with a splendid ardour. Is there, for example, in the whole range of English literature a better tribute by one liberal spirit to another than Brailsford's twenty-page essay on Thomas Paine? The opening paragraph sounds like a tocsin:

'Where Liberty is, there is my country.' The sentiment has a Latin ring; one can imagine an early Stoic as its author. It was spoken by Benjamin Franklin, and no saying better expresses the spirit of eighteenth-century humanity. 'Where is not Liberty, there is mine.' The answer is Thomas Paine's. It is the watchword of the knight errant, the marching music that sent Lafayette to America and Byron to Greece, the motto of every man who prizes striving above enjoyment, honours comradeship above patriotism, and follows an idea that no frontier can arrest.

It was that same watchword which sent Brailsford himself to enlist in the Greek forces in the war with Turkey in the 1890s. He was always a knight errant in Socialist politics, whether the battlefields were real or imagined. Never did a man so completely subordinate his own personal interests to the cause in which he believed. Rarely has anyone striven so persistently and so passionately to translate word into deed, to make the one inextricable from the other.

He was, and remains, the greatest Socialist journalist of the century, or at least, the greatest of those who wrote in the English language. His only competing claimant for the title is Robert Blatchford, and perhaps the fair way to apportion glory between the two is to invent two different competitions. Blatchford doubtless made more Socialists than Brailsford; indeed my guess is that he probably made more than all the other Socialist propagandists rolled into one. He spoke more directly to the heart of his English working-class readers than anyone has done since, and, in his spare time, or rather as a principal accompanying preoccupation, he was an unrivalled popular educator. How many millions did he teach to read, to love books, to imbibe their Socialism, almost unconsciously, between the lines? Brailsford did not have that gift, at least not in Blatchford's overflowing measure. He had not the common touch of unfailing readability, the quality of Blatchford or, say, Daniel Defoe, or William Cobbett, or Thomas Paine himself. But in most other qualities he was supreme. He had an intellectual passion to which Blatchford never aspired; a determination to ransack the truth from any situation and to tell it with all the power at his command; a combination of honesty and courage and astringency which put all rivals in the shade; an individual streak of mordancy which gave his own character to everything he wrote. Shamefully, his journalism or substantial sections of it have never been properly collected and republished as it should be. However, his books, a few of them masterpieces, do convey the same sense of urgency and exhilaration with which his journalism was impregnated. He could write about Shelley or Thomas Paine or the Levellers as if they were his own living comrades. He could turn the pages of history into modern battlecries. Within him the past and the present were fused into a single revolutionary force.

And yet, before these high claims may be accepted, it is necessary to remove some legitimate objections or misapprehensions. Hardly ever in his life did he receive unqualified acclaim. He was always just out of step, even with his closest associates. He was rarely, if ever, the foremost spokesman of a particular campaign. He repeatedly devoted his whole soul to lost causes. Such features of his political record may give the momentary impression that he must have been argumentative, priggish even, too fastidious in his choice of means and allies, and ready to set sectarian purity above rough victory for the ideals he cherished. Did he not even perhaps have a taste for martyrdom? But any such suggestions must be swept aside at once and for ever. In personal dealings he was diffident, modest, and exquisitely gentle. He had a soft, precise, insistently courteous manner of speech which made the epigrammatic flashes all the more startling. His scruple about forms of political action had a peculiar combined derivation; he had a non-conformist conscience and a Marxist imagination and a romantic Shelleyan faith in the perfectibility of man and, more especially, woman.

When I first encountered him, at the time the Socialist League was formed in the early thirties or a few years later when *Tribune* was first published, the individuality of his political stance was marked with especial sharpness. He had only recently broken with his old friends of the Independent Labour Party, whose paper the *New Leader* he had once edited with a distinction which made it nationally, indeed internationally, famous. His breach with them was not due to any new-found respect for what he derided as 'the slouching leadership' of the official Labour Party. He, like most other Socialists of the time, had had to pick their path between the Right-wing of the Party which had only escaped from 'MacDonaldism' by the narrowest of margins and a variety of Left-wing lurches towards sectarian impotence or the Communist Party. As the horrors, and the opportunities, of the decade unfolded—the rise of Fascism, and the rise too, as is customarily and conveniently forgotten, of a predominantly Socialist opposition to the assault on the most elementary standards of human decency—Brailsford with his boundless romantic faith in Socialism as an international creed was better qualified than anyone to give the necessary summons to resistance. He did so, with all his eloquence and courage, as the European crisis mounted to each fresh climax; when, for example, Dollfuss machine-gunned the Socialists in Vienna, when Mussolini invaded Abyssinia, when Franco invaded Spain. Yet all through these years of agony he conducted, single-handed in the British Left-wing press, a persistent criticism of the Stalin show trials in the Soviet Union.

Almost the entire Labour movement in Britain, Left, Right and Centre, was blindly, vehemently eager to be pro-Russian and pro-Stalin. Brailsford himself had written tens of thousands of words defending the Russian Revolution; more than almost any other Western Socialist journalist he had seen the early years of the Soviet Revolution with his own eyes and his own faith. The moment of the thirties was not inviting for anyone to step out of the popular Left line, particularly after the spring of 1936 when Spain was afire, and the flames might engulf all Europe. Militant Socialism moved to the tramp of the International Brigade. How deeply the Left craved to give the benefit of all the doubts to Moscow! No one who did not live through that decade can quite appreciate how overwhelming that craving was. If Juan Negrin, the valiant, inspired, highly discriminating leader of Spanish democracy knew the necessity of embracing his Soviet ally, who were the rest of us to cavil?

But Brailsford would not be budged from his allegiance to his own first principles. He had been the friend of many of those called 'the traitors and the wreckers', Radek, Bukharin, and many more. He would not betray them and the finest ideals of the Soviet Revolution itself. 'One begins by suppressing Mensheviks, one ends by suppressing Trotsky', he wrote. Week by week in his articles in *Reynolds News*, he struggled against the flood, and the Socialist defence of freedom which he asserted more bravely than anyone else had a significance for the whole future of Socialism. A Socialism which did not embrace freedom as it most precious strand was for him no Socialism at all. In him, the best and only the best of the liberal heritage became intertwined with the exposure of capitalist economics. Voltaire stood beside Marx in his gallery. (His *Voltaire*, also in the Home University Library, is another classic).

Brailsford drew his richest inspiration from English sources, but, unlike so many English Socialists, he never weakened in his appreciation of the greatness of Marx. Rather, he saw him, like his other heroes, in a spacious international context. He wrote in *Property or Peace?* (published in 1934):

> The world may one day come to join in the honour that Russia pays to Marx. But the world will then be a medieval monastery, unless, while it honours him, it is free to doubt and deny every word he uttered. On no other terms can the human reason live. Religious faith is vital just in so far as it dare listen to an atheist. Socialist conviction is genuine, only in so far as it will open its ears to the classical economists. In so far as any society departs from this principle, it lessens its own intellectual vigour and betrays the spirit of science.

The extreme terms in which Brailsford stated his intellectual allegiance to Marxism should be constantly reiterated: thus, beneath the darkening shadows of Nazism and Stalinism, he contributed something of the purest nobility to Socialist thought and history. In a sense, it was his finest hour. He was almost alone in combining such a perception of all the monstrous horrors of the age with an unwavering determination still to act—alone certainly in the eloquence with which he both analysed the scene and issued the call to action. Yet, thanks to that perception, to which no power on earth could prevent him from giving utterance, it is *his* writings on those mighty themes which can better endure scrutiny three-quarters of a century later than those of any other Socialist of the age. It was not his last service to the cause of Socialism, but it is one that still shines with a matchless splendour.

Yet it may be objected: Brailsford's critique of Stalinism, indispensable, courageous and far-seeing though it may be, was still a by-product of his thought and of events. What of a larger Socialist theme which necessarily figures more prominently in his writings, and which he had made peculiarly his own, and where his power of prophecy, his interpretation of Marxism, can be exposed as a most misleading instrument and guide? The question cannot be dodged. As a journalist—for many years, for example, the editor of the Independent Labour Party's weekly the *New Leader*—he was required, as Socialist editors always are, to write on every subject under the sun and moon. Long before Keynes and Beveridge and with much more acknowledgement to his tutor, he had grasped and applied J. A. Hobson's analysis of the causes of capitalist slump, deduced no doubt from Marx's *Das Kapital*. But he also learnt from Hobson (Lenin also was not too proud to do), how Marxist economics could and should be extended to establish a full-scale critique of imperialism—a thesis developed most famously in *The War of Steel and Gold*, published first of all a few months before the outbreak of the 1914 war, and then in the later years in such volumes as *Rebel India* or *Property or Peace?*, and it merged too into his frequent articles and pamphlets on the origins of the 1914–1918 war and on the role of Germany both in those pre-1914 years and thereafter. He was not, and he never became, as some of his pamphleteering opponents at the time had alleged, an apologist for German policy and German imperialism; that was merely the vicious taunt to which he exposed himself by his persistence in attacking the policies of the Entente powers before 1914 or the Versailles powers after 1918. Maybe, in striving to adjust the balance, he did trap himself into an illegitimate pro-German sentiment. But that is not the core of the controversy. The question is: did his neo-Marxism, his neo-Hobsonism, his elevation of imperialism into the central place in his theory, lead him and others into a false appreciation of the causes of the two world wars of the century—no trifling criticism for sure, if indeed the charge can be driven home?

The criticism has been delivered most formidably by A. J. P. Taylor, once in his volume on the pre-1914 years* and again in his lectures, *The Troublemakers*, and in one of these the contest seems to be initiated with a knock-out. There, a conclusion from *The War of Steel and Gold*, published in March 1914, is quoted:

The dangers which forced our ancestors into European coalitions and Continental wars have gone never to return . . . It is as certain as

---

*The Struggle for Mastery in Europe 1848–1918, Oxford.

anything can be, that the frontiers of our modern national states are finally drawn. My own belief is that there will be no more wars among the Six Great Powers.

Clearly, when the next edition of the same book appeared in 1915, some modification was called for. The last sentence quoted above was omitted, but another was inserted in a preface thus:

> It seems to me doubtful whether [questions of nationality] could have made a general war, had not colonial and economic issues supplied a wider motive for the use of force.

And then again in the postscript:

> War could never have come about save for these sordid colonial and economic issues . . . France is defending the colonies and especially Morocco. Germany is attacking and the Allies are maintaining the present distribution of colonies and dependencies. The stakes lie outside Europe, though the war is fought on its soil.

By contrast, it is hardly overstating the case to say that A. J. P. Taylor's historical verdict, after the most scrupulous, modern and original examination of the evidence, reaches the exactly opposite conclusion. The decisions of the great powers were shaped not by any estimate of the stakes outside Europe but by calculations or miscalculations about the balance of power in Europe itself. Marxism, for all its much-trumpeted world-vision, or Marxism as interpreted by Brailsford, attributed too much discernment and rationality to the leaders of 'finance capitalism' who controlled events. Strategy, not economics, governed diplomacy, and the strategy might have no more decipherable aim than diplomatic gain in 'the perpetual quadrille of the balance of powers'. So fears, often unfounded, bred wars. Taylor insisted:

> The war of 1866, like the war of 1859 before it and the wars of 1870 and 1914 after it, was launched by the conservative power, the power standing on the defensive, which, baited beyond endurance, broke out on its tormentors. Every war between great powers [between 1866 and 1914] started as a preventive war, not as a war of conquest.

No fair-minded student of this controversy can deny that Alan Taylor does make a considerable dent in the Brailsford case; but does that admission also mean that his many books on this subject are robbed of their potency and appeal? If this theoretical heart is knocked out, what life can possibly remain in the rest of the work? The curious answer is, I believe, that, thanks to the fact that Brailsford was only superficially writing in strict economic terms, the value of his books is scarcely touched. He was never much attracted by the supposed inexorable necessities of Marxism. He was never entranced by the all-consuming dominance of economics, Marxist or any other. He was much more concerned with the victors and the victims in the class war; no one could doubt *that* reality. He was outraged by all the indecencies and savageries inflicted on human beings in the name of Empire and its trappings, and no Marxist theory was needed to instil that sense in his mind and heart. Whenever he wrote about imperialism his words scorched. 'Property must go armed', he said, and the aphorism ranks with the greatest of Marxist revelations. The spectacle of imperialist oppression in every guise or disguise unloosed within him a scorn, a fury, a passion which no soft excuses could ever abate. If his theory and nature did not accord due weight to the calculations of diplomacy in the pre-1914 or the pre-1939 periods, the balance is much more than restored by his deeper imaginative understanding of the spirit of revolt which in this century has shaken to their ruin all the old empires, and a few of the new ones too. When he set out on his first anti-imperialist odyssey in 1897, almost all those old elaborate imperial courts and structures, even the Turkish one, looked strong, well-nigh invincible; when he died in 1958, they had all, without exception, vanished from the world stage. And his pen was one of the weapons which had assisted in their disappearance. Revolutionaries in every continent where the English language prevailed—in India, above all—read Brailsford. He had translated Shelley and Voltaire and Karl Marx into sentences they could all understand.

Impossible indeed to write about any aspect of Brailsford's life without invoking his inheritance from the past; it was his constant, treasured companion. And here was one reason why he, in the service of another of his great causes, the pre-1914 fight for women's suffrage, could set the struggle in its proper setting. The suffragette movement was looked upon by some at the time, and much less excusably has been treated by some historians since, as a distraction from the great historical mainstream of democratic emancipation. Brailsford knew better; he was steeped in the writings of John Stuart Mill and Mary Wollstonecraft, and indeed of Shelley and Thomas Paine who had been pioneers of this cause along with the others. Hurling himself into the struggle with all his customary zest, he was soon horrified to discover that he was thrust into controversy with some of his closest liberal associates. He was working at the time on the *Daily News*; a Liberal newspaper then in its greatest days, edited by a great Liberal editor, A. G. Gardiner. But when Brailsford, with his colleague, H. W. Nevinson, was confronted at last with the fact that their newspaper was ready to condone the forcible feeding of suffragettes in prison, they wrote to *The Times*—on 5 October 1909—a letter which concluded with these paragraphs:

> At the outset the Government treated the movement with blind contempt. The movement grew under persecution. Exasperation begat violence, and with suffering came a bravery and a spirit of self-sacrifice which no penalty can crush. The weeks as they pass are bringing us nearer to the phase of mortal tragedy. To our minds the graver responsibility will fall on the members of a nominally democratic party who have turned their backs upon a gallant movement of emancipation, and, above all, on 'the great leader', (that is, the Prime Minister, Asquith) whose obstinate refusal to the appeals even of the constitutional women has made at each repetition a multitude of converts to violence. Lest we should seem in our strictures on Liberalism and its organs in the Press to be guilty of inconsistency, we wish to take this opportunity of stating that, despite our warm approval of the Budget [Lloyd George's People's Budget, of course], we have resigned our positions as leader-writers on the *Daily News*. We cannot denounce torture in Russia and support it in England, nor can we advocate democratic principles in the name of a party which confines them to a single sex.

Thereafter Don Quixote turned his energies, without a moment's delay or relaxation, to the pursuit of the cause. He campaigned on suffragette platforms. He crossed lances with the new Home

Secretary, Winston Churchill, and won the contest so unmerci-
fully that more than half a century later Churchill's biographer,
Randolph, was still wisely unwilling to risk renewing the
argument. He worked mightily behind the scenes to replace the
danger of fresh violence with conciliation. He became secretary of
the so-called Conciliation Committee. And the cause came so
near to victory. On 12 May 1912, at the Connaught Rooms in
London, Brailsford made the speech celebrating the 'Second
Reading Majority' of a few days before:

> I am not nervous about the result. And that is not because I am
> naturally of a sanguine disposition. I think, in point of fact, that the
> only service I may have been able to render to this cause came from a
> certain cynicism of disposition which taught me to see that while you
> were talking about your emancipation, the only thing that concerned
> the House of Commons was not your freedom, not your elevation,
> not the future of the human race, but simply, solely their own
> constituencies, their own fortunes, their own party calculations.

And that, be it not forgotten, was the great pre-war Liberal
House of Commons, but Brailsford continued:

> The honour has fallen to me of proposing the toast of 'Votes for
> Women' but I am not going to identify that toast with the Bill before
> the House of Commons. It is a compromise. It has the greyness and
> inadequacy of every compromise. I listened throughout the debate
> last week to the discussion on the political status of women, and as it
> went on I asked myself whether you and I and all of us had not been
> perpetuating a sort of practical joke. We have dreamed our dreams
> while we have talked about something so relatively small as this
> matter of parliamentary voting, so modest in this Conciliation Bill.
> But I question if the men on whose decision your fortunes rest fully
> realise that what is at stake is anything larger than their own future
> and the fortunes of their party. I do not think it has yet dawned upon
> them that what is really at issue is nothing less than a revolution in
> European civilisation. It will be achieved half-consciously amid the
> pettiness of partisan debates. But we at least know what it means. We
> know what it means for the cause of the poor and the sweated, for the
> widows and the women of the slums. But above all we know that it
> means a transformation in the mind and spirit of every human soul
> which comes into the world a woman. It means the removal from

every growing mind and every developing spirit of the shackles which would otherwise have bound her brain, fettered her limbs. It is a mental emancipation and a moral awakening that lie at the root of this great cause of ours.

And so it was—after a few more years of unconscionable delay. Even the compromising Conciliation Bill, despite its Second Reading victory, was still blocked by male obstinacy, fear and stunted imagination, and perhaps even more by Asquithian double-talk and double-dealing. The romantic Brailsford had foreseen the future so much more clearly than the foremost Liberal statesmen of his time.

Brailsford's magnificent gesture of resignation from the *Daily News* was made when he was thirty-six years old; he never secured a regular job on a daily newspaper again. That was another of his finest hours; they were constantly recurring. Perhaps he later had doubts, or at least it became clear how painful were some of the choices he did make. For, thirty years later, on 6 August, 1938, he wrote me a most generous letter about a quarrel I was having with *Tribune*, and here are a few extracts which recalled his own experience:

> [I had to resign] three times in my journalistic career, and each time was in some difficulty until I found other work. So I know it has to be done sometimes, and may cost a lot . . . I had to face a motion demanding my resignation at almost every Board meeting through four years, when I edited the *New Leader*. It wasn't pleasant and in the end I was defeated. But I had the satisfaction of making what I, anyhow, thought a pretty good paper. One may be too subjective— that's in the Liberal-Non-conformist tradition— and forget that to run a good paper matters more than to perform prodigies of conscience. (I too came out of that tradition, and it has poisoned most of my life. One never wholly liberates oneself. It is a great inheritance—to throw away).

Startling sentences indeed, and they still leap from the faded manuscript when I read them. Did he truly mean it? I knew nothing of his personal life, and it was to this I believe he must have been referring. Anyhow, the Brailsford who so brazenly suggested that he had tossed aside his non-conformist conscience, presumably in deference to the masterful, objective Marxist voice overpowering him, was at that very moment defying all the popular storms and temptations on the Left to instruct Socialists on the historic evils of Stalinism—in the years 1937 and 1938, I repeat, long before most of us had heard of Koestler or Orwell or Silone.

However, whatever crises of conscience may have afflicted him in other fields, he never wavered an inch in his allegiance to the cause of women's rights. It was not just a question of a desirable reform; it was a democratic necessity. The dominant sex, he would insinuate, always had some other dominant issue which should be allowed to push the campaign for equality off the agenda altogether. For him, 'Votes for Women' had never been an odd Edwardian affair suddenly blazing across the skies and then vanishing to leave no mark on the politics of the century. It was a major campaign in the great war of liberation in which he never ceased to enlist, and it was fitting that his last service of all took the form of an adventure into the origins of English democracy itself. For long he had contemplated the task, and during the last decade of his life he applied himself devotedly to it. Two years after his death, the wonder appeared: *The Levellers and the English Revolution* by H. N. Brailsford. Edited by Christopher Hill. Cresset Press. Brailsford himself had not been able to apply the finishing touches, and, since he was such a perfectionist in points of literary style, we cannot be sure that the text is all he would have wished. But it speaks for itself.

Who *were* the Levellers? All the great Whig historians, including the last of them, G. M. Trevelyan, had been content to dismiss them in a paragraph or a footnote. 'A few visionaries' was S. R. Gardiner's phrase. Even those sympathetic to their ideas had found it difficult not to be influenced by these serried judgements. John Lilburne had often been regarded more as a brave and endearing eccentric than a figure of historical significance. The ancient sneers of the Royalist writers helped to fortify the usual portrait of a bunch of cranks, men centuries ahead of their time who intruded upon no more than the fringe of great affairs. 'The name of the Levellers', one wrote:

a most apt title for such a despicable and desperate lot to be known by, that endeavour to cast down and level the enclosures of nobility, gentry and propriety, to make us all even, so that even Jack shall vie with a gentleman and every gentleman be made a Jack.

How inconsiderable must these men have been in the stupendous struggle between Roundhead and Cavalier! What dwarfs in the shadow of a Cromwell!

The first big achievement of Brailsford's book was that it shattered this assumption for ever. Never again could the history of the Civil War and the Commonwealth be written in the old terms. 'Enough has come to light in recent years', said Brailsford, 'to compel a revision of the classical story of the Revolution. Not in ideas only but in action, the initiative during this critical phase came from the Levellers. They led the struggle against clericalism and intolerance; they challenged the ascendancy of Holles and his class; they set the Army marching.' Modestly Brailsford did not claim the credit for the discovery; but the beauty of his mind, the sweep of his narrative, the detailed, scrupulous proof he offered in seven hundred massive pages carry conviction for his high claims. What Clarendon did for the Cavaliers, and what Carlyle did for Cromwell, Brailsford did for the Levellers and their associates, and in any proper English library the volumes of these three should be placed on the same shelf.

Of course, a few objections may be heard. In particular, as the devoted editor of Brailsford's volume, Christopher Hill, pointed out, Brailsford may have been wrong in his assertions that the Levellers were demanding *manhood* suffrage; the full democratic claim had not yet been tabled. Alas, too, not even for Brailsford's benefit, could it be claimed that they were demanding *woman-hood* suffrage, and yet he did place special emphasis on the fact— which other historian had ever stopped to do so?—that in 1849 ten thousand women had signed one of the first Leveller petitions and that one thousand of their number had presented it to the House of Commons insisting:

> Have we not an equal interest with the men of this nation in those liberties and securities contained in the *Petition of Right*, and the other good laws of the land?

Certainly no qualifications can alter or injure Brailsford's two main themes. First he showed how much more formidable than anyone had conceived before was the Leveller organisation; how deeply the Army was infected by the doctrine that 'our being soldiers hath not deprived us of our rights as commoners'; how at so many moments of crisis Cromwell was more their servant than their master. And secondly, and more expectedly, in the realm of ideas, he showed how various, how humane and far-seeing, were the anthems which Lilburne and his colleagues could play on their 'eternal trumpet of defiance to all the men and devils in earth and hell'. If he exaggerated the all-embracing nature of their democratic faith, it is still true that they were the first organisers of a democratic party and a citizen army, the first advocates of a secular democratic Republic, the first consistent champions of a genuine tolerance for everyone, for Catholics and Jews no less than good Puritans. 'What is done to anyone may be done to everyone', said Lilburne, and upon that rock he built a programme of reform which most of the free world still has not shown the will to execute. And, bless their revolutionary souls, they called their weekly newspaper, the first of its type, the ancestor of the *New Leader* or *Tribune, The Moderate*, to put all future moderates in their place.

These despised, irresponsible moderates were seeking to pierce the mysteries of the universe as daringly as they argued about society and strategy with their officers in Putney Church. 'They were freemen of the century of Galileo, Harvey and Newton.' Who but Brailsford could have made that claim? It is hardly less bold than his insistence on their direct week-by-week political influence. But the proof was offered in the most perceptive examination of the Levellers' writings ever undertaken; Brailsford knew what qualities weekly immoderate journalism could require. In the end they were crushed. But their sea green ribbons were never trailed through the mud. When Cromwell set out on his terrible mission to Ireland, they would have no part of it. They raised the first English banner against the crime of imperialism as they had set the fashion in so much else. 'It will be no satisfaction to God's Justice', wrote William Walwyn, 'to plead that you murdered men in obedience to your

General.' Here indeed, deeper than in his Marxism, was Brailsford's fury against imperialist oppression traced to its source.

The Levellers is a glorious book. Not only did Brailsford add a new dimension to seventeenth-century history; presented in this context, a whole long list of men acquire a new stature and step forward to enrich still further the richest pages in our history. Richard Overton ('A wit always pays a heavy penalty for amusing Anglo Saxons; he is classed among the not quite respectable'), William Walwyn, Edward Sexby, Henry Marten, Thomas Rainsborough, John Lilburne himself and many more, not overlooking Elizabeth Lilburne or Katherine Chidley and her 'practised pen'. Brailsford would not look upon any scene in our history without asking what the women were doing; the habit started opening before him archives still scarcely scratched by others. Altogether, at last, after three centuries these names begin to get their due and should recover in the eyes of their countrymen the place of honour they once held among 'the plain men' of Cromwell's armies and the London mob. Henry Noel Brailsford was their truest descendant, a knight errant fit to take his place in their company. When he died his friends talked of a monument for him. Here with *The Levellers* it is, an imperishable work of passion, scholarship and art.

EIGHT

The New Machiavelli

He loved Italy as the saints love God.

G. M. TREVELYAN on Garibaldi.

WHEN IGNAZIO SILONE DIED at the age of seventy-eight in a Geneva hospital, in the year 1978, he was given respectful English tributes in a few, a very few, obituary columns. Naturally in Italy more was said and written, although for some reason not easily discernible he is one of the prophets who was never accorded proper honour in his native land. Yet taking the man and his books together, and they can never be separated, he is one of the great men of the last half-century, of the whole Fascist-Communist epoch in human history. Machiavelli died penniless, was condemned to do most of his work in exile and never saw his great writing published in his lifetime; and yet his became a household name the world over. Ignazio Silone may achieve a similar posthumous conquest in Italy and beyond; his greatness, I believe, is on the same scale. He shows a comparable combination of insight into the tumult of his own age, together with an enduring vision of the heights and depths which human nature can attain, and he combines with it too a splendour and fortitude in his own character which, in some degree, Machiavelli had too.

Silone's first novel, scarcely more than a short story, *Fontamara*, published in 1934, told how Mussolini's Fascism came to a medieval Christian village in the Abruzzi, the scene of all his writings from which he never wished or sought to escape. The plain picture of poverty and cruelty, of the heroism of the rebel and how resistance is born, survives better than most of the rhetoric and poetry of the thirties. Unlike loftier exponents of the anti-Fascist case, Silone never had anything, not a single syllable, to qualify or retract. He never forgot what poverty meant in humiliation of the individual. Years later he was still asserting, with all the passion at his command, that the claptrap about the virtues of poverty is an odious falsehood. In any case, there were no words to spare in *Fontamara*. Only a great mind dares to express itself simply, said Stendhal, and Silone, himself a student of Stendhal, is the best modern exponent of the latter's practice and precept.

The same lack of any necessity to disavow his earlier words and deeds applies to Silone's disillusion with Communism, which he explored in his later novels and expounded best of all in that little-known classic, *The School for Dictators*, the one among his writings which truly deserves its place alongside Machiavelli's *Prince*. Silone at least did see his masterpiece published, but the precise moment and method of publication were wretchedly devised. *The School for Dictators* first made its appearance in 1939, just after a British Prime Minister had been toasting Mussolini in Rome, and just before Stalin made his Pact with Hitler. Most political leaders of that pusillanimous age did not want to learn the truth from anybody, least of all from an Italian exile, an ex-Communist denied entry into Britain.

Moreover, Silone fitted easily into no party or definable group; his every sentence bristled with his own brand of independence. Most members of the legion of literary ex-Communists beat their breasts, and deserted the revolutionary camp altogether, following a well-smoothed track to comfort and complacency. Silone instead purified his Socialist faith, made it an instrument of sharper metal and never lost the dignity and ardour which he had seen in his peasant heroes. Indeed, even in this restricted category of anti-Communist literature, it is too easy to forget what an originator he was. He first found the path which writers like George Orwell and Arthur Koestler were to follow later, and both of them, to their credit it should be quickly added, were later to acknowledge his example.

None of Silone's anti-Communist writings, taken singly, ever achieved the success of Orwell's *Animal Farm* or Koestler's *Darkness at Noon*; none of them could lay claim to the same artistic triumph. But taken together they stated, no less effectively the Socialist answer to Stalinism, and some of the scenes he has described will never fade from the history books.

It was, according to his own description, way back in 1922, as he was leaving Moscow on one occasion, that Alexandra Kollontai had jokingly warned him: 'If you should read in the papers that Lenin has had me arrested for stealing the Kremlin's silverware, it will mean simply that I have not been in full agreement with him on some problem of agricultural or industrial policy.' And it was a year or two later again that another ineffable exchange occurred in Moscow which should surely have shaken the universe. Confronted with a dilemma of tactics posed by the British Communist Party, a Russian expert offered a simple if Jesuitical solution, whereupon the British Communist delegate interrupted: 'But that would be a lie.' Then follows Silone's great scene—'This naïve objection,' he wrote,

> was greeted with a burst of laughter, frank, warm, interminable laughter, the like of which the gloomy offices of the Communist International had certainly never heard, laughter which rapidly spread all over Moscow, since the Englishman's incredibly funny answer was immediately telephoned to Stalin and the most important offices of State, leaving new waves of astonishment and hilarity in its wake, as we learned later. 'In judging a regime it is very important to know what it finds amusing', said Togliatti, who was with me.

But why and how, after moments such as that, did it take so long for the world to unearth the truth? Silone was the most incorruptible of witnesses. Togliatti was a politician of genius. And both, incidentally, had been trained on Machiavelli and Mazzini as well as Marx. A host of the most intelligent and selfless men and women of that age or any other saw what happened in the Kremlin—until, for example, Silone was prompted to ask Togliatti: 'Do you suppose that's the way they do things in the Sacred College of Cardinals? Or in the Fascist Grand Council?' How could Stalinism survive such an inquisition, pressed at a time, be it noted, when Trotsky was still alive and kicking in Moscow?

Silone's simple answers ring truer than any elaborate treatise. He understood why the Communist Party was 'school, church, barracks, family'; he knew that 'consciences are not synchronised like traffic signals'. And he knew why his own brother, tortured to death by the Fascists, proclaimed himself, falsely, a Communist, to honour the creed of defiance, learnt in the Abruzzi. Even when he was risking his life to swear eternal war on the monstrous evil unmasked before him, Silone could not or would not forget the human face of Communism which had first inspired himself and his young comrades.

He once wrote a fierce criticism of modern British writers, accusing them of shirking the great themes, and whether that stone was well-aimed or not, no one can reply that it was thrown from a glasshouse. Silone himself could breathe only on the highest altitudes. He was obsessed by the perpetual interaction of morals and politics, thought and action, ends and means, the flesh and the spirit. He could not stoop. He would castigate not only the gaolers and executioners of totalitarian states, but the literary tradesmen who pandered to the lowest tastes, particularly those who trafficked in eroticism in the name of liberty. For the liberty he treasured, in his work and with his life, was something inexpressibly richer and nobler. Since it had had to be wrested from Fascist thugs and Communist dogmatists, how could it not be? It was not a word but a thing. Indeed, in Silone's hands, many other dusty abstractions regain, like polished silver, a gleaming brightness and purity: honour, conscience, courage, faith. And on a similar reckoning, he saw, as Orwell saw, how human misery can derive from the debasement of language, what stark horror can breed beneath Byzantine pomposity, how words like poverty and slavery must not be allowed soft edges, just as freedom must keep its revolutionary force.

The words and the man perpetually merge; every Silone aphorism seems sharpened by his personality. He was truly a saint, and yet saints who devote their lives to politics can prove to be the most dangerous persecutors of all. Silone knew that better than any of his potential critics, and had devoted his wit to expose the peril. 'This ordinary man', he wrote in *The School for Dictators*,

is a hotch-potch of desires. He likes eating, drinking, smoking, sleeping, keeping a canary, playing tennis, going to the theatre, being well-dressed, having children, stamp-collecting, doing his job, and many other things besides. This is the reason he remains a nobody; he spreads himself over so many little things. But the born politician wants nothing but power and lives for nothing but power. It is his bread, his meat, his work, his hobby, his lover, his canary, his theatre, his stamp album, his life-sentence. The fact that all his powers and energies are concentrated upon one thing makes it easy for him to appear extraordinary in the eyes of the masses and thus become a leader, in the same way as those who really concentrate on God become saints and those who live only for money become millionaires.

Fortunately, this man who guarded his cherished ideas from all assaults with such saint-like fanaticism also possessed the mordancy of a Machiavelli, and he brought this quality to its peak in *The School for Dictators*. Here Thomas the Cynic explained to an aspirant from the United States how to establish a dictatorship in that country ('How can I save America from the Red Menace, if the menace doesn't exist?'). The aphoristic arrows are fired off in all directions and few escaped unscathed: no dictator has ever had trouble finding Civil Servants; if a party calls itself 'radical' it's bound to be moderate; the height of the art of government for our contemporary democratic statesmen (1939, don't forget) seems to consist in accepting smacks in the face to avoid having their posteriors kicked; America, as you know, never had an Age of Enlightenment, and was therefore spared Socialism and the struggles of political ideologies; a sincere orator only feels inconsistent when he is silent.

And yet it is his imagination and his courage, even more than his wit, which will make him so powerful a voice in the years to come: especially for Socialists, to whom he continued to the end to address his strictures, his warnings, his invocations, and his hopes. Socialism, he was convinced, would outlive Marxism, and he said that as one who knew how human and inspiring, no less than corrupting and explosive, Marxism could be:

I cannot conceive of Socialism tied to any particular theory, only to a faith. The more Socialist theories claim to be 'scientific', the more transitory they are. But Socialist values are permanent. The distinction between theories and values is still not clearly enough

understood by those who ponder these problems, but it is fundamental. A school or a system of propaganda may be founded on a
collection of theories. But only a system of values can construct a
culture, a civilisation, a new way of living together as men.

A few have sought, like Silone, to remodel their faith in
democratic Socialism in the light of the experience of Soviet
Communism which has afflicted the East and what Silone calls
'the leprosy of nihilism' which has afflicted the West. But no
other Socialist writer has refashioned the call to action so nobly as
Silone. He never allowed himself to be overwhelmed by cynicism
or lassitude; he kept to the end just as he had infused all his
writings with the spirit of resistance he had learned in the
Abruzzi. 'I don't believe', he said, 'that the honest man is forced
to submit to history,' or, again: 'No predicament, however
desperate, can deprive us of the power to act.' The kinship
between the old Machiavelli and the new one looks closer still.
The old Machiavelli refused to submit to history, much in
accordance with Ignazio Silone's admonition, and yet his books
survived to play a foremost part in reshaping the Italy he loved.

NINE
Vicky

Cold and shrewd philosophers! How compassionately they
smile down at the self-tortures and crazy illusions of poor
Don Quixote; and in all their school-room wisdom they do
not mark that this very Don Quixotism is the most precious
thing in life—that it is life itself—and that Don Quixotism
lends wings to the whole world, and to all in it who
philosophise, make music, plough and yawn!

HEINRICH HEINE.

OVER A PERIOD of some fifteen years up till two days before his
death I met Vicky more and more frequently; he became, I
supposed, just about the closest friend I had. We had fixed a
standing Monday lunch date and often met in the evenings too.
We could resume an argument in the middle of a sentence; I
thought I really knew him. Then one cold afternoon, Charles
Wintour, editor of the *Evening Standard*, rang up and told me he
was dead. I had barely understood at all. Despite persistent
conversations on the fringes of the subject, I had no comprehension of how near his mind was to the end of its tether.

One person at least did comprehend—James Cameron, truly
Vicky's closest associate over a few decades. Their response to
events was continuously and uncannily the same. They often
found themselves, in Cameron's phrase, 'poised between hilarity
and despair'. Incredibly for two such complicated anatomies,
their hearts beat as one. Moreover, for Vicky, James Cameron
always was, as for many of us he remains, the prince of modern
journalists, the reporter who can best place each individual scene
and spectacle in the world-wide drama. He could place Vicky's
death amid that drama too; for Vicky was a casualty of the
Vietnam war and its kindred enormities, not forgetting the

sophistries with which those much nearer home, within his own adopted country and his beloved, wayward Labour movement, excused their part in the holocaust. And if he had lived, which of us would have escaped the lash?

He was a twentieth-century Don Quixote and honoured the mournful knight just as his adored Heinrich Heine, fellow artist, fellow Jew, and kindred spirit, had done before him. Heine wrote:

> My colleague mistook windmills for giants; I, on the contrary, see in our giants of today only ranting windmills . . . I must constantly fight duels, battle my way through untold misery, and I gain no victory which has not cost me something of my heart's blood. Night and day I am sorely beset, for my foes are so insidious that many of them, whom I have dealt a death-blow, still show the semblance of life and appear in all shapes and molest me day and night. What agonies I already have had to endure from these perfidious ghosts!

And that was Vicky too. He had painted a Daumier-like painting of his knight-errant hero, and was justly proud of the technical skill it displayed; wherever he moved, it was given the pride of place on his wall. No doubt was possible; his Don Quixote was a tragic figure. Yet, naturally enough at those lunches, the hilarity quickly subdued the despair, and it was not until after his death that a conversation with his wife, Inge, cast a most curious retrospective glance on their therapeutic effects. Whenever I had sought, born, blind, boneheaded optimist that I was, to cheer him in his most despondent moments, he would come home to dinner more despondent than ever. But when Jimmy had been there, to deepen the darkness from the outset and at every turn in the argument, the balm would take effect and he would return with a renewed light in his eye, the same indeed which, if only I had had the sensitivity to see it, had helped to shed a few gleams into Jimmy's hell. James Cameron, like Vicky, was sometimes derided for his Don Quixotism. Perhaps this was the only form of journalism fully suitable for the age of Auschwitz, and Hiroshima, and Vietnam, and Afghanistan and all such horrors. Together, the two of them, Vicky and Cameron, lifted the old trade to a new level.

Vicky made himself the best cartoonist in the world, the one

proper successor of David Low, a student and example of the
greatest tradition of caricature. It could be argued that others
might equal or occasionally surpass him in draughtsmanship. He
more than restored his pre-eminence with his humour, his
fertility, his diligence, his political insight and instinct. Few
observers have ever studied the English political scene with more
persistence and acumen. He knew every corner of the workshop,
every twist in the game, every shade of character. In this sense his
equipment as a cartoonist was unique. It is hard to believe that
any of his famous predecessors, Gillray, Rowlandson and the rest,
understood the internal operations of British politics as Vicky
made it his business to comprehend them.

And, of course, this extraordinary knowledge was not easily
acquired. If he had not been a genius anyhow, he would have
become one by taking pains. When he arrived in London in the
thirties and got a job on the *News Chronicle* he had none of the
uncanny understanding of English habits, pastimes and idioms
which became one of his strengths. He set about learning them,
by reading, listening and the range of his all-perceptive eye.
Gerald Barry was his first editor and mentor, and Vicky was
always eager to acknowledge the debt. Richard Winnington, and
later James Cameron and Tom Baistow, were his intimate
journalistic confederates. Somehow the greatest days of the *News
Chronicle* were associated with Vicky, and when he left—after
some of his cartoons had been refused publication by Barry's
successors—the Liberal journal seemed preparing for its own
doom.

Then came more strained and strenuous years on the *Daily
Mirror*. Here freedom was complete. Vicky had won the opportunity to say exactly what he wished to a vast national audience.
But year by year his own doubts and anxieties tortured him, to
the amazement of his employers and friends. Somehow he needed
to preach to the unconverted. Somehow he needed to awaken his
enemies. He sought a new context for his message, and found it in
the *Evening Standard*, signing a contract guaranteeing his
freedom more secure than any cartoonist before him, even Low,
had ever had. Little Vicky had become an independent power,
almost the Fifth Estate of the Realm.

Most men who wield such power become corrupted, but here was one of his secrets. He was incorruptible, the most incorruptible man I ever knew. Neither money nor other material offerings could sway him from what he considered the course his conscience dictated. All the other more subtle seductions were equally pushed aside, rejected without reckoning. He could not be bought, browbeaten, or bulldozed. He stood against the world, the proud unshakable anarchist who knew there was a force more explosive than bombs and who, knowing so well how power corrupted others, stayed miraculously immune himself. Above all, he had an abiding compassion, drawn from his heart and nurtured by his love of music, literature and beauty. Some of his victims may find the claim baffling, but if ever they dare breathe a word of dissent, a host of *their* victims from the underworld of the defeated, the forgotten and the maligned, could rally from the depths to defend their champion. Vicky felt for those who suffered, the casualties of war, poverty and persecution, as if the strokes fell across his own back. 'No one ever lost an inch of sleep from any public worry', said Dr. Johnson. Vicky utterly disproved the thesis. He hardly had a full night's rest for most of his adult life, and one cause of his unsettled mind was undoubtedly that he felt more sharply than most of the rest of the human race. He had no armour to protect himself against the twentieth-century horrors.

It was a good day for Britain when he came to these shores. It was even better, the day after and thenceforward, when he resolved to take us at our best liberal word—when he assumed that he would have the right to say what he thought, though the heavens fell and however much all the undercover totalitarians and skin-deep democrats might scream. Curiously, the little Hungarian became a great English patriot, upholding the finest traditions of this land, our most precious treasures of free speech, free thought, the right to laugh at the mighty, the duty to appease the pains of the weak.

When he died tributes flowed in from all over the world to Vicky the artist, the incomparable master of political humour, and some of us in Fleet Street bowed our heads in remembrance of the most lovable companion we ever knew. But the proper epitaph for Vicky was that which Heinrich Heine, whom Vicky so greatly honoured, had asked to be accorded him when he died. He wrote:

> I doubt that I deserve the laurel wreath, for poetry has always been merely an instrument with me, a sort of divine plaything. If you would honour me, lay a sword rather than a wreath upon my coffin; for I was, first of all, a soldier in the war for the liberation of humanity.

Vicky and Heine, divinely gifted, lovers of peace, haters of tyranny, belonged to the same army.

TEN

Randolph

It doesn't matter what you do as long as you don't do it in the street and frighten the horses.

MRS. PAT CAMPBELL, whose comments on many matters were recited with much relish by Randolph Churchill. She was the heroine of another of his favourite tales; how, having safely transformed one of her innumerable suitors from a lover into a husband, she remarked, 'Ah, the peace of the double-bed after the hurly-burly of the *chaise longue*.'

RANDOLPH CHURCHILL and I would wake up every morning, for several weeks on end, polishing the thunderbolts which each hoped to unloose on the unbowed head of the other before the night was done. I was the Labour candidate for Devonport, dourly defending my home town against a Churchillian carpet-bagger. He bustled in like something not merely from another world, but another century, talking as if the place belonged to him, as the Churchills have often done, from the great Marlborough and his Duchess onwards. The brilliant cascade of abuse poured forth in all directions, sometimes drenching his own supporters. They say that the joists and beams of Conservative clubs in Devonport still quiver at the name of Randolph.

Then suddenly, when he learned that he had lost, in the agonising seconds which only parliamentary candidates can appreciate, the storm subsided and all was sweetness and charm. 'I thought you took that marvellously', I felt compelled to acknowledge. 'Yes', he replied, 'I've had plenty of practice.' He had indeed. He lost all the parliamentary contests he ever fought.

(When he actually got in he was unopposed).* Considering his boast at the age of twenty that he might emulate William Pitt and become Prime Minister at twenty-four, considering the family background and the expectations of his doting father, his whole political life might be seen as a crushing defeat.

He did not bury his talents; rather he scattered them in a riot of political profligacy. Way back in the early thirties he tried to batter his path into Parliament *against* the massed power of the Conservative Party machine. He turned up at a famous by-election in Wavertree, Liverpool, as an Independent Conservative. I happened to be present at one of his packed meetings when, mimicking his father, he perorated on the menace of Baldwin's India policy to the Lancashire cotton trade. The periods soared until he was shot down in mid-flight. 'And who is responsible for putting Liverpool where she is today?' he cried, whereupon a voice from the back recalled the devastating blow inflicted upon

---

*I had, during the war, taken the liberty of celebrating these events in a blasphemous document which was designed only for private circulation; here it is:

The Apostles' Creed

Then shall be sung or said the Apostles' Creed by the Minister, and the people standing . . .

I believe in Churchill the Father Almighty, Dictator of Heaven and earth; And in Randolph, his only Son, Who entered politics at Wavertree, Contested the Toxteth division of Liverpool, Fought at Ross and Cromarty, Was roundly defeated, rejected and forgotten: He descended into the Army; The third day he rose again from obscurity; He was returned unopposed for Preston, And sitteth on the right hand of Churchill the Father Almighty; From thence he and his descendants shall continue to govern us through eternity.

I believe in Bracken the Holy Ghost; the Holy Ministry of Information; the Communion of Yes-Men; The Forgiveness of all Churchill's sins; The Resurrection of the Conservative Party, And the tenure of office everlasting. Amen.

And after that these Prayers following, all devoutly kneeling: the Minister first pronouncing with a loud voice,

> *The Lord be with you*
> ANSWER: *And with thy spirit*
> MINISTER: *Let us pray. Lord, have mercy upon us.*
> *Christ, have mercy upon us. Lord, have mercy upon us.*

the city on the previous Saturday; 'Blackburn Rovers!' It almost seemed that the campaign floundered from that moment. But Randolph's achievement was truly amazing. He collected 10,000 Independent votes in a few days and handed the seat on a platter to the Labour Party. And the machine never forgot or forgave, even when his father had helped lead the nation and, more especially, the Conservative Party, cowering beneath his shield, through the valley of the shadow of death.

Not that Randolph never contributed to his own misfortunes, the ostracism, the constantly repeated thud of blackballs; no one could ever say *that*. At Eton he was beaten for some crime he had never committed. When he protested his innocence with customary volubility, the Captain of Games refused to relent: 'Anyway, you have been bloody awful all round—bend down, you're going to have six up.' The words have an authentic ring. 'Bloody awful all round' is the kind of comprehensive verdict which others who had dealings with him were always searching for—politicians, newspaper proprietors, editors, reporters, TV interviewers and, alas, some less able to answer back. Often in Fleet Street I have heard a fellow-journalist, still reeling from the impact, recall how Randolph had set the Thames, the Hudson, the Tiber or the Danube on fire with his boiling intoxicant invective. In how many places, in how many hemispheres, I wonder, did he stand there, unterrified and untameable, while the insults and the champagne bottles hurtled all around?

There were those days in 1938 and 1939, at Beaverbrook's house when he metaphorically coshed any Munichite Minister whom his host had been ill-advised enough to invite to the party. Or the splendid occasion when he turned the Foyle's luncheon table at the Dorchester upside down, knocked Hugh Cudlipp's and Lord Rothermere's heads together, gave his own award to the Pornographer Royal, and launched a one-man campaign to stop newspaper bosses from selling the equivalent of filthy postcards on the street corner. Sunday journalism has never quite been the same since, or rather it was only quite a number of years after he was safely in his grave that the Murdochs and his craven imitators dared to creep out again so brazenly from beneath the stones. Randolph would have stamped upon them.

Invective was his strongest suit but he had real wit too. When an editor of the *Evening Standard* spiked one of his articles on the grounds that it was 'obscure', Randolph replied: 'To the obscure all things are obscure.' When Lord Beaverbrook's valet, who normally referred to his master as 'The Lord', informed Randolph that 'The Lord was walking in St. James's Park,' he insisted: 'On the water, I presume?' Then there was the early hours session in the startled salon in the Marrakesh Hotel when, half-dead, he poured scorn on all the bronzed weaklings who escaped from his entrancing monologue to their beds. A couple of days later after he had been operated upon in London for cancer, my wife found him sitting up, smoking, drinking and protesting to one of the most eminent physicians in the land: 'Stop treating me like an invalid.'

Somehow it is such incidents, senseless or grotesque, which stick in the memory. Somehow his character compensates for all offences and explosions. One feels it was all his own work, achieved against hopeless odds; the spoilt child, the staggeringly handsome adolescent; the illusion that this Adonis could also talk as sparklingly as his father's beloved F. E. Smith, or write as readily as his father's model, Macaulay.

By the age of thirty or earlier, all his juvenile ambitions were shattered. Every time he attempted a political comeback he met fresh rebuffs. Every way he turned he faced the jibe that when nature makes a genius she breaks the mould. But he would not be beaten. He would retire to the garden he loved. He made himself a most formidable journalist, the trade he had never bothered to learn before. He made himself the biographer of his father and set the style for a great book; the father with whom he could quarrel but whose political cause he served with selfless loyalty.

He was outrageous and endearing, impossible and unforgettable, a Churchill who scarcely ever tasted victory, and what super-Churchillian courage that must have called for. Along with his honesty ('Lies are so dull', he would say) and his streaks of kindness, it was this reckless courage which shone most brightly. It could make him magnificent in political controversy, as he had once shown himself on the battlefield.

Friends and enemies would look on, admiring or aghast. Both

enjoyed the witticism when someone said that he was the kind of person who should not be allowed out in private. But it was the private Randolph whose memory many of us treasured. He was a friend and enemy worth having.

ELEVEN

The Greatest Exile

His pen continued an overmatch for the whole brood . . .

RICHARD CARLILE,
imprisoned in 1823 for selling
Paine's *Rights of Man*.

WHEN THOMAS PAINE died in New York on 8 June, in the year 1809, no one took much notice. A Quaker watchmaker, an old Frenchwoman alleged (falsely, as far as we know) to be Paine's mistress, her two little boys and two Negro pall-bearers were the only people at the graveside. Next day the leading New York newspaper supplied an epitaph: 'Paine had lived long (he was seventy-two), done some good, and much harm.'

Few of his legion of enemies spoke in so temperate a tone. Since his return to America in 1802 he had been denounced from the pulpits as the most wanton of blasphemers. Shortly after his death a full-length biography appeared in which accusations of drunkenness, lechery and dirtiness in all his personal habits were added to the charge-sheet. 'He had no country in the world, and it may truly be said that he had not a friend. Was ever man so wretched? Was ever enormous sinner so justly punished?' Three years before his death he was stopped at the polling booth when he went to cast his vote; the men in power chose to deny his claim to be a citizen of the Republic—he who had first dared to use the words *'the United States of America'*. So he died in contempt, poverty and squalor.

It has taken generations to wipe away the mud. For years, on both sides of the Atlantic, publishers went to prison for attempting to reprint his books. By some inscrutable Stalinite censorship, whole histories of the American Revolution were written without mentioning the American Trotsky. A century after his death Theodore Roosevelt could still dismiss him as a 'filthy, little atheist'. Even now he is sometimes written down as a crank, a busybody, a third-rate taproom philosopher. And yet, judged by the test of his impact on his own generation and many since, Thomas Paine was the most far-seeing Englishman of the eighteenth century. He was the greatest exile ever driven from these shores. In the teeth of all the slanders and the libels, he remains the major prophet of democracy and representative government, the much-vaunted creed of our Western world. Today, Presidents and Prime Ministers, even Queens on Christmas Day, make obeisance before the central theory of Thomas Paine, the English outlaw and the outcast in the land of his adoption.

In all history, there is no more curious story than that of Paine's blaze to fame, his pitiable fall, and then the slow but assured recovery in his reputation. Strangely, that recovery itself is chiefly his own achievement; it is due to the persistent potency of his pen. No master of the English language—with the exception of H. N. Brailsford in one brief, classic essay—has written his biography.* It is Paine's own writings which have made his name survive while the forgotten historians were busy expurgating it from the records; almost every great democratic statesman or writer has found his way back to the source books.

---

*This sentence is not intended as a reflection on Moncure Conway's excellent and well-researched two-volume work which, published in 1892, started the work of rehabilitation, after Paine and the Painites had had to endure nearly a century of defamation on both sides of the Atlantic. And here for sure was an attempt by an American to repay the debt to 'the Englishman', who wrote *Common Sense* and so described himself on the front page of the first edition. But Conway's book, for all its many virtues, does not place Thomas Paine's life in its full world-wide setting, and none of the others who have written about him would claim to have achieved that spacious feat. He has not received the historical treatment accorded to all the other founders of the American Republic. Neither the United States nor the other country of his adoption nor his England have given him his due. No single country and no exclusive creed can claim him as their own; that is part of his greatness.

And yet even on this reckoning, as a writer, Paine has seldom had his due. American Tories who disliked his arguments found fault with his grammar. Hazlitt was scoffed at for calling him a great writer. More often than not since then, any reference to his literary claims is compressed into a few patronising paragraphs. While he lived his pamphlets probably had a bigger sale than anything published since the invention of the printing press, second only to the Bible. Since his death they have been reprinted and reprinted again in almost every language. Momentary best-sellers can be dismissed; but how can the critics deride the verdict of so mammoth an electorate?

Certainly, his pamphlets sometimes seem ill-constructed and uneven. There is none of the smooth perfection of Swift, although Paine, like Hazlitt and Cobbett, had obviously soaked himself in Swift. There is indeed a grating, metallic flavour in some of his writing. All the mysteries of the universe are quickly made to fit into his mechanical symmetrical system. The lack of subtlety and colour can begin to pall. But then, suddenly, the whole surrounding landscape is lit up by another streak of lightning. These are the real riches of Paine's prose, the abundance of his aphorisms, sharp, hard and glittering, like diamonds. How the gorgeous eloquence of Edmund Burke on the tragedy of Marie Antoinette withers before Paine's most famous epigram: *he pities the plumage, but forgets the dying bird*. More perhaps than all the others who revolted against the English prose style of the eighteenth century, Paine changed the fashion. He is still read because he is still modern. He is, therefore, also, a foremost figure in the history of English literature.

The curiosity is that his immortality could so easily have been foreseen. All the historians had to do was to let his contemporaries bear witness. In an age when it took weeks to cross the Atlantic, he gained an international notoriety such as only pop stars have today. News of the spirit he had aroused around the American campfires spread fast across the civilised world. Little children in Philadelphia and New York knew the name of 'Mr. Common Sense'. A song specially composed in his honour—'He comes, the great Reformer comes'—was sung in the London taverns. He was appointed an honorary member of the French

Convention. When he set foot at Calais the whole town turned out to see him, and pretty girls presented him with cockades all the way to Paris. Hazlitt wrote:

> In 1792 Paine was so great, or so popular an author, and so much read and admired, that the Government was obliged to suspend the Constitution, and to go to war to counteract the effects of his popularity.

Of course the exaggeration was intended, but was it really so wide of the mark? The real crime of Thomas Muir, sentenced to Botany Bay for fourteen years, was the circulation he had given to Paine's *Rights of Man*; twenty-six years later Richard Carlile was put away to solitary confinement in Dorchester gaol for a similar offence. And even today no historian has fully unravelled how large a part was played by fear of the English Jacobins—with Paine as their most effective spokesman—in sending the England of William Pitt to war with revolutionary France. 'A statue of gold ought to be erected to you in every city of the universe', said Napoleon who searched out the old rebel in some Paris back-street. Napoleon claimed, no doubt lyingly, that he slept with the *Rights of Man* under his pillow. Paine was not deceived by the flattering 'French charlatan', but Napoleon's measure of the man and his influence surely offers some proof of his signifi-cance.

Finally, the greatest American of the age never wavered in his opinion. Thomas Jefferson always paid honour to Thomas Paine. He knew how Paine had shaped and captured—and refused to betray—the spirit of 1776. That was his supreme moment. Paine was not the very first to use the word but he more than any other had made the Americans unafraid to declare their *independence*. 'The debate is ended', he insisted; America must fight. It was as if in the Britain of 1940 the Churchill resistance speeches had been made not by a national leader but by an unknown journalist who suddenly forced his way to the centre of the stage.

Indeed, in another sense, it was so much more difficult for Paine to give the summons to battle. It was not merely that he made Americans see the prize of independence as something within their grasp; not merely that he personified their frustrations in his picture of George III, the 'Royal Brute of England', the 'hardened, sullen-tempered Pharaoh'. He had also to persuade the aristocratic experts and fainthearts that an upstart pamphleteer understood the English political system better than they. It was not true that the King was the unwilling prisoner of his Ministers, that a message of magnanimous reprieve and reconciliation would miraculously arrive by the next boat. Paine never had the advantage of studying Namier, but he knew how the structure of politics in the reign of George III really worked. He explained how the King and his Ministers distributed their *loaves and fishes*. He knew the contempt in which 'the colonists' were held. He knew, while most Americans would not face it, that America must fight. Jefferson was only nineteen at the time, but he never forgot the man who performed this service to his country.

How grotesque, then, in the face of all these contemporary tributes is the tale that Paine's reputation was something of a bubble. His strength was that he saw with shining clarity the forces changing his world. History offers few examples of such confident and breathtaking foresight. He always believed that the words he had written in some desperate garret forecast the shape of things to come. No cloud of uncertainty crossed his horizon— neither when he walked amid Washington's bedraggled and beaten armies nor when he was being hunted out of England for his high treason with William Pitt's policemen on his heels, nor even, on that most macabre occasion, when he waited in one of Robespierre's prisons to be taken to the guillotine. That was an hour of disillusion and despair if ever there was one. He, the most merciless exposer of monarchy, had pleaded for the King's life in the name of mercy; and when his own life was at stake even his beloved America would not breathe a word to rescue him. Yet with his great argument on earth gone temporarily awry, Paine turned to put heaven to rights. He settled down in his over-crowded cell to write *The Age of Reason*.

Of course, such faith was fanaticism, but it was the fanaticism of genius. Always, once he had become a public figure, Paine was proud, cocksure, incorrigibly combative and vain; vain, in particular, about his writings. (Who wouldn't be when all his major works sold at least 100,000 copies within a matter of months?) Nothing could shake his conviction that within his own lifetime or shortly afterwards—and thanks largely to his own Atlas-like exertions—the world would be turned upside down. He knew he possessed the implement which could work the miracle—the power of free speech, free writing and free thought. Nothing could induce in him a hairsbreadth of doubt; the bigger the bonfires they made of his books, the bigger would be the sales. No other figure in history can ever have believed in the *power* of freedom—and not merely its virtue—with Paine's single-minded intensity. That was his secret. 'Mankind', he said with his grand simplicity, 'are not now to be told they shall not think, or they shall not read.' And, incredibly, he was proved right, as near as mortal man can be.

Thus if the historians malign Paine himself, they are still forced to acknowledge the victory of his opinions. Our modern spacious histories of his times, written with all the advantages of hindsight, portray the American Revolution, the French Revolution and the movement which led to the English Reform Bill as three parts of the same whole. Each reacted on the other and each is incomprehensible without the other. A few Englishmen realised that the cause of English freedom was at stake in the American revolt. A few Englishmen realised that English freedom might be forfeited in the war against revolutionary France. A few Americans realised America's interest in the triumph of the French Revolution. Paine had seen that the same battle was being fought in all three countries. He was the link between the three convulsions. He, an Englishman (and thus he signed anonymously his great American pamphlet, *Common Sense*) was given the key of the Bastille by Lafayette to take across the Atlantic and lay on Washington's table. He wrote:

> That the principles of America opened the Bastille is not to be doubted, and therefore the key comes to the right place. I am returned from France to London, and am engaged to return to Paris when the Constitution shall be proclaimed and to carry the American flag in the procession. I have not the least doubt of the final and

complete success of the French Revolution. Little ebbings and flowings, for and against, the natural companions of revolution, sometimes appear; but the full current of it is, in my opinion, as fixed as the Gulf Stream.

The England which had denounced Paine as a traitor could not remain immune; it was washed by the same sea. William Blake had helped him to escape from London. William Cobbett, once his most ferocious assailant, admitted: 'at his expiring flambeau I lighted my taper'. All the other English rebels who raised the ferment which led to the Reform Bill pored over his forbidden pages. 'Government is for the living not for the dead', had been Paine's reply to Burke in 1791; forty years later, England marched on, in company with France and America, along the road which Paine, not Burke, had mapped out for her.

Enough of achievement for one man, surely—to understand the three great revolutions of his age before they happened, to bring politics home to the common people, to build a bridge of common idealism across the Atlantic and the English Channel (as firm as the real iron bridge which he invented in his spare time). Yet this was not all. Scattered through his writings we can find hints, often much more than hints, of the other ideas which have given vitality to the democratic movement for the past hundred and fifty years.

Almost a century before Lincoln he sought to write into the American Constitution a clause against slavery. Long before even John Stuart Mill, he championed the rights of women. He was among the very first of English writers to espouse the cause of Indian freedom. Well ahead of my old friends, Dick Crossman or Barbara Castle, he had a good plan for old age pensions. And how men in all our modern parties might tremble at his proposals for land nationalisation; he wanted new laws for marriage and divorce. International arbitration, family allowances, maternity benefits, free education, prison reform, full employment—yes much of the future the Labour Party has offered was previously on offer, in even better English, from Thomas Paine. Note how true these single syllables ring with the triumphant organ note of that last final word: 'It is wrong to say God made *rich* and *poor*;

He made only *male* and *female*; and He gave them the earth for their inheritance.'

It was not until more than 150 years after his death that a statue to Thomas Paine was erected in England. (After a protest, in the year 1963, from a Thetford Conservative Councillor: 'A monument to Thomas Paine on the Market Place would be an insult to the town'). The French and the Americans were less churlish. Paine himself, for all his vanity, would probably agree with Cato who said he would prefer people should ask why he had *not* a monument erected to him than why he had. Even so, surely it is time to make amends. Or can it be that our Establishment, meticulously ticking off those items in his programme still unachieved, feel that no unnecessary chances can be taken? The man still lives. *Rights of Man* still sells some 5,000 copies a year and even that 'Devil's Prayer Book', *The Age of Reason*, can still be read, if not to bring down thunderbolts from heaven, at least to prove that the 'filthy little atheist' was not an atheist at all.

TWELVE
Daniel Defoe, Feminist

> On any monument worthy the name of monument the
> names of *Moll Flanders* and *Roxana*, at least, should be
> carved as deeply as the name of Defoe. They stand among
> the few English novels which we can call indisputably great.
>
> VIRGINIA WOOLF

SOMETIME IN THE SUMMER of the year 1660 (the exact date is unknown) a Cripplegate butcher and his wife brought forth a prodigy—Daniel Defoe, author of almost the first and still the most famous novel ever written. But the world had still to wait more than half a century for *The Life and Strange Surprising Adventures of Robinson Crusoe, of York, Mariner*. It was not until his fifty-ninth year—in 1719—that Defoe turned his aching hand from journalism and sat down in his Stoke Newington retreat to produce his masterpiece.

Success was instantaneous. 'There is not an old woman', wrote one jealous competitor, 'that can go to the price of it, but buys the "Life and Adventures," and leaves it as legacy with the "Pilgrim's Progress," the "Practice of Piety" and "God's Revenge Against Murther" to her posterity.' Everybody was snatching for it, even those who sneered. So Defoe swiftly scribbled off a sequel. He went on scribbling at an unaccountable pace for the remaining ten years of his life, churning out newspaper articles, manuals on manners, marriage, economics and every conceivable topic, with a new novel roughly every twelve months. Three more at least—*Moll Flanders, Roxana, A Journal of the Plague Year*—must be classed as masterpieces alongside *Robinson Crusoe*. During that last decade, indeed—particularly between the years 1719 and 1722—the genius of Defoe suddenly sprouted into a winter blossom unexampled in the whole range of literature.

No one at the time foresaw his immortality. Alexander Pope recognised the excellence of *Robinson Crusoe*, but his tribute had a touch of patronage. No one believed that Defoe would surpass in fame all the other great men of the age, the Addisons and the Steeles, with Swift alone surviving as his one acknowledged master. Defoe, to his contemporaries, was a Grub Street hack who could never aspire to real literary eminence. And Defoe himself, despite his abounding vanity, half shared the general opinion. The erratic promptings of his old Puritan conscience made him apologise for writing 'mere fiction'. *Robinson Crusoe* and *Moll Flanders*, he claimed, were moral tracts, like so much else he had written. He was prouder of his *True-Born Englishman*, the doggerel verse he had produced twenty years earlier. The fact was he wrote for bread, and the *True-Born Englishman* had sold 40,000 copies, making him for a moment the most widely read poet in the English language.

Even when he died—he was still on the run from his creditors whom all the royalties from *Crusoe* could not fend off—none of the obituaries mourned the founder of the English novel. On the burial register they got his name wrong: 'Mr. Dubow.' And the register of St. Giles, Cripplegate, recorded quite simply and falsely: 'Mr. Defoe, Gentleman.'

Whatever else he was, he was never that. He was by turns a tradesman, an adventurer, a radical pamphleteer and agitator, a reporter, a spy, a gallant crusader, a crawling sycophant, a man accepted in court circles and once the confidant of the King and then able to plunge with equal zest into the lowest life of London; for months or even years on end, his diligent biographers cannot track him down through those murky, labyrinthine lairs. Half his life he seemed to be bombarding Ministers with far-seeing schemes for new trading projects, for founding new colonies, for military expeditions, for old-age pensions and marine insurance, for establishing academies for education or asylums for the insane. Through the other half he was getting practical acquaintance with 'that worst of devils, poverty'.

He was a preacher and a moraliser, too, obsessed with the religious controversies of his time. Often he reads like an eighteenth-century Samuel Smiles. But often again all the smugness is shattered with one sharp blow from the Defoean hammer for hypocrisy.

> To be reduced to necessity is to be wicked; for necessity is not only the temptation, but it is such a temptation as human nature is not empowered to resist.

Who could believe, after this, that some of his biographers would strive to reduce him to a plaster saint, a little bourgeois Bunyan?

Even those two halves of his life were nothing more than fragments; so many other lives as well remain to be explained. Apart from the great merchant sailors themselves, he was the foremost traveller of his age; searching out, as he claimed, every nook and corner of England, the first English writer to discover Scotland, knowing Italy, France and Spain besides and still, with it all, staying the most obvious and knowledgeable of Londoners. He called himself a native of the universe; and he explored his own city as ruthlessly as Hogarth or Dickens.

He was, too, the most prolific writer of his age, and perhaps of any other. Only when forty years old did he set out on his full career as a journalist, but then he went to work with a stupendous will and energy. He devised his own shorthand. He established some sixty correspondents or agents all over the country. For nine years he ran his own *Review*, producing the whole of it two or three times a week and still finding time to write for other journals (not omitting to commend their most percipient articles from his own anonymous hand in his own *Review*) and pour forth a deluge of pamphlets and satirical poems interspersed with full-length histories and biographies. Every night of those hectic years, after his day in the saddle, Defoe must have been writing several thousands of words.

He wrote:

> The unhappy People are deluded, are impos'd upon, are fermented, their Spirits disorder'd, *and how?* By raising false Reports, affirming forg'd and barbarous Allegations, raising Scandalous Surmises, and

pushing about absurd, ridiculous and incongruous Whymsies among the well-meaning but ignorant People.

Daniel Defoe undertook to turn back the flood single-handed. The father of English journalism, like the later founder of the English novel, did not care a straw for academic theories about his art. He had to feed his wife and eight children.

Above all, he was at war. He was himself, of course, 'a man of peace and reason', set upon from every quarter by devils. How wrathfully he insisted on liberty for himself and how complacently he watched restraints imposed on his licentious competitors. Apart from his clear distinction, he never worried his head about drawing the ineffable line between liberty and licence. Doubtless he was right; no one since has discovered where to draw it, either. For thirty years Defoe was in the thick of the journalistic hurly-burly at a time when it raged with more ferocity than in almost any other epoch. In one sense the struggle must have been more wearing for him than most of the others; for he was alone, a member of no party at a time when party affiliations were being drawn as sharply as battle lines. Although a life-long supporter of the Protestant settlement of 1688, Defoe was never able to enlist wholeheartedly under the flag of its most loyal upholders, the Whigs. Always his unfailing curiosity, ingenuity and inventiveness were forcing him to stray from the beaten track. All he would be able to claim with certainty on the Day of Judgement, in extenuation of his twists and turns, was that he had never actually been a Tory; was he not one of the first of English writers to explain the origin of those party labels and had he not further gleefully explained how the nicknames served their purpose 'till at last the word Tory became popular, and it stuck so close to the party in all their bloody proceedings, that they had no way to get it off?'

Defoe was, in fact, sent to Newgate Prison and made to stand in the pillory by the highest of high Tory Ministers for his satirical pamphlet, *The Shortest Way With Dissenters*, which outraged the bishops without comforting the dissenters. But then, within a few years, it seemed that, for all his disavowals of the horrific charge, he was content to do the bidding of a Tory Ministry. The suspicion grew that he was not merely a hack, but a treacherous paid hack at that. The suspicion was well-founded, although we have had to wait until the archives were opened to clinch it. In Newgate, Defoe's spirit wilted.

> I agreed to give the Court No Trouble but to plead Guilty to the Indictment, Even to all the Adverbs, the Seditiously's, the Maliciously's and a Long Rhapsody of the Lawyers et Ceteras; and all this upon promises of being used Tenderly.

The man who got him out was Robert Harley. Harley, like Defoe, was a middle-of-the roader, but he became more and more encoiled in the manoeuvres of the Tories and lived to be the head of the most explicitly Tory Administration which Britain had yet known; indeed, the first man in history to be called Prime Minister in the parlance of the day. This was another piece of English history which Defoe helped to make; the term had first been used in one of his letters to Harley. Defoe was ready to serve his hero with uncritical devotion. 'Intelligence', he wrote, 'is the Soul of all Publick Business.' He showed an incredible assiduity in supplying it. 'If you'll allow the Vanity of the Expression, *If I were a Public Minister*, I would if Possible kno'what Every body said of me.' Harley, it seems, was the first politician who, with Defoe's help, paid proper attention to his press cuttings.

It might have been thought that all Defoe's other multitudinous activities were enough. He was a merchant as well as a journalist, dealing at one time and another in bricks, tiles, hosiery, cheese, oysters, and heaven knows what else and bankrupting himself to the tune of £17,000 at the age of thirty. But in his busiest decade, when he worked for Harley and wrote his *Review*, he was also secret agent and propagandist-in-chief for the man who had saved him from prison and might still save him from his creditors. For his chosen Prime Minister he performed all the duties now severally discharged by Downing Street Public Relations Officers, Durrant's press cutting agency, the research students of the Conservative Central Office and the leader writers of the *Daily Telegraph*.

Small wonder that his fellow practitioners in Grub Street

pursued him with a special venom. One of the ablest, Abel Boyer—as a journalist and historian quite a match for Defoe himself—ripped aside the mask at every available opportunity. Defoe, the man of moderation, retaliated by calling Boyer a sodomite. The daggers were out in those last years of the Queen and the early years of the new King.

Defoe stooped or was driven to the depths. Switching back his allegiance to the Whigs, he was ready to be assigned by the government spies to a Tory newspaper, there to pass himself off as a Jacobite, doctor the editorials in the government interest and play the informer against his unsuspecting editor. 'Thus I bow in the House of Rimmon', said the man who had once so bravely, in his dissenting youth, marched out to fight under the green banners of 'King Monmouth' at Sedgemoor, challenged the silly boasts of racial superiority with his satire *The True Born Englishman*, and paid for his detestation of religious persecution in the pillory. It seemed a pitiable end but the end had not quite come.

Those biographers of Defoe who try to wipe away the dirt from his political apostasies and subterfuges cannot adequately explain the glorious flowering of his final years. The miracle of Defoe remains his sudden and belated mastery of a new form of writing in *Robinson Crusoe* and *Moll Flanders*. The world would not have had either if their creator had not been forced by the screw of money and politics from desperation to dishonour. If Swift had never descended into the mire of English politics *Gulliver's Travels* would never have been written. Defoe never achieved Swift's corrosive indignation and contempt for the conventional thought of his day. But he learnt enough to take the edge off his complacency and transform the self-righteous polemicist into a great novelist.

The jaunty, inquisitive, bubbling, so self-confident, moralising bourgeois adventurer, which is the face Defoe so often presents, had also seen with his own eyes and knew in his own heart how relentless the devil of poverty could be. Like Moll, if not so frequently, he had yielded to temptation. Once he turned to fiction he could tell the whole truth; all the half-lies and the devious cheatings and devices he had felt compelled to employ in his journalistic career enabled him to do it with a special relish.

Robinson Crusoe was a moral tract in a way, but not in the way that Defoe tried to commend it to his prudish public. If anyone wants to see how an incipient agnostic in a religious age tries not to shirk while still camouflaging his doubts, let him study Crusoe's lame efforts to make Man Friday a good Protestant. And yet *Robinson Crusoe*, despite all its marvellous invention and suspense, is not the finest of his works. As the best of his biographers, Mr. James Sutherland, has suggested, there is more of Defoe in Moll Flanders than in any other of his characters. Here he returns to the radicalism of his youth. Once in his young days he wrote a pamphlet called *The Poor Man's Plea*, some passages of which could have been written by a Leveller around the camp-fires of Cromwell's army. Here, in *Moll Flanders*, the Poor Man's Plea is heard again; even more the Poor Woman's Plea, for *Moll Flanders* is also a feminist tract, justifying the ways of woman to God and man.

'There are more thieves and rogues made by that prison of Newgate, than by all the clubs and societies of villains in the nation.' Moll was born in Newgate; she ought to know. She knows much else besides:

> She is always married too soon who gets a bad husband and she is never married too late who gets a good one; in a word, there is no woman, deformity or bad reputation excepted, but if she manages well may be married safely one time or another; but if she precipitates herself, it is ten thousand to one she is undone.

If anyone could doubt that moral embedded in this most immoral of tracts, *Roxana* came a few years later to clinch the case even more impudently.

But, most of all, *Moll Flanders* displays the art, the insight, the mind, the humour—a quality which he shows only in occasional flashes—the unquenchable optimism amid despair and disgrace of Defoe himself. We are told in the Preface:

> When a woman, debauched from youth, nay, even being the offspring of debauchery and vice, comes to give an account of all her vicious practices, and even to descend to the particular occasions and

circumstances by which she first became wicked, and of all the progressions of crime which she ran through in three score years, an author must be hard put to it to wrap it up so clean as not to give room, especially for vicious readers, to turn it to his disadvantage.

However, the fact underlined in that superb Defoean sentence is that at last Defoe did not feel the need to wrap it all up. The truth he had bottled up within himself for so long poured out in golden spate.

Postscript

In August 1959, the House of Commons passed a so-called Street Offences Act designed to fulfil that part of a Committee of Inquiry which proposed means of moving prostitutes off the streets.

Daniel Defoe had always been fascinated by this subject. Hence *Moll Flanders, Roxana* and many other references throughout his writing. Here is how he, or rather Moll Flanders, his favourite creation, might have viewed the 1959 Act.

An incident with a constable

I was walking down one of those streets near Soho fields as cool and jaunty as can be imagined, decked in some finery and with my head held high but with at least one eye well cocked to study what might befall, when a young constable (he could not have been above twenty years and was handsome enough, I swear, to be my own son by my Lancashire husband) approached me in a manner too insolent to be mentioned.

'You're a common whore,' he said without so much as a by-your-leave; 'and I'll have you in front of the magistrate and into Newgate prison before you can say Robinson Crusoe.'

My distress, you may suppose, was something considerable. Never before had I been confronted in such a manner in a public place, not to say privately.

Readers of my earlier misfortunes will recall that never once had I been so indelicate to transact my business on the streets;

except on that one occasion when I went to Bartholomew Fair and met the gentleman extremely well dressed and very rich whose name I was mannerly enough not to record; and, then, you may agree, something must be allowed for the quality of the gentleman, the quantity of drink he had taken and the merry time of year: not that any of these matters are advanced to reduce the fervour of my penitentials. I offer no opinions and recite only facts.

'Indeed,' says I to the constable with as much spirit as you may guess; 'and what gives you the right to accost honest gentlewomen in this style? Save your insults for your own sex and save your daring to deal with those thieves and pickpockets who, with so little to fear from the bold guardians of the law, threaten and terrify hard-toiling traders. Begone, you dog, before I must report you for your pranks to your grieving mother.'

'Not so fast, Mrs. Flanders,' says he, with a scoff. 'Not so hasty, Moll.' This was indeed a strange address. Few knew my name, at least in those outlying villages. But I was granted no time for cautious reflection. Did I not read the public prints? Did I not know the new law? 'Madam,' says he, affecting the stiffest decorum, 'I find you don't know what it is to be a constable now; I beg of you, don't oblige me to be rude to you.'

In short, the whole tale came out. He had the power, so he insisted, to clear the streets and bundle us all into Newgate.

I had a mind to tell him, and had already started, of my own mother and how she had only escaped from that terrible place by pleading her belly; how Newgate was a house to make whores, not to cure them; how in that roaring, swearing clamour, amid that stench and nastiness, thieves and murderers, let alone women sadly neglectful of their virtue, were bred in legions too vast to be apprehended by all the constables in Christendom; and such like and so forth and much more.

But by now a considerable company had assembled. 'They've got you now, Molly,' jeered one who could not have known me from Eve. 'Take her away,' said another. The rest were not so churlish. 'Leave her alone; what's she done to you?' they cried.

And so the buzz became louder every minute. However, as luck would have it, the press was so great, that several sturdy citizens of Soho had wedged themselves between myself and the constable. I decided to run for it, never stopping until I had reached my governess's house and slammed the door behind me.

My governess had always acted the true mother. She cried with me and for me. She put me to bed. And then, with my breath recovered, she told me to tell her plainly all that had happened and everything the constable had said. She followed all I had to recount with many an 'indeed,' many 'Oh Fies!' and such-like expressions.

I did not refrain from appealing to her with the woman's rhetoric of tears. But now my governess who, as I have told you, had treated me more amiably than anyone else in my life, showed a mood more curious than anything I had ever known. At first, I thought she was sobbing at the affront offered to her comrade in so many adventures. But no; these were not sobs. She was shaking with mirth and not so long after she broke into peals of laughter.

'Mrs. Flanders,' says she. 'We shall help your handsome brave constable to clear the streets. We shall do it for him. I did not tell you, dear Moll, when first you came to entrust yourself to my care, what was the exact nature of my calling or profession. But now that it is blessed by the Secretary of State, by the House of Commons, by the House of Lords, by the full bench of Bishops and high society, I need blush no longer.

'Others, I fear, may not treat you as gently as I. We shall have every rogue and escaped felon fit for Tyburn competing in our trade. But then, consider the gain for honest folk too fastidious to believe their own eyes; you always had the tenderest thoughts for gentlemen and gentlewomen, never reckoning your affairs so different from theirs, since all you ever did (apart from that visit to Bartholomew Fair in the Springtime) was to make matrimony a matter of fortune.

'Sleep soundly, dearest Moll. Spare yourself, if you can, any nightmares about Newgate. Tomorrow or the day after both of us shall be rich beyond our dreams; and, along with us, every lord and lady, every gentleman and gentlewoman in the land, may give praise to the authors of the Brothel Keepers' Charter.'

THIRTEEN

In Defence
of the Duchess

'I am afraid that we must expect things to go from bad to worse in England so long as a woman is in charge. She lets herself be led by many wrong-headed people . . .'

Prince Eugen of Savoy, to the Imperial representative in The Hague, January 1710.

'A BOOK WITHOUT A WOMAN', said Jill, my wife, more on a note of scorn than anything else, and in our household the offence, if true, was especially reprehensible. The room of her own, the room where she works, when she is not cooking, gardening, shopping, cleaning, making beds, entertaining and the rest, is a feminist temple, a shrine dedicated to the cause of women's rights. Every book on every shelf, every picture, every inch of wall space helps to tell the story of how, mostly, women had to liberate themselves, what mountains of male tyranny and imbecility they had to move to achieve it, what agonies of subjection they endured; how indeed the true role of women in history and in literature has been twisted and bowdlerised beyond all reckoning, and how only now, and still most diffidently, has the task of discovering the truth begun; and yet, with it all, how the liberation of women is always properly to be seen as part of the wider liberation of mankind and womankind in general: a splendid, spacious theme, if ever there was one, with endless permutations.

An error, then, not to have included even one woman in a title role in the original cast, and I thought for one swift moment that an easy riposte might be found by adding up the number of males and females which Virginia Woolf, the princess of modern feminists, includes in her two volumes of one of our favourite companions, *The Common Reader*, but that argument does not quite hold. (The figure, if anyone still wants to know, is seventeen women subjects out of the full list of thirty-eight.) So I was driven back on the fragile defence that women of one kind and another, conspicuous if not actually liberated, played their part in the lives of all the chosen heroes, and a brief backward glance at the list may reveal how the original error was merely compounded.

My mother ruled every roost where she and my father ever alighted; she knew something of women's rights, but still had little enough time to enjoy them, having to rear seven children, five of them males, each with his streak of armour-plated male aggressiveness which she condemned in theory and unwittingly encouraged in practice: so no sign of rescue appeared there, and, thereafter, the case seems to weaken further. William Hazlitt deserted two wives, or two wives deserted him, and his affair with Sarah was, from the woman's point of view, a romantic fiasco. Thomas Paine left, or was left by, only one actual wife, but mostly over his relations with women a veil is drawn, and by his own hand. Bertrand Russell left several and, as one of them, Dora, has explained, he was not quite, as he appeared to outside admirers like myself, the strict practitioner of his own precepts. Bonar Thompson, it must be sadly admitted, although happily married, was a fierce, explicit enemy of the women's movement in his time. As for Max Beaverbrook and Randolph Churchill, they were raging, rampaging male chauvinists long before the term had ever been considered sexually apposite. And even little, endearing Vicky had his marital and sexual disasters; not that they, by themselves or in any combination, can clinch the feminist case, but he can hardly be listed as a firm recruit in the opposite camp.

So where does that leave us—or me? Has some revealing manual been unwittingly compiled by a series of Freudian slips, by this time almost a Freudian avalanche? Can the others come to the rescue? The sex life of Jonathan Swift, the mystery of his relationship with Stella and Vanessa, has been for years a prime subject of scholarly studies; but here too there is an awkward case to answer. James Joyce was a devoted Swiftian, honouring his writing by every form of allusion, imitation and assimilation. But he also made a direct attack on Swift's character. Once he and Frank Budgen engaged in a conversation about Swift's 'secret grief'.

'I suppose', said Budgen, 'that the proud, sensitive man needed love but that pride robbed him of the power of self-surrender that love demands of man or woman.'

'Maybe', said Joyce, 'but that isn't enough. The reason must be not latent but manifest. Anyway, the man was a strong and stingy sentimentalist. He meddled with and muddled up two women's lives.'

Let that terrible indictment stand for just a moment. Three at least out of the full complement here can be impregnably registered as champions of women's rights without any question or qualification whatever. One is Daniel Defoe, almost the first, if not *the* first, male spokesman in the cause. The second is H. N. Brailsford, the most eloquent male spokesman in the pre-1914 struggle, with his friend, H. W. Nevinson, as his only rival claimant to the title. The third is Benjamin Disraeli who expressed his feminism, to use the word anachronistically, more in thought and word than in deed, but whose long allegiance to the idea is all the more remarkable in the light of his other political interests and affiliations.

Where did he learn it? The newly discovered Disraeli novel, *A Year at Hartlebury or The Election*, published in March 1834, contains a passage in which a fine old Dame, Dame Harrald, laments outside some almshouse door the fact that women have not the vote. 'In this world', she protests, 'the men have it all their own way.' Here is an early suffragist or suffragette demand, it might be thought, considering that women did not get the vote until ninety-odd years later, and considering that even the Chartists in their confabulations at the time, in that very same decade, could not finally agree to include votes for women in their demand for parliamentary reform. Yet the idea was not so entirely novel. 'I dined with Bulwer *en famille* on Sunday, "To meet some truffles"—very agreeable company,' wrote Disraeli to his sister Sarah in 29 January, 1833. 'His mother-in-law, Mrs.

Wheeler, was there; not so pleasant, something between Jeremy
Bentham and Meg Merrilies, very clever, but awfully revolutionary. She poured forth all her systems upon my novitiate ear,
and while she advocated the rights of women, Bulwer abused
system-mongers and the sex, and Rosina played with her dog.'

Anna Wheeler's political assault upon, or seduction of, the
young Disraeli—she looks very much like the model for Dame
Harrald in *Hartlebury*—was just one of her minor casual
triumphs. More serious and significant was her association with
the early Socialist writer, William Thompson, who wrote in 1825
and dedicated to her his *Appeal of One Half of the Human Race,
Women, against the Pretensions of the Other Half, Men, to restrain
them in Political and thence in Civil and Domestic Slavery.* Anna
has some claim to be the biggest woman figure in the movement
of woman's emancipation between Mary Wollstonecraft and
Emmeline Pankhurst. But who knows anything about her? Who
writes about her? Where can we read of her? She finds no place in
the Dictionary of National Biography. Her name and fame are
suppressed, forgotten, hard now to disinter from the man-made
mausoleum of history.

The monstrous suppression will not last for ever, and mostly of
course the women achieve their own historical and literary
discoveries. But sometimes the men assist in rolling away the
boulders. 'When I read history, and am impressed by any deed or
occurrence', wrote Heinrich Heine, 'I often feel as if I should like
to see the woman concealed behind it, as the secret spring. The
women govern, although the *Moniteur* only mentions men: they
make history, although the historians know only the names of
men.' And lest anyone imagines that Heine, writing a century and
a half ago on the subject, was soon to be overtaken by the modern
age or modern historians, let us recall the verdict of one of the
most eminent of modern English historians, Professor J. H.
Plumb, Professor of Modern English history at Cambridge
University:

> How very few women have left an indelible mark on English
> history—a queen or two, a novelist or two, a couple of nurses, maybe
> a brace of actresses, but the list is a short one, and perhaps only Sarah,

Duchess of Marlborough gets into it by sheer flaming temperament. What a virago she was!*

The word *virago* is now being transmuted by a most excellent publishing firm into a term of approbation and honour, like *Leveller* or *Suffragette* itself; but it was not always so, and certainly it was never so intended by Professor Plumb. And how mean and miserable is his fiercely truncated list of the names which are known, and how aggressively oblivious he is of the legions who are unknown or half-known, and how wretched are the conditions upon which Sarah is admitted to the English pantheon inhabited well-nigh exclusively by males. Nothing much but her screaming tantrums to recommend her! Thus history is reduced to the level of something concocted by gossip columnists.

The only excuse for such churlishness in the estimate of Sarah's character at this late date is that the same misapprehension has occasionally been shown, not only by her sworn enemies but even across the centuries by the supposedly magnanimous Churchills. The first Duke of Marlborough loved the Duchess and, probably, never wavered in his affections, despite her furious allegations to the contrary. Yet the extraordinary fact is that he never grasped the scale of her political intelligence. Not all her huge progeny of sons, daughters, sons-in-law, daughters-in-law, grandsons and granddaughters, shared that devotion; indeed if the tally is properly made she quarrelled with them all. Yet politics lay at the root of much of this dissension, and if the first great Duke could not see the wisdom of her prescriptions, why should these lesser figures in the family show a greater perspicacity? All through her long, cantankerous widowhood—she survived the Duke by twenty-two years—she unloosed what looked like spleen on almost everyone within range, with a special spatter of venom for

---

*Professor Plumb's words are taken from his review of two books on the Duchess published a few years ago, one *Sarah, Duchess of Marlborough* by David Green (Collins, 1967) and the other *Rule of Three: Sarah, Duchess of Marlborough and her Companions in Power* by Iris Butler (Hodder, 1967). Both are reasonably friendly to the Duchess; both are well worth reading; but neither succeeded in altering the assumptions about the Duchess, of which Professor Plumb's comment was all too typical.

members of the family. Most of Marlborough's biographers, including Sir Winston Churchill, felt little obligation to come to her rescue. Rather, she can be made the scapegoat for the Duke's political setbacks. Most of his letters to her are preserved; most of hers to him are gone. So it is his case which is readily available to historians. Moreover, despite that deep love between them, there is the ugly fact, which obviously stuck in Sir Winston's gullet, that her charge of infidelity against him was made just at the moment when he was preparing to march across Europe to Blenheim and eternal fame. How can her reputation ever blossom beneath his shadow—even if we may dare to whisper that he was not actually put off the march or the glory? Finally, to descend from these heights, I may be permitted to recall that the Winstonian view of Sarah was adopted by Randolph (*our* Randolph, of this century) in an extreme form. He could not sit silent and hear Sarah praised. Nothing else mattered but military victory, and her single womanly duty in life was to protect the Duke's interest at Queen Anne's court. This influence, for whatever reason, she had forfeited, and judgement upon her must be pronounced accordingly—which final rite Randolph performed with mounting wrath, thus proving, as I believed, before our eyes that Sarah's sulphurous blood still ran in his veins.

Could it be, can it be, that the Plumb portrait is accurate after all? Contemporary pamphleteers saw her villainous profile:

> On the Right Hand an oldish woman, of a fair countenance, in youthfull Dress; her chin and nose turning up, her Eyes glowing like Lightning; blasted all she had power over with strange Diseases— Out of her nostrils came a Sulphurous Smoak, and out of her Mouth Flames of Fire. Her hair was grisled and adorn'd with Spoils of ruined People. Her neck bare, with Chains about it of Dice, mixed with Pieces of Gold, which rattling, made a horrid noise; for her Motions were all fierce and violent. Her garment was all stained with Tears and Blood.

And another pamphleteer, not so anonymous then and not at all since, Jonathan Swift, compiled a whole anthology of abuse designed to deluge this single head 'Three Furies', he said to summarise, 'reigned in her breast, the most mortal enemies of all softer passions, which were sordid Avarice, disdainful Pride and ungovernable Rage.'

But let judgement be reserved. One of the strongest strands in Sarah's character, the one I suspect which especially provoked the blindest fury from her legion of enemies, was that she mastered many of the arts in which women were not supposed to dabble. She despised the backstairs ('I think anyone that has common sense or honesty must needs be very weary of every thing that one meets with in courts'), and wanted to capture other arenas altogether. She conducted, even apart from her battles on behalf of Marlborough, a one-woman liberation.

She made herself, as she herself said, 'a kind of author'. It is hard to know which to marvel at the more, the modesty of the claim from one not normally modest or its truth—especially since in her early years she had accepted the orthodox doctrine of the time about the non-education of girls. 'I am no scholar', she came near to boasting, 'nor a wit, thank God', or on another occasion: 'An ounce of mother wit is better than a pound of clargy.' Her mother wit and her other charms were quite sufficient to enable her to capture young Churchill at the time of her choosing; she needed no assistance from any other art. True, women authors were beginning, just at that time and soon after, to make something of a name in Grub Street or elsewhere: Mary Astell, for example, a true pioneer among woman writers or Mrs. Riviere Manley who was there to prove that the malice would not be left to the men. But why should radiant court beauties who had already set out, with the aid of other gifts, on the path to fame, fortune, and great estates, worry their pretty heads about learning how to use pens? Sarah soon did, and what she must have absorbed for the purpose is a wonder in itself. 'I am of the simple sex', she once said, incredibly, 'and I tumble my mind out on paper without any disguise.' Who will believe it was just quite like that? Mostly she would scorn any disguise in any situation anywhere, but her downright simplicity of style was not so easily acquired. The books on the shelves in her libraries at Blenheim or later St. Albans included Burton, Burnet, Clarendon, Milton, Cowper, Dryden, Spencer, Shakespeare, Ben Jonson, *Don Quixote*, Montaigne, Cowley, Waller, St. Egremont, Plutarch and Epictetus in translation, several volumes on medicine, architecture and theology, with Swift and Addison to add the final contemporary touch. No doubt most of these shelf-fuls in great houses, even in those days, were intended for display, and Sarah herself would not allow that she was deeply read; but she did take one or two favourites to her heart, notably *Don Quixote* and Montaigne, and one of her correspondents was driven to remark: 'In your letter that lyes now before me, one part is written exactly after Montaigne's manner, so much has your Grace profited by those few Books which you say you have read.' No bookworm, for sure: what she wanted was action, but that she did read is proved in her own writing. Anyhow, she had plenty to divert her from Queen Anne's royal 'twitell-twatell'.

Alas, huge stacks of what she wrote herself, in her correspondence to Marlborough in particular but to many others besides, were destroyed on her own orders. Yet mountains remain—some six hundred volumes have recently arrived from Blenheim at the British Library, and out of it all a new vindication of Sarah may come. Yet for some reason her published writing, her own book *The Conduct**, together with the portraits of some of her contemporaries, has rarely received the credit it deserves. Horace Walpole condemned it, at the time of publication, as 'the annals of a wardrobe rather than a reign', and neither she nor her admirers have ever been able quite to remove the effects of that sneer. It is true that she managed to recount the events of that age, including even how King William would gobble his dish of peas, without even mentioning the Battle of Blenheim. Must she not be convicted, then, from her own mouth, as a woman of constricted mind, an incorrigible gossip herself, confined by the Horace Walpole sense of proportion? Maybe; and who is Horace Walpole to complain? It is hard not to suppose that in dealing with the Duchess he was just avenging his father for her ancient feud against him. But *The Conduct* is truly a much better book than that. It is fresh, glowing with life, lit up by the political

---

*An Account of the Conduct of the Dowager Duchess of Marlborough. From her first coming to Court to the Year 1710 In a letter from Herself to MYLORD published in 1842.

flames of party strife which rose so high in Queen Anne's time but which scarcely still smouldered when the book was published thirty years later. The language in which it is written has a force and fury of its own; sharp, hard, belligerent, immediately intelligible, and yet not in any sense naive. She wanted everyone to know—a good reason for writing.

And she always had the sense to realise there was a battle on. Never had she had any patience with those, her husband included, who hankered always for some uneasy accommodation above party strife. The facts could not be altered; the beginning of wisdom was to face them. From her earliest days of introduction to the political scene she had imbibed Whig principles, a hatred of 'the gibberish' of the Tories 'about non-resistance and passive obedience and hereditary right', a splendid contempt for 'the High Church nonsense of promoting religion by persecution'. As it happened, when King William III first arrived he heaped hardship on the Marlborough family, but that could not drive Sarah into the opposite camp:

> As I was perfectly convinced that a Roman Catholic is not to be trusted with the liberties of England, I never once repined at the change of government, no, not in all the time of that long persecution I went through.

When William had sent Marlborough to the Tower, she still did not waver. To a friend who offered bail she replied that 'one of his best friends was a paper that lay upon the table which I had often kissed, the Act of Habeas Corpus'—and Sarah, be it not forgotten, was only then nine years old when Habeas Corpus was enacted. England was at that time the only country in the world where such a protection for individual rights existed; how much of English liberty do we owe to those who treasured it as Sarah did. Marlborough would go off and fight, and win, the wars; no one appreciated that necessity better than Sarah. But there were other unavoidable battles to be fought and indispensable victories to be won here at home, where Sarah grasped the reality so much more firmly than Marlborough himself, and how infuriating it must have been when the doors were slammed in her face. 'I am confident', she asserted (and who would ever doubt it?), 'that I would have been the greatest hero that was ever known in the Parliament House, if I had been so happy as to have been a man.'

How nearly the men on the larger stage, in the Parliament House without her assistance and outside, came to casting aside all that had been won at home and abroad. How foolish they were not to recognise her simple proposition. If English and European liberties depended on victory, Marlborough would need to make terms with the men who truly believed in them, the party which had burnt its boats and staked its whole future on the Protestant succession. This was the gospel which she preached in season and out of season, to the Queen, to the Duke and to the whole of her entourage. And who can say that she was wrong? Terribly late and by *force majeure* Marlborough himself was brought to the same conclusion. At last he too realised that his fate was interlocked with that of the great Whig Lords. But how much safer his base at home would have been if he had recognised the fact earlier, and had pursued the aim of an alliance with the Whigs from the beginning of the reign with something of Sarah's rock-like determination.

Sarah foresaw the future more plainly than most of her contemporaries, especially those of her own class. She recognised that the Whig grandees, denounced by Anne and Marlborough as factious self-seekers, were the real custodians of the spirit of the age, the unwitting protectors of the English liberty she loved. They alone could safeguard the achievements of the English Revolution against Stuart counter-revolution. She strove to rally all her friends, including her husband, to this cause, and everyone would have been saved a lot of trouble if her advice had been accepted sooner. She was a modern, independent woman, and, judged by her ideas and manners, the citizen of a new century into which Marlborough, with his fear of public opinion and open debate, survived only as an anachronism.

So there was a political clash of temperament between them, arising partly from her feminism, to use the word even more anachronistically than in the case of Disraeli, and how little it has been allowed for by even the greatest of the Duke's biographers may be seen in the famous story of her retort to the Duke of Somerset's proposal of marriage delivered, of course, long after

Marlborough was dead and when she was a ripe but still devastatingly beautiful sixty-three. The historian William Coxe, a near-contemporary, had one majestic version which Sir Winston grandiloquently and excusably reiterated:

> If I were young and handsome as I was instead of old and faded as I am, and you could lay the empire of the world at my feet, you should never share the heart and hand that once belonged to John, Duke of Marlborough.

Magnificent, but not Sarah! In more recent times a copy of the actual letter of refusal was discovered in the Blenheim archives and a review in *The Times Literary Supplement* described it as 'more prosaic and more probable'. More probable and less romantic, for sure: but prosaic is not precisely the term to describe this declaration of independence which was surely directed not to the Duke but to mankind in general:

> I am confident that there is very few women (if any) that would not be extremely pleased with what your grace proposes to me; but I am resolved never to change my condition, and if I know anything of myself I would not marry the Emperor of the world tho I were but thirty years old . . .

Such was the woman to whom Professor Plumb will attribute greatness only on account of her viragoish temperament. What great men could survive similar discrimination—to see all their political aims and accomplishments submerged beneath domestic embroilments and vanities. What would happen, on such a condition, to Lloyd George's fame or Lord Palmerston's, and how many more? Even Henry VIII managed to pass himself off as a Renaissance prince, a Protestant hero, a Tudor statesman, and that, moreover, at the hands of Victorian historians. How pitiful by comparison is the dispensation customarily allowed poor Sarah, and the caricature largely sketched by Professor Plumb would not have been recognised, even in her rancorous old age, by some of her bitterest critics and former enemies. For, strangest of all, this Lady Macbeth *manqué* had a sense of humour which kept on breaking out at the most unlikely moments and right to her dying day. Voltaire came to call on her, wanting to see her Memoirs before publication, but she insisted: 'Wait a little; I am altering my account of Queen Anne's character. I have come to love her again since the present lot have become our governors.'* At the age of eighty-one she exchanged enchanting letters, part flirtatious, part remonstrative, with Alexander Pope who had once attacked her and her Duke almost as furiously as Swift but who became so captivated that, enfolded in a character-sketch of her of excruciating perception, were his last words, almost: 'What a girl you are!' Almost, but not quite. Pope, allegedly, lampooned her as Atossa in his *Moral Essays*. Almost certainly the allegation was false; he had another beauty on his list. Enough damage had been done, in her estimate, however, to restore him to the status of 'that crooked, perverse little wretch at Twickenham'—quite a kindly rebuke in the circumstances. And happily no such last-minute cloud befell an even more remarkable literary recon-ciliation. She was 'in raptures' over *Gulliver's Travels*, and sat up in bed lamenting—if only *he* had been on our side in the old battles of Queen Anne's time. She 'grew prodigiously fond of him', and 'could easily forgive him all the slaps he has given me and the Duke of Marlborough'. And she could flick aside anyone she wanted with the lightest touch of one of those old arthritic fingers. I like this epitaph on a great man otherwise quite forgotten:

> Lord Scarborough voted with the minority, and spoke, though he has something so very particular, that I can't be sure he will go on, for he is always splitting a hair; but there is now, I think, no hair to split.

One of the great questions of politics which politicians do not always appreciate is to discern the moments when there are no more hairs to split. In the great age of Queen Anne, Sarah knew

---

*A recent, most substantial and perhaps definitive life of Queen Anne—*Queen Anne* by Edward Gregg (Routledge, Kegan Paul, 1980) has rehabilitated the Queen at the expense of the Duchess, and some reviewers have rushed in to damn the Duchess afresh. But it is pleasant to note here how Sarah had antici-pated them.

that better than anyone else. It was the men, *pace* Prince Eugen at the head of this chapter, who had allowed things in England to go from bad to worse, and Sarah, given her magnificent head, could have saved it all.

FOURTEEN

Round the next corner: the pursuit of Jonathan Swift

Oh, when shall we have such another Rector of Laracor!
—William Hazlitt

JONATHAN SWIFT was born in Dublin in the year 1667 (the exact circumstances and the details of parentage are all part of the endless mystification which still surrounds his name), and three hundred years later proper and lavish tercentenary celebrations were conducted in Trinity College, Dublin, where he was educated and which he had left in the year 1686, not exactly 'under a cloud', yet without the slightest hint of the world-wide fame which was one day to be his. Any writer anywhere who had shown any interest in Swift was invited to the occasion, and this was already a guarantee of a mass attendance. At the opening ceremony in the Public Theatre the Roman Catholic Bishop from University College talked as if Swift, with a few nods and adjustments, might almost have been a Catholic, and the Presbyterian Provost from Trinity itself managed to make no embarrassing reference to Swift's unprintable views about Presbyterianism. The only speaker who attempted to attain Swift's own standard of candour, renouncing all traces of hypocrisy whatever, was the President of the Irish Republic at that moment, Eamon De Valera. It was wonderful to see him in his eighties, almost blind, being guided to the rostrum, to put the assembled worlds of scholarship, literature and religion in their respective places. He explained his own difficulties in accepting Swift as a true Irish patriot. He described how the snatches of information which he had learned about Swift in his childhood had not originally been convincing; and how hard it was to suppose that any good thing could come out of such a stronghold of the English ascendancy as Trinity College. A whiff of Easter, 1916, wafted through the hall. And yet it was Swift's slogan, we were told at last, which had touched the heart of Mr. De Valera: 'Burn everything English but their coal'—the most successful example of sanctions in history, enforced by the Irish against the English, according to the directions of a disappointed would-be Anglican bishop turned revolutionary.

We must go to Ireland to appreciate Swift in the fullest measure. There he was born, there he was exiled or self-exiled, there he died, but there he scaled the highest peaks of his greatness, and there he was rescued during his lifetime, and on numerous notable occasions thereafter, from his English defamers. There the true Swift is still guarded today. In England he is a great writer; in Ireland he is part of the folklore. You can walk beside St. Patrick's Cathedral and imagine, as Yeats said, that you see him round the next corner, being cheered through the streets by the people, riding respectably in his carriage with Stella and Mrs. Dingley or sneaking off to an assignation with Vanessa. In Dublin, for some twenty years during his lifetime, they lit bonfires to celebrate his birthday, and three hundred years later not a single one from the host of critics, for all their other controversies on every other aspect of his life and work, could question his devotion to the cause of Irish freedom. And it was at the height of his Irish popularity, let it never be forgotten, that he wrote *Gulliver's Travels* and unloosed within the human mind a tumult which has never since subsided.

Gulliver's Travels, like most of the other great books of the world, has been freshly interpreted from age to age. Cherished alongside *Robinson Crusoe* as a children's book, it has, quite unlike *Crusoe*, been the subject of furious debate among historians, philosophers and literary critics. Many of its pages are devoted to direct political satire, but we may safely guess that not one in ten thousand of its appreciative readers is aware of even the most patent particular references. Writers claiming to do no more than appraise its philosophical content have been driven to paroxysms of denunciation. Somehow the foremost exponent of lucidity in the English language has left as his chief legacy a grotesque enigma.

The author protests at the outset that 'the style is very plain and simple'. And so it is. In accordance with his custom, Swift read large chunks aloud to his servants, to make sure that every sentence attained his rigorous standard of simplicity. It is possible, with much enjoyment, to skate over the surface, most of it as smooth as ice, without noticing the dark chasms underneath, and this no doubt is what children do with their expurgated editions. But no one can deceive himself for long. Gentleness, playfulness, irony, finely-poised argument and lacerating invectives are so carefully enfolded one within another that it is evident Jonathan Swift created the endless mystery on purpose.

Part One, A Voyage to Lilliput, is the fantasy about the giant in the land of midgets told in such unchallengeable, precise, matter-of-fact terms that it has become a household word and idea in every civilised tongue throughout the world. Yet through this section in particular runs a long, weaving stream of topical innuendo about the forgotten politics of the reign of Queen Anne. Part Two, A Voyage to Brobdingnag, is Lilliput in reverse, but it also offers some of Swift's fiercest assaults upon the behaviour of his fellow countrymen and the nearest effort he ever made to describe his own notion of an ideal state. Part Three, A Voyage to Laputa, etc., is evidently directed against the scientists and philosophers of his own age, but how up to date these gentlemen appear. Part Four, A Voyage to the Houyhnhnms, has been regarded as a vile or corrective satire on human nature itself, but any attempt to compress its meaning into a sentence becomes an absurdity. In the country of the Houyhnhnms, the ground trembles beneath our feet; a storm beats about our heads; terrifying shafts of light and darkness are thrown backwards across the rest of the book, into every corner of the human mind.

Gulliver's Travels is a perpetual, unfinished argument, one from which flatly contradictory morals have been and still can be extracted. And, wondrously, no reader need be deterred by the experts from forming his own judgement. On this subject, some of the most eminent authorities have made the most eminent

asses of themselves, a development which Swift foresaw and
invited. He says in the last chapter that he hopes he may
pronounce himself 'an author perfectly blameless, against whom
the tribe of answerers, considerers, observers, reflecters, detec-
ters, remarkers, will never be able to find matter for exercising
their talents'. By which, of course, he meant the opposite. One of
the fascinations of *Gulliver's Travels* is that, although every
phrase seems immediately comprehensible, the whole subject
matter is endlessly complex.

When the book was published, anonymously, on 28 October
1726, success was instantaneous. One report said that ten
thousand copies were sold in three weeks. Immediate translations
were made into French and Dutch, weekly journals started
printing pirated extracts, and Swift's friends in London com-
peted with one another in dispatching glowing reports to the
author in Dublin. Dr. John Arbuthnot, the closest friend of all,
wrote:

> I will make over all my profits to you for the property of Gulliver's
> Travels; which, I believe, will have as great a run as John Bunyan.
> Gulliver is a happy man, that, at his age [Swift was fifty-nine], can
> write such a merry book.

Alexander Pope and John Gay wrote jointly: 'From the highest to
the lowest it is universally read, from the cabinet council to the
nursery.' Thus soon was the volume accepted as a classic
simultaneously from the cradle to the corridors of power. The old
Duchess of Marlborough, once the victim of Swift's harshest
abuse, was said to be 'in raptures at it; she says she can dream of
nothing else since she read it'. And Swift's own fears were set at
rest. He had told Pope a year before that publication would have
to wait until 'a printer shall be found brave enough to venture his
ears'; in those days authors at odds with the authorities risked the
pillory or imprisonment as well as mere poverty. He had warned
the publisher, to whom the manuscript was deviously delivered,
that some parts of what he had written 'may be thought in one or
two places to be a little satirical'. But all was well. No hint of a
prosecution, such as had often threatened Swift before in his

pamphleteering career, was heard. 'It has passed Lords and Common's *nemine contradicente*, and the whole town, men, women and children are full of it', was Pope's reassurance. One of the few expressions of protest at the time, heralding what was to follow later, came, curiously, from a member of Swift's intimate circle, Lord Bolingbroke; 'he is the person', continued Pope, 'who least approves it, blaming it as a design of evil consequence to depreciate human nature.' But this might have been no more than a joke at Bolingbroke's expense, comparable with that told of the old gentleman who, when lent the book, was alleged to have gone immediately to his map to search for Lilliput, or of the Bishop who said it was 'full of improbable lies, and, for his part, he hardly believed a word of it'. Pope, the Roman Catholic, and Swift, the militant Church of England or Church of Ireland man, needed no excuse to poke fun at Bolingbroke and his deistical, or even atheistical, deviations from the Christian faith. 'A merry book' by a man gay-spirited and greatly loved as well as feared—that was the general view of Swift's contemporaries. Stomachs were stronger in the reigns of Queen Anne and George I.

Fifty years later, in his *Lives of the English Poets*, Dr. Johnson gravely recalled the publication of the already famous volume:

> A production so new and strange that it filled the reader with a mingled emotion of merriment and amazement. It was received with such avidity, that the price of the first edition was raised before the second could be made; it was read by high and low, the learned and illiterate. Criticism was for a while lost in wonder; no rules of judgement were applied to a book written in open defiance of truth and regularity.

Thereafter, Johnson applied his own rules. Boswell tells how the assault upon Swift was renewed on all available occasions, despite his own valiant efforts to withstand the deluge of nonsense. Johnson thought that Swift's political writings were inferior to Addison's, that his most brilliant pamphlet, *The Conduct of the Allies*, was a mere bundle of facts, that *Gulliver's Travels* might be assigned to its proper place thus: 'when once you have thought of the big men and the little men, it is very easy to do all the rest.' A good Johnsonian joke, maybe, but it still leaves us wondering whether, apart even from his critical judgement, he ever got past the first two books and the disappearance of the big men and the little men from the scene.

More insidiously effective, however, than the criticism of Swift's talents was the denigration of his demeanour and character. A man of muddy complexion, of sour and severe countenance, deficient in both wit and humour, one 'who stubbornly resisted any tendency to laughter', was Johnson's summary. The beloved friend of Arbuthnot and Pope, the drinking companion of Addison and Steele, recedes, and a grim twisted specimen begins to take his place. Dr. Johnson even recalls, with some relish and too faint repudiation, the false tale that Pope entrusted to his executors a defamatory Life of Swift which he had prepared in advance as an instrument of vengeance to be drawn from its scabbard if provocation arose; the implication being, presumably, that Swift might have savaged Pope or at least that Pope considered him capable of it. The historical evidence is different. Never in our literary annals has there existed between two prominent figures a purer friendship and one so untinged by the slightest strain of jealousy or envy as that which prevailed between Pope and Swift. All Pope's superabundant venom subsided in the presence of Swift, and Swift's devotion, in particular it could be said, never wavered or weakened to the end of his days. Yet the tale-bearers spread lies about Swift's disloyalties, his eccentricities, his furies, his diseased nature, his madness. 'The merry book' was quite forgotten; it had become something sinister. Indeed, the strangest fate overtook Swift's general reputation. When he died in 1745, he had already, in the words of a recent critic, Professor Ricardo Quintana, 'ceased to be understood by the eighteenth century . . . No English writer of corresponding stature has been repudiated so persistently and so fiercely by immediately succeeding generations'.

How the change occurred, from the first exultation that the human mind had produced a delight and a marvel to such frantic fear or hate, is not easy to discern. Some responsibility may rest with the ineffectualness of Swift's early biographers who purveyed silly gossip about him with ponderous assiduity. But the heaviest burden of guilt must still rest on Dr. Johnson. True, ever-

growing multitudes of readers continued to read Swift despite
Johnson's condemnation of his manners and his morals. True,
some years later, a few stray voices were raised openly in
defence—William Godwin, William Cobbett, William Hazlitt.
But these were literary no less than political outcasts, quite
beyond the pale of the early nineteenth-century literary Establishment, rabid apologists for, if not actual advocates of,
revolution after the French style. Defence from that quarter
damned Swift more than ever.

And who truly wished to defend him? Sir Walter Scott, a
kindred Tory and fellow spirit, it might be thought, made the
effort valiantly. He produced a collected edition of Swift's works,
greatly admired his poems, read the *Journal to Stella* with a
fresh, sympathetic eye, and wrote a compassionate, intelligent
Life. Yet he recoiled from *Gulliver's Travels*:

> Severe, unjust and degrading as this satire is, it was hailed with
> malignant triumph by those whose disappointed hopes had thrown
> them into the same state of gloomy misanthropy which it argues in its
> author.

If this was how Swift was to be defended by his political friends,
what could he expect from his enemies? Francis Jeffrey, in his
Edinburgh Review article on Scott's book, made a momentary
effort to distinguish between the literary achievement and the
character, and then launched into a brilliant libel in which the
victim might have been a composite Tory figure of Jeffrey's own
age. Macaulay, in 1833, went much further. He conjured up in one
ferocious sentence a vision hard to dispel:

> the apostate politician, the ribald priest, the perjured lover, a heart
> burning with hatred against the whole human race, a mind richly
> stored with images from the dunghill and the lazar house.

The portrait of the monster was now widely accepted, and, in
1851, Thackeray unloosed an invective which, even when its
more flamboyant passages are dismissed as hysterical, leaves no
doubt about what had become the settled verdict of Victorian
opinion.

Dr. Johnson, wrote Thackeray (it was always safe to ride into battle behind that shield),

> could not give the Dean that honest hand of his; the stout old man puts it into his breast, and moves off from him . . . As fierce a beak and talon as ever struck, as strong as ever beat, belonged to Swift . . . One can gaze, and not without awe and pity, at the lonely eagle chained behind bars . . . The 'saeva indignatio' of which he spoke as lacerating his heart, and which he dares to inscribe on his tomb-stone—as if the wretch who lay under that stone waiting God's Judgement had a right to be angry—breaks out from him in a thousand pages of his writing, and tears and rends him . . .

Thus the prelude on Swift's character has prepared the way for the cool appraisal of his book:

> Mr. Dean has no softness, and enters the nursery with the tread and gaiety of an ogre . . . Our great satirist was of the opinion that conjugal love was inadvisable, and illustrated the theory by his own practice and example—God help him—which made him about the most wretched being in God's world . . . As for the humour and conduct of this famous fable, I suppose there is no person who reads but must admire; as for the moral, I think it horrible, shameful, unmanly, blasphemous; and giant and great as this Dean is, I say we should hoot him . . . It [the fourth book of Gulliver] is Yahoo language; a monster, gibbering shrieks and gnashing imprecations against mankind—tearing down all shreds of modesty, past all sense of manliness and shame; filthy in word, filthy in thought, furious, raging, obscene.

And thus—but there is much more of it—in the name of everything the nineteenth century considered holy, Thackeray anticipated the Day of Judgement. The merry book had become a work of the devil.

A few decades later, some lesser figures than Macaulay and Thackeray struggled to retrieve the century's critical reputation. A series of writers attempted the serious work of biography previously neglected and the more they assembled facts in their proper context the more the picture of Swift, the ogre, began to dissolve. Leslie Stephen in his volume (1882) and Churton

Collins in his (1893) surveyed the work already done in rectifying glaring injustices, but even so, both quailed before the later sections of *Gulliver's Travels*. Leslie Stephen called them 'painful and repulsive' and 'a ghastly caricature':

> Readers who wish to indulge in a harmless play of fancy will do well to omit the last two voyages; for the strain of misanthropy which breathes in them is simply oppressive. They are probably the sources from which the popular impression of Swift's character is often derived. It is important therefore to remember that they were wrung from him in later years, after a life tormented by constant disappointment and disease.

Churton Collins's reactions were similar:

> It [*Gulliver's Travels*, he wrote] has no moral, no social, no philosophical purpose. It was the mere ebullition of cynicism and misanthrophy. A savage *jeu d'esprit*. And as such wise men will regard it . . . At no period distinguished by generosity of sentiment, by humanity, by decency, could such satire have been universally applauded. Yet so it was. The men and women of those times appear to have seen nothing objectionable in an apologue which would scarcely have passed without protest in the Rome of Petronius.

So even strong Swift defenders seemed unable to repel the weight of the attack. Augustine Birrell, reviewing Churton Collins's biography in the 1890s, could write:

> It is a question not of morality, but of decency, whether it is becoming to sit in the same room with the works of this divine . . . Thackeray's criticism is severe, but is it not just? Are we to stand by and hear our nature libelled, and our purest affections beslimed, without a word of protest?

Somehow *Gulliver* could not be treated as a book at all; it was unfit for human consumption.

Twenty-five years later, to his credit, Birrell had recovered a sense of proportion. Partly he had been studying Swift's new biographers, although these, as we have seen, were still on the defensive about *Gulliver*. Partly he attributed the conversion to a warm-hearted lecture in defence of Swift, as the enemy of injustice and oppression, delivered by Charles Whibley at Cambridge in 1917. But, more obviously, he himself had been reading—and writing a Life of—William Hazlitt, and Hazlitt could have saved all concerned a century of trouble and defamation. For in the year 1817—exactly a century before Whibley's apologia—Hazlitt had delivered a lecture which both replied to Dr. Johnson and leaped forward to adopt a modern view of *Gulliver's Travels*. Little notice was taken of it at the time, except by an unknown John Keats, then twenty-two years old. Leslie Stephen and Churton Collins, disinterring Hazlitt's case as if they had made some recondite discoveries, both acknowledged its force, but found it too extreme for acceptance. It must be pardonable to quote a part of the passage at length and to marvel that Hazlitt, Macaulay, Thackeray and the rest were supposedly talking about the same man and the same book.

Whether the excellence of *Gulliver's Travels* is in the conception or the execution, [wrote Hazlitt] is of little consequence; the power is somewhere, and it is a power that has moved the world. The power is not that of big words and vaunting common places. Swift left these to those who wanted them; and has done what his acuteness and intensity of mind alone could enable any one to conceive or to perform. His object was to strip empty pride and grandeur of the imposing air which external circumstances throw around them; and for this purpose he has cheated the imagination of the illusions which the prejudices of sense and of the world put upon it, by reducing everything to the abstract predicament of size. He enlarges or diminishes the scale, as he wishes, to shew the insignificance or the grossness of our overweening self-love. That he has done this with mathematical precision, with complete presence of mind and perfect keeping, in a manner that comes equally home to the understanding of the man and of the child, does not take away from the merit of the work or the genius of the author. He has taken a new view of human nature, such as a being of a higher sphere might take of it; he has torn the scales from off his moral vision; he has tried an experiment with human life, and sifted its pretensions from the alloy of circumstances; he has measured it with a rule, has weighed it in a balance, and found it, for the most part, wanting and worthless—in substance and in shew. Nothing solid, nothing valuable is left in his system but virtue and wisdom. What a libel is this upon mankind! What a convincing proof of misanthrophy! What presumptions and what *malice prepense*, to shew men what they are, and to teach them what they ought to be! What a mortifying stroke aimed at national glory, is that unlucky incident of Gulliver's wading across the channel and carrying off the whole fleet of Blefuscu! After that, we have only to consider which of the contending parties was in the right. What a shock to personal vanity is given in the account of Gulliver's nurse Glumdalclitch! Still, notwithstanding the disparagement of her personal charms, her good-nature remains the same amiable quality as before. I cannot see the harm, the misanthrophy, the immoral and degrading tendency of this. The moral lesson is as fine as the intellectual exhibition is amusing. It is an attempt to tear off the mask of imposture from the world; and nothing but imposture has a right to complain of it.

There! Swift, one feels, would have cheered. At last someone had understood. In the next paragraph, Hazlitt, at the distance of a century, took it upon himself to forgive Swift for having been a Tory, and Swift, if he had read this encomium, would surely have repaid the compliment and forgiven Hazlitt for a lifetime's dedication to his rebel faith. Across the gulf of time and politics, there was a kinship between their spirits, and the common strand runs through *Gulliver's Travels*.

It is curious that Augustine Birrell, the biographer of Hazlitt, did not record his debt to that passage, and curious too that, in the period of the so-called Whibley revaluation, he did not take into account an essay by H. W. Nevinson far more telling than Whibley's and written some years earlier. Nevinson, the rebel and the intimate friend of rebels, like Hazlitt, recognised Swift as one of the same tribe. The rebel streak was not the whole of Swift, but it was part of him.

It was not [wrote Nevinson] any spirit of hatred or cruelty but an intensely personal sympathy with suffering, that tore his heart and kindled that furnace of indignation against the stupid, the hateful and the cruel to whom most suffering is due; and it was a furnace in which he himself was consumed. Writing while he was still a youth in *A Tale of a Tub*, he composed a terrible sentence, in which all his rage and pity and ironical bareness of style seem foretold: 'Last week,' he says, 'I saw a woman flayed, and you will hardly believe how much it altered her person for the worse.'

How has it ever been possible to think that the man who wrote those words lacked a heart, and could anyone but the author of *Gulliver* have written them?

The man and the book; the two become inextricable, however open to objection such a method of judgement may be. It is peculiarly difficult to discuss Swift's writings, insisted F. R. Leavis, without shifting the focus of discussion to the kind of man that Swift was:

> For instance, one may (it appears), having offered to discuss the nature and import of Swift's satire, find oneself countering imputations of misanthrophy with the argument that Swift earned the love of Pope, Arbuthnot, Gay, several other men and two women; this should not be found necessary by the literary critic.

Yet did Dr. Leavis abide by his own rule? Having reached the conclusion that Swift's greatness 'is no matter of moral grandeur or human centrality: our sense is merely a sense of great force', he added: 'And this force, as we feel it, is conditioned by frustration and constriction: the channels of life have been blocked and perverted.' The man-monster peeps out again, and before proceeding farther it must be discovered how valid the apparition may be.

Was *Gulliver's Travels*, or at least the Voyage to the Houyhnhnms, the product of a perverted, diseased mind? Was Swift a gloomy misanthrope who never laughed, a tormented hater of all men and, more particularly, all women, consumed at last in the furnace of his own fury? Did he, in short, go mad? Altogether, the charge of madness has been made by the following, among others: Dr. Johnson, Walter Scott, Macaulay, Thackeray, Aldous Huxley, W. B. Yeats possibly, D. H. Lawrence probably, George Orwell, Malcolm Muggeridge and A. L. Rowse. A reviewer of Professor Rowse's major book, *Jonathan Swift: Major Prophet** Mr. Michael Gearing Tosh in the *Sunday Times* in January 1976 wrote: 'Swift was a Christian who hated mankind. This must have created a fierce tension whose outcome,

---

*Published by Thames & Hudson, 1975.

if suicide were excluded by faith, could hardly have been other than madness. And Swift became insane.' Q.E.D. 'The odds are', we were coolly told a few years earlier, on the combined medical and scholarly authority of Malcolm Muggeridge, a delighted and delightful admirer of Swift, 'that the illness which struck him down was GPI, doubtless due to syphilis, contracted when he was young and addicted to what he called low company.' Maybe literary critics should not be concerned with such trifles. But if the author did in truth go mad, it would be hard to deny that some support is given to the Johnson, even the Thackeray, view of the book. Moreover, in the list of accusers tabulated above appears the potent name of Yeats. If he, the great Irish poet of the twentieth century, was willing to pass such a judgement on his great Irish predecessor, must not others be excused? Yeats wrote a play in which the subject was Swift's supposed premonition of madness, and he had a vision of

Swift beating on his breast in sibylline frenzy blind
Because the heart in his blood-sodden breast had dragged him down
into mankind

True, Yeats also turned into poetic form Swift's epitaph which he called the greatest ever written, and there is no element of madness to be discerned there. Yet it is hard, once the phrase is uttered, ever to expunge the thought of that sibylline frenzy.

Swift, it must be acknowledged too, has offered much testimony against himself. Someone called him, justly, an inverted hypocrite because he often seemed to paint himself in undeservedly harsh colours. 'I shall be like that tree, I shall die at the top', he said and the prophecy has been quoted a hundred times, out of context, as a key to his personality. 'Principally I hate and detest that animal called man . . .' runs another half-sentence of self-conviction. He bequeathed his small fortune to found an asylum in Dublin and wrote the famous lines on his own death:

He gave the little wealth he had
To build a House for Fools and Mad.
And shew'd by one Satyric Touch,
No nation needed it so much.

Have we not here intimations of his sympathy for those who suffered his own fate? He resented his enforced exile in Ireland and talked of dying 'in a rage, like a poisoned rat in a hole'. There is, alas, plentiful evidence from various witnesses of the scarcely endurable pains and miseries which bore him to the grave. Is all this, then, plus the horrific passages of *Gulliver's Travels*, not enough to clinch the case?

It is not, and nothing like it. Most of the real evidence available strongly suggests that Swift did not go mad, and that the story of an appalling end compounded of rage, violence and fatuity was a myth at first maliciously spread and then much too readily adopted and disseminated by Dr. Johnson, who rounded off a verse with the charge that Swift became, in his last years, 'a driviller and a show'. The medical case was examined a couple of decades ago by one of Britain's most distinguished brain neurologists, Lord Brain, who confirmed that most of his life Swift must have suffered from what is defined as Bilateral Meniere's disease, and that this would have accounted for his bursts of giddiness, vomiting and deafness. Eventually he also suffered from senile decay, as most of his accusers have or will. All these matters were properly surveyed by Professor Irvin Ehrenpreis in his book *The Personality of Jonathan Swift* (published in 1958, Methuen), and there is no reason to dissent, or rather there can be no means of escape, from his conclusion:

> Swift, from birth to death, was insane by no medical definition. He was no more eccentric or neurotic than Pope or Johnson, and probably less so. The tradition of his madness has been rejected for forty years by every qualified scholar who has bothered to look into the question.

As for the verses on his own death now cited as an illustration of Swift's awareness of his own fate, no claim could be more ludicrous. They were written some thirteen years before his death, long before the first time when the most virulent of his enemies has thought to suggest that he showed signs of insanity. To argue, even to hint, that they reveal a premonition of madness is to wrench four from the 486 most cheerful lines Swift ever wrote. It might indeed be the shortest cure for those who still talk of Swift's madness—better even than Lord Brain's diagnosis or Dr. Ehrenpreis's scholarship—to compel them to read the verses on the Death of Dr. Swift right through. They have some claim to be the gayest poem in the English language.

And what, we may wonder, was Yeats's verdict on this poem and this whole spacious arena of Swift's mind which they represent? He never attempted to tell us. Moreover, Yeats, when he talks or writes of Swift, must always be treated with some circumspection, to use no harsher word. He himself has described how, at some Irish Literary Society meeting in London in the 1890s, he in turn would attack 'the dishonest figures of Swift's attack on Wood's halfpence, and, making that my text, had argued that, because no sane man is permitted to lie knowingly, God made certain men mad, and that it was these men—daimon possessed as I said—who, possessing truths of passion that were intellectual falsehoods, had created nations',* An astonishing passage indeed; why, two hundred years and more after the event, should Yeats be so eager to reopen in dubious terms, it must be said, the arithmetical argument about Wood's halfpence? And Yeats must be surely the first person, certainly the first Irishman, who would attempt to trace such a direct, unbreakable connection between insanity and patriotism. Maybe Swift was 'dragged down into mankind' more readily than Yeats himself.

However, the case of Swift's madness, or rather of the determination of some of his enemies or critics or admirers to believe in it in the teeth of all the evidence, has a glaring feature all its own. His rescue from the charge does not depend solely on the latest neurological knowledge, valuable though that may be. Way back in the year 1846, a Dr. Mackenzie of Glasgow wrote to his medical friend W. R. Wilde, FRIA, FRCS of Dublin—later Sir William and later too the father of Oscar Wilde—suggesting that some of the medical assumptions of Swift's biographers were questionable, to say the least. Sir William obliged with three years of intelligent research and reached the firm conclusion:

---

*W. B. Yeats, *Memoirs* Macmillan 1972.

as we trust a fair examination of his case will show, Swift was not, at any period of his life, not even in his last illness, what is understood as mad.

The first edition of the book, *The Closing Years of Dean Swift's Life*, was published in Dublin in 1849 and received widespread and justified critical acclaim in Ireland principally but in some degree in England too. A second enlarged edition—with the epigraph added on the title page, 'I am not mad, most noble Festus'—was published in the same year. It contains a detailed examination of the evidence available, including of course Swift's own comments on his own health:

> Neither in his expression, nor the tone of his writings, nor from any examination of any of his acts, have we been able to discover a single symptom of insanity, nor aught but the effects of physical disease, and the natural wearing and decay of a mind such as Swift's . . .

The examination continued, as best the scrupulous Doctor could continue it, throughout the period when guardians had to be appointed to protect Swift in his senility, as has been required in the case of many others with no charge of insanity being preferred. Only at the end did the Doctor seek his revenge. He had given a glancing rebuke to Dr. Johnson, 'the most malevolent of all Swift's biographers', but even the more kindly Walter Scott could not be spared altogether:

> Sir Walter Scott's edition of Swift's works, [wrote Wilde] contains the following notice of his last poetical effusion. The exact date of the circumstance has not been recorded, but it appears to have been subsequent to the appointment of guardians of his person. 'The Dean in his lunacy had some intervals of sense, at which his guardians or physicians took him out for the air. On one of these days, when they came to the Park, Swift remarked a new building which he had never seen, and asked what it was designed for? to which Dr. Kingsbury answered "that Mr. Dean, is the magazine for arms and powder for the security of the city"—"Oh! Oh!" says the Dean, pulling out his pocket-book, "let me take an item of that. This is worth remarking: 'My tablets', as Hamlet says, 'my tablets—memory put down that!' "

Which produced these lines, said to be the last he ever wrote:

> *Behold! a proof of Irish sense;*
> *Here Irish wit is seen!*
> *When nothing's left that's worth defence,*
> *We build a magazine.*

Now if this proves the insanity of its author the reader is to judge.

And we may add: nothing frenzied could be detected in such an attitude, sibylline or otherwise.

It is insufferable that any subsequent biography of Swift should have been written without account being taken of William Wilde's examination, especially since a few of the latter-day nineteenth-century biographers did recognise its significance. Yet this has been the treatment in many twentieth-century biographies, including Professor Rowse's. Time and again Dr. Wilde's findings are neglected or overturned without a scrap of fresh evidence being offered. And what in any case has this two-and-a-half-century old debate about the last few years of Swift's life to do with *Gulliver's Travels*? 'A man's life', wrote Hazlitt in another connection, 'is his whole life, not the last glimmering snuff of the candle.' If Swift had gone mad in the last years, here would have been a sufficient retort. For *Gulliver's Travels* was published about twenty years before Swift's death; it was mostly written earlier still; the especially offensive voyage to the Houyhnhnms, the scholars reckon, was not the last part of the book to be compiled. It is just not true, as even the appreciative Leslie Stephen had inferred, that the last chapters were the outpouring of 'a diseased condition of his mind, perhaps of actual mental decay'. It is just not true, as Scott asserted, that when he wrote of the Yahoos he was suffering from 'incipient mental disease'. When he finished the book Swift was fifty-nine years old, still fully active, in complete possession of his faculties. If what he produced then, by far the most ambitious literary achievement of his life, was morbid and demonic, then the whole man was morbid and demonic. And such is often still the claim which must be considered.

Yet before attempting the ascent to this higher philosophic

ground, it is impossible to avoid the other personal questions. What of the perjured, syphilitic lover; the treacherous or impotent suitor of Stella and Vanessa, not to mention those more shadowy beauties, Varina and Betty Jones, and not to forget Mr. Muggeridge's low company? It is the seemingly inescapable conjecture about his treatment of Stella and Vanessa which leave so sickening a taste on the palate; the most formidable charge, in the words delivered by James Joyce, that he had destroyed two lives with his sentimental muddling. Biographers at one stage tended to divide themselves into Vanessa-ites and Stella-ites, but in the tercentenary year of 1967, at the hands of Mrs. Le Brocquy, an assault was made upon him on behalf of Vanessa *and* Stella, a most formidable combination, and a heavy blow for a man to receive as a tercentenary birthday present. Moreover, even these accusations may be considered mild in comparison with some others. D. H. Lawrence deduced from the scatological poems that the fellow suffered from 'a terror of the body', and Aldous Huxley was no less excited by the discovery that he hated the word *bowels*—'It was unbearable to him that men (and women even more, no doubt) should go through life with guts and sweetbreads, with liver and lights, spleens and kidneys'; he was an incurable romantic, one who resented the world of reality and would never dare face it. After such stuff, it is a relief even to arrive at Dr. Rowse. Professor John Kenyon, reviewing Dr. Rowse's book in the *Observer* wrote: 'All the evidence suggests that Swift was a latent homosexual, deeply frightened of women . . .', but 'all the evidence', not even Dr. Rowse's, suggests nothing of the sort. Dr. Rowse himself, having informed us at the start, without even a pretence at hinting at any substantiating evidence whatever, that the young Swift suffered from 'complete sexual repression', later excuses what may be supposed to be the outward expression of this disability by the difficulties all males must encounter from 'typical female unreason'. Later we are told, again without a shred of evidence, that the iron control which he sought vainly to impose on his sexual nature broke out in a reeking self-pity, 'as it did in the comparable exemplar of self-repression in our time, Lawrence of Arabia'. And, finally, to win sympathy for Swift (or, more likely, his biographer) which, in

defiance of all self-pitying allegations, Swift himself never invited,
Vanessa is dismissed as an importunate, infatuated bore, 'a
hopeless case'. Vanessa, the twin subject of Swift's most delightful poem, 'a hopeless case'! Stella had every excuse for her deadly
comment: that Dr. Swift had been known to write matchlessly on
any subject, even a broomstick. But not even the most sex-
addicted author should be allowed the same licence. And Swift
had his own final word on the point:

> For who could such a Nymph forsake
> Except a Blockhead or a Rake?

The best cure is to read Swift himself, to return afresh and
in particular to the seemingly inexhaustible sources of his comic
invention. He could make any company he was in laugh or smile;
he could lash any opponent, worthy or unworthy, with his wit;
and most of both the humour and the wit can still work their
magic today when the audience and the victims are no more. One
from that array of beautiful women was Mrs. Finch who, under
the more bewitching title of Ardeliah, was lauded for her prowess
in outwitting Apollo.

> The Nymph who oft had read in Books
>   Of that Bright God whom Gods invoke,
> Soon knew Apollo by his looks
>   And Guest his Business ere he Spoke
>
> He in the old Celestial Cant,
>   Confest his Flame, and Swore by Styx,
> What e're she would desire, to Grant,
>   But wise Ardeliah knew his Tricks.
>
> Ovid had warn'd her to beware,
>   Of Stroling Gods, whose usual Trade is,
> Under pretence of Taking Air,
>   To pick up Sublunary Ladies.

Apollo might be resistible, but not the irreverent Vicar in such a
mood. It is hard to believe that such faculties could be invoked at
will by a monster scarcely fit to associate with the rest of human
kind. However, a few more particular replies to the charges listed

above may be offered, not in the hope that the whole case may be clinched but rather to illustrate how wretched is the attempt to constrict Swift's genius in any narrow limits whatever. 'To discuss the colossal mind of the great Dean of St. Patrick's', wrote Lytton Strachey, 'would be no unworthy task for a Shakespeare. Less powerful spirits can only prostrate themselves in dumb worship, like Egyptian priests before the enormous effigies of their gods.' But the Swift-haters or the Swift-detractors have no such humility. His personal life, the scatalogical poems, the Stella-Vanessa imbroglio in particular, provide them with material which has been digested and regurgitated, from Dr. Johnson's day to Dr. Rowse's. No great writer, except Shakespeare himself, has had to endure more from the biographers or critics who would fasten on their subject their own vices or supposed virtues.

Nothing, for example, could be more pitiful than Dr. Rowse's attempt to foist upon Swift his own contempt for women. Poor Swift, of all people in his generation, would have squirmed to be defended thus, and Stella and Vanessa would have arisen, united in this if nothing else, and sustained by a vast assembly of their women contemporaries, to repudiate the indictment. He adored the company of women and they adored his; he was one of the very first to insist that women should have the same education as men ('my Master among the Houyhnhnms thought it monstrous for us to give the Females a different Education from the Males'); he could deride the notion of male superiority; by the cramped standards of his time he was almost a women's liberator. And similarly, and scarcely less conclusively, we can dismiss all the downright charges of perversion. One of the great Swiftian scholars dealt with at least two of these—the Huxley theory and the Lawrence theory—several decades ago, and no good reasons exist for reviving them. Herbert Davis explained how Huxley had stumbled on a Swiftian phrase in a letter to Stella—'I hate the word bowels'—and then attempted to construct upon it his notion of how Swift also hated the bodily functions. But Huxley had failed to notice that the word bowels, in its seventeenth or early eighteenth-century sense, meant something quite different from his assumption. And Lawrence's charges too may be equally discarded. He had argued that Swift's prudery had arisen partly from 'having taboo words'. Yet whatever other crimes he may have committed, Swift was guiltless on that count; he used all the words which Lawrence dared to utter a few centuries later. 'The whole significance of these poems (the ones selected by Lawrence and Huxley for attack)', wrote Herbert Davis, 'lies in the fact that Swift hated the ordinary romantic love-stuff.' It is scarcely credible that sentimentality should still figure on the charge-sheet. Indeed, in a sense the assault can be carried into the opposite camp. The best modern essay on Swift's scatalogical propensities is Norman O. Brown's *The Excremental Vision*, in which he expounds how 'if we are willing to listen to Swift we will find startling anticipations of Freudian theories about anality, about sublimation, and about the universal neuroses of mankind'. The thesis is driven home with Swiftian force. No longer is it necessary to consign the extensive excursions of Swift into scatalogy to some bluebeard's chamber. Norman Brown has nothing but contempt for those who would 'domesticate and housebreak this tiger of English literature'. He never commits the same error himself. But his tiger is a real live animal, not some figure of evil and of shadowy omen.

So with all idea of perversion, mild or monstrous, set aside, let us return to the Vanessa-Stella mystery. No solution is offered here—except the simplest: that is, that he loved them both and that his heart was torn between the two. It is hard to read of his long years with Stella, the poems he wrote to her, and the *Journal*, without believing he loved her; and if it wasn't love, it was something of his own invention very like it. As for Vanessa, it is impossible to read the poem to her without believing it was love, and that he must in some way have avowed it. If not, the last famous lines were too tantalisingly cruel to be imagined, and there is not even the faintest tinge of cruelty in the rest of the poem, and no sign indeed that Swift was ever cruel to his friends; he saved that for his assortment of well-chosen enemies. And why should it be difficult to accept the simplest explanation? Swift, for all his devotion to truth, could be defensive and secretive. He insisted upon his independence and privacy, even to his life-long companion, Stella. The nearest we can come to intimacy with him appears to be through his letters to her ('diurnal trifles', as Dr. Johnson fatheadedly called them), and yet these cover only a few years of his life and all but the most oblique reference to Vanessa is excluded from them. If he had *not* loved Vanessa, Stella and Mrs. Dingley back in Laracor, and the world at large ever since, would have been told much more about her. But we would never have had the love poem: *Cadenus and Vanessa* would never have enfolded its riveting mysteries in the language of grace and tenderness.

The most plausible elaboration of the simplest conclusion—not proof, of course: that will surely never be available—was supplied in Denis Johnston's *In Search of Swift* (published in 1959 and based on an article which he had written in *The Dublin Historical Record*, in June 1941). This is no place to recite the complicated details; but if it is true, as Johnston argues, that Swift was Stella's uncle, and that he discovered this at some date we do not know, then so much in his relation with Stella is explained. It explains the strange business whereby they were never known to meet alone in the same room and the terrible story of Swift demanding Stella's removal from the Deanery before she died. He could not live with Stella as man and wife, if those were the facts, without provoking or risking an intolerable scandal—intolerable for her as well as himself. As for Vanessa's endearing importunities, in Mr. Johnston's words: 'When cruelty was the only thing that could have saved her, he should have been cruel. She was wronged through the demonic pity that was the keystone of his character.' But that does not make him any form of monster or sex maniac or even Joyce's muddled sentimentalist. Denis Johnston concludes: 'He was a perfectly normal man, of colossal proportions, motivated by two of the most universal, the most lovable and the most dangerous of all human emotions—Pride and Pity.' It is intolerable at least that anyone should still write, as many have done, about Swift's life without considering Denis Johnston's formidable theory; intolerable too—even if the precise details of the Johnston theory are not accepted—that the shades of Stella and Vanessa should still be summoned from the grave to bring fresh damnation upon him. Thackeray talked as if it were Swift's treatment of the divine

Stella which stirred him to his highest pitch of fury; surely a combined piece of impertinence and vanity if ever there was one, since he, like the rest of us, did not know the intimate detail of Swift's relationship with the apparently uncomplaining Stella and since we are obviously intended to admire the gallantry with which Thackeray rushes to her aid. But Stella or Vanessa or anyone else, male or female, whom Swift is alleged to have used badly, serves the same purpose—to feed the insensate hostility which he beyond all other great writers seems to provoke. The reason must lie deeper in the doctrines he made peculiarly his own.

However, let us draw back again from any such ascent or descent. Let us glance at a few other items on the charge sheet. He spent a large part of his time—much more than a man of genius ought to waste—in seeking, scheming for, preferment in the Church, and that in turn meant toadying to politicians. It is, alas, true; that is what he did do, for a considerable part of his life. He devoted himself to becoming what he called that 'apt conjunction of lawn and black satin we entitle a Bishop'. He learnt the tricks and necessities of politicians in his own soul. In that world he noted that 'climbing is done in the same posture as creeping'. And some people tend to deplore the whole of this part of his career, but quite wrongly. If he had never descended into Grub Street, *Gulliver's Travels* could never have been written. And not only in *Gulliver's Travels*, but in many of his writings, he offers excellent advice for the treatment of politicians. He said, when he wrote to Stella: 'If we let these Ministers pretend too much, there will be no governing them.' And yet, at the same time when he said that, he also wrote a great defence of Grub Street and the journalists, which must be quoted at rather greater length. Maybe there are journals of the present age, possibly *Private Eye*, which would find comfort in painting these words on their walls.

In the Attic Commonwealth, [he wrote] it was the privilege and birthright of every citizen and poet to rail aloud, and in public, or to expose upon the stage, by name any person they pleased, though of the greatest figure whether a Creon, an Hyperbolus, an Alcibiades, or a Demosthenes; but, on the other side, the least reflecting word let fall against the people in general, was immediately caught up, and revenged upon the authors, however considerable for their quality or merits. Whereas in England it is just the reverse of all this. Here you may securely display your utmost rhetoric against mankind, in the face of the world . . . And when you have done, the whole audience, far from being offended, shall return you thanks, as a deliverer of precious and useful truths. Nay, farther, it is but to venture your lungs, and you may preach it in Covent Garden against foppery and fornication, and something else: against pride, and dissimulation, and bribery, at Whitehall: you may expose rapine and injustice in the Inns of Court Chapel: and in the city pulpit, be as fierce as you please against avarice, hypocrisy and extortion. 'Tis but a ball bandied to and fro and every man carries a racket about him, to strike it from himself, among the rest of the company. But on the other side, whoever should mistake the nature of things so far, as to drop but a single hint in public, how such a one starved half the fleet, and half poisoned the rest; how such a one, from a true principle of love and honour, pays no debt but for wenches and play; how such a one has got clap, and runs out of his estate; how Paris, bribed by Juno and Venus, loth to defend either party, slept out the whole cause on the bench; or how such an author makes long speeches in the senate, with much thought, little sense, and to no purpose; whoever, I say, should venture to be this particular, must expect to be imprisoned for *scandalum magnatum*; to have challenges sent to him; to be sued for defamation; and to be brought to the bar of the House of Commons.

No better defence of the journalistic craft has been written since that day.

Yet Swift's politics—the truth can no longer be blurred—left much to be desired. He himself made the confession playfully:

> *He was an Honest Man, I'll swear—*
> *Why, Sir, I differ from you there.*
> *For, I have heard another Story,*
> *He was a most confounded Tory.*

It is true. Search as we may, it is impossible to refute it. He did believe in a form of static society. He ranged himself against the moderns. He sneered at scientists. And what he would have said of the white heat or the black heart of the technological age passes comprehension. He believed that the hierarchical forms

of society should be left untouched. Walter Scott, certainly
no advanced thinker himself, talked of the antiquated and
unpopular nature of Swift's politics. Indeed Swift was inclined to
curse *all* politics. He put his verdict into the mouth of the King of
Brobdingnag. When Gulliver was in Brobdingnag, he explained to
the King how politics worked in England, and Swift wrote:

> The prejudices of his education prevailed so far, that he could not
> forbear from taking me up in his right hand, and stroking me gently
> with the other, after an hearty fit of laughing, asked me, whether I
> were a Whig or a Tory.

He was opposed to the idea of progress. He was inclined to be
extremely pessimistic about human nature. Which brings us to
the even more familiar charge: that he was a misanthrope; that he
was anti-life; that *Gulliver's Travels*, and especially the last book
and the picture of the Yahoos, is a vile satire on the whole human
race; almost the most terrifying ever written. That is the charge
which has been sustained over centuries. Before seeking to answer
it, however, it is necessary to pose the other side of the mystery.

If Swift was such a Tory, if he was so dedicated a champion of
the doctrines of original sin, why has he commanded such interest
and allegiance on the Left in British politics, and from the
romantic revolutionaries of later times who believed in the
perfectibility of man? It is no exaggeration to say that, for
considerable periods since Swift's death, the protection of his
reputation has rested almost entirely with people on the Left.
Tories and Whigs have reviled him, Dr. Johnson, the greatest of
the Tories, and Lord Macaulay, the greatest of the Whigs. But the
extreme radicals rallied to his defence. Before asking why they did
it, let us substantiate the claim.

Swift's defence of 'the whole people of Ireland' naturally made
him the enemy of the English Establishment, and he became a
great popular writer and a popular symbol. During John Wilkes's
fight on behalf of the free press against the King and the House of
Commons, there were riots and political demonstrations throughout London. One of them occurred outside the Rose and Crown
in Wapping, and it is recorded that an Irish voice above the

tumult was heard to greet Wilkes thus: 'By Jasus, he's a liberty boy—like Dean Swift.' And coming a little later, to the epoch of the French Revolution and its aftermath, when England was near revolution too, evidence of how influential was the liberty boy is startling. William Godwin, father of English anarchism, and husband of Mary Wollstonecraft, mother of English feminism, was a devotee of *Gulliver's Travels*. So was Thomas Holcroft, tried in 1794 at the famous Treason Trial. When Edmund Burke denounced all would-be revolutionaries as the 'swinish multitude', a penny news-sheet was produced by Thomas Spence called *Pig's Meat*. It was stuffed with Swift; whenever the editor had a hole to fill, more Swift was used to plug it. When Leigh Hunt wanted a name for his radical newspaper, he called it after Swift's old paper, *The Examiner*. And William Cobbett, as a boy, bought for threepence a copy of *A Tale of a Tub* and kept it as his Bible. Swift has told us, he said, not to chop blocks with razors. Swift was Cobbett's tutor. Cobbett understood Swift's dictum which should be inscribed on the wall of every political journalist: 'Use the point of the pen, not the feather.'

It was people on the Left in English politics who came to the aid of Swift, when he was being attacked from quarters where he might have expected defence, and most significant and comprehensive was the defence of Swift against all comers by William Hazlitt in his 1818 London lecture delivered at the Surrey Institution, just across from Blackfriars. That, as we have seen, was a literary occasion. There he defended Swift as a writer, became the first critic to recognise his greatness as a poet, and was even prepared to forgive him for having been a Tory. Yet how well he knew what he was doing; how safe, from the viewpoint of his own political dreams, the encouragement might be. Hazlitt was addressing the stolid English; in Ireland they had seized the point more quickly and partly no doubt because Swift's style was sharpened for the purpose. It became colder, clearer, harder still. The common people—a phrase Swift would use himself as a compliment—understood. In Dublin he became an even more popular writer than he had ever been in London. Irishmen read him even more eagerly than the English. Henry Grattan and Thomas Davis hailed him as their patriotic guide; Wolfe Tone

and James Fintan Lalor sought to adopt his pamphleteering
style, and Michael Davitt, the truest patriot and wisest and most
selfless leader of them all, saw him as the prophet of the land war
and the supremacy of moral force. John Redmond declared: 'He
did as much as any man in history to lift Ireland into the position
of a nation.' In Ireland throughout the whole nineteenth century
and beyond he was overtly and effectively a revolutionary figure.
And yet he rarely addressed his words to the Irish alone. He
wrote, as he often laughingly said, for the universal improvement
of mankind.

Some of his more recent and reputable critics can admit his
qualities, as if they were making a grudging confession, or accuse
him of vices which seem the exact opposite of those which could
ever be attributed to him. George Orwell, for example, accepts
that Swift was 'a diseased writer' and that he solved his dilemmas
by blowing everything to pieces in the only way open to him, that
is, by going mad, and then cudgels his brain to discover how a man
with 'a world view which only just passes the test of sanity' can
still have such appeal to so many, himself included. He offers no
sufficient answer, and given the diseased mind as the unalterable
factor in the situation, the failure is not surprising; men do not
gather grapes of thorns and figs of thistles. Aldous Huxley, as we
have seen, is even more startling, with his accusations about Swift
being an incurable sentimentalist and romantic, one who resented
the world of reality and would never dare face it. And Dr. Leavis
concluded that 'he certainly does not impress us as a mind in
possession of its experience'. These, from three such powerful
and independent minds, seem the oddest conclusions. Surely the
author of *Gulliver*, whatever else he was doing, was consciously
compressing his whole life into one book and stripping aside all
sentimental impurities.

George Orwell's essay, however, offers some useful signposts
to other conclusions. 'Why is it', he asks, 'that we don't mind
being called Yahoos although firmly convinced that we are not
Yahoos?' His own reply is unconvincing, and perhaps a better one
is that Swift does *not* call us Yahoos; Lemuel Gulliver does, but
he is not Swift. Orwell also remarks, as others have done, how
dreary is the ideal world of the Houyhnhnms. 'Swift did his best

for the Houyhnhnms', says Dr. Leavis, 'and they may have all the reason, but the Yahoos have all the life.' This undeniable effect of the last book in *Gulliver* is commonly attributed to the failure of all writers to produce a tolerable ideal. All Utopias are too dull to be lived in; the perfection, the immobility, become suffocating. But suppose Swift knew that as well as, or better than, we. Suppose he intended the ideal world to be dreary, its inhabitants too good to be true. Suppose he wanted those who might rise above that brutish Yahoo level to be quite endearing creatures, despite their assortment of obvious defects. Suppose it was his purpose to expose the insufficiency and the insipidity of the Augustan virtues of Reason, Truth and Nature which the Houyhnhnms allegedly exemplify. Suppose the Houyhnhnms are not the heroes and heroines of the book. Suppose (and a fair hint of it is given in the last chapter of the Voyage to the Houyhnhnms) it is the wise and humane and 'least corrupted' Brobdingnagians and their kind-hearted king who represent Swift's positive standard for erring man. Suppose, in short, that *Gulliver's Travels* is not the work of some indefinable demon operating in the decaying carcase of the infamous Dean of St. Patrick's but the deliberate contrivance of his intense, luminous, compassionate mind.

The view crudely summarised in these suppositions is expounded at length with something approaching Swiftian grace and lucidity in the book *Jonathan Swift and the Age of Compromise* by Kathleen Williams (Constable 1959). It is fortified in the conclusions reached by Professor Irvin Ehrenpreis in *The Personality of Jonathan Swift* and the three-volume Life on which he has been engaged. Swift, insists Miss Williams, refused to simplify; as a moral being and a political being, man is a complex creature, and only a process of compromise can produce in any sphere a state of things which will do justice to his complexity. She makes a startling comparison between Swift and Montaigne, and at first thought any alleged common characteristics between the two may seem absurd. How can the meandering ruminations of Montaigne be likened to Swift's fierce polemical thrust? But she notes how Montaigne must have been one of Swift's favourites; 'your old prating friend' was Bolingbroke's taunt.

And there is another fact more clinching than any literary allusion. Swift gave a copy of Montaigne to Vanessa.

'Both [that is Swift and Montaigne] search among ideas, rather than assert ideas', writes Miss Williams, 'feeling their way among a multiplicity of conflicting and assertive doctrines . . . but for Swift the search is a thing of urgency, and he cannot exist calmly in the life of suspense.' It is tempting to lift one quotation after another from her book, especially as she sees the Voyage of the Houyhnhnms as summing up all Swift's writing, the most complete expression of his moral, political and social outlook. But since her views are complex to match Swift's, quotations impair the complete effect. One may be given, since it offers a fresh approach to the perpetually changing interpretation of *Gulliver's Travels*:

> Our first impression, in Swift's work [she writes] is of the elusive brilliance of the attack; a glancing, dazzling mind appears to be concerned solely with the presentation of absurdity or of evil, shifting its point of view constantly the better to perform its task. But as we grow accustomed to his ways of thinking and feeling we become aware that at the heart of Swift's work are unity and consistency, and we see that the attack is also a defence, that tools of destruction are being employed for a positive and constructive purpose. The inventiveness and resourcefulness of his satiric method is seen as arising directly out of the necessities of his mind and of his age: the changing complications of his irony are the necessary expression of an untiring devotion to the few certainties that life affords. For all his elusiveness and indirection, his readiness to compromise or change his ground, few writers have been more essentially consistent than Swift, but for him consistency could be sustained only by such methods as these. Balance in the state or in the individual mind could be kept only by an agile shifting of weights.

It may be added that there was nothing accidental in Miss Williams's return to the estimate Swift's contemporaries made of him, for her method is to discover and describe the exact context in which he wrote.

Swift, then, as a militant Montaigne! One can almost hear the snort of derision from Dr. Johnson or Dr. Leavis. Pope, Gay,

Arbuthnot and Bolingbroke might have found it easier to recognise the likeness. They knew how sane he was and how cheerful he could be, and did he not write to them about *Gulliver* and say:

> I desire you and all my friends will take a special care that my disaffection to the world may not be imputed to my age . . . I tell you after all, that I do not hate mankind: it is *vous autres* who hate them, because you would have them reasonable animals, and are angry for being disappointed.

Swift's scepticism never went so far as Montaigne's. His pessimism about man and his sinful nature and the possibilities of improvement by human effort stayed close to that of orthodox Christianity. But it did not reach the depths of black despair which is supposed to have issued in his madness, nor did it prevent him from declaiming, denouncing, preaching and exhorting with all his skill and might—occupations which certainly would have been senseless if man's condition were incurable.

No one indeed has ever lashed the brutalities and bestialities which men inflict upon one another with a greater intensity. He had a horror of state tyranny and, as George Orwell has underlined, an uncanny presentiment of totalitarianism and all the torture it would brand on body and mind. He loathed cruelty. He was enraged by the attempts of one nation to impose its will on another which we call imperialism. He exposed, as never before or since, the crimes committed in the name of a strutting, shouting patriotism. Gulliver doubts whether our 'conquests in the countries I treat of, would be as easy as those of Ferdinando Cortez over the naked Americans' (where did he learn that, except from Montaigne?), and then comes an outburst as topical as the news from Cambodia or Kabul in the year 1980:

> But I had another Reason which made me less forward to enlarge his Majesty's dominions by my discoveries. To say the truth, I had conceived a few scruples with relation to the distributive justice of princes upon those occasions. For instance, a crew of pirates are

driven by a storm they know not whither; at length a boy discovers
land from the top-mast; they go on shore to rob and plunder; they see
an harmless people, are entertained with kindness, they give the
country a new name, they take formal possession of it for the King,
they set up a rotten plank or a stone for a memorial, they murder two
or three dozen of the natives, bring away a couple more by force for a
sample, return home, and get their pardon. Here commences a new
dominion acquired with a title by *divine right*. Ships are sent with the
first opportunity; the natives driven out or destroyed, their princes
tortured to discover their gold; a free licence given to all acts of
inhumanity and lust, the earth reeking with the blood of its
inhabitants: and this execrable crew of butchers employed in so pious
an expedition, is a *modern colony* sent to convert and civilise an
idolatrous and barbarous people.

Above all, he hated war and the barbarisms it let loose. War, for
him, embraced all other forms of agony and wickedness. *Gulliver's
Travels* is still the most powerful of pacifist pamphlets. And, of
course, it is these aspects of his iconoclasm which have won for
him such persistent allegiance on the Left. It is not surprising that
Hazlitt, Cobbett, Leigh Hunt and Godwin, in the midst of
another great war when spies and informers were at work in the
interests of exorbitant authority, in the age of the press gang and
Peterloo, treasured *Gulliver's Travels* as a seditious tract. It
spoke the truth at that hour called high treason. It sounded the
trumpet of anarchistic revolt when others who did so were being
dispatched to Botany Bay. It assailed the Establishment, Whig
and Tory (what Cobbett called 'The Thing'), and reduced the
whole pretentious bunch to their proper stature. Small wonder
that stout patriots like Dr. Johnson, Sir Walter Scott, Macaulay
and the rest, found the meat too strong for them. But they might,
in their various epochs, have hit upon a more creditable retort
than merely to call the man mad. Not even we today, in the
twentieth century, regard a hatred of slavery, oppression and war
as infallible signs of insanity.

Enough, by any reckoning, to have established Swift's claim as
a revolutionary figure—to have assailed in frontal attack the war-
makers and the empire-builders at the supreme moment of their
power, in England and in Ireland: the first voice to be raised in
this ferocious tone. Yet, miraculously, there is more, and much

more. He marked the clash between 'the common people' and their rulers, their landlords, their oppressors. He saw that 'Freedom consists in a People being governed by Laws made with their own Consent; and Slavery on the contrary'. He saw that 'Poor Nations are hungry and rich Nations are proud', and Pride and Hunger will ever be at variance. He saw what real politics are about. He prophesied what would happen if the new moneyed class, the new economic man, should rule the community. 'Swift's special distinction'—the words of F. W. Bateson—'is that he exposed *laissez-faire* capitalism, and all that it stood for, while it was still no bigger than a cloud the size of a man's hand.' *The Modest Proposal for Preventing the Children of Ireland from being a Burden to their Parents or Country* was not solely addressed to the Irish. It was 'the actual language of Cheapside and Threadneedle Street'. It was the most tremendous curse on the money lenders since Jesus of Nazareth drove them from the temple.

Hazlitt had noted, earlier than anyone else, earlier than such excellent modern critics as Bateson, what service Swift, properly invoked, could do for the cause of the people against their rulers. He wrote a letter to *The Examiner* on 25 August, 1816, which shows how closely Swift always stood at his side:

> Sir,—One reason that the world does not grow wiser is, that we forget what we have learned. While we are making new discoveries we neglect old ones. Mr. Burke had certainly read *Gulliver's Travels*, yet in his invidious paradox, that 'if the poor were to cut the throats of the rich, they would not get a meal the more for it', he seems not to have recollected what that very popular Author says on this subject. In the sixth chapter of the Voyage to the Houyhnhnms, is the following passage, which may show that Swift's Toryism did not, like Mr. Burke's Anti-Jacobinism deprive him of common sense. . .

And then, under the simple class war title, *Rich and Poor*, the great passage followed, showing that the last Voyage is not solely concerned with high philosophical themes:

> My master was yet wholly at a loss to understand what motives could incite this race of lawyers to perplex, disquiet, and weary themselves by engaging in a confederacy of injustice, merely for the sake of

injuring their fellow-animals; neither could he comprehend what I meant in saying they did it for *hire*. Whereupon I was at much pains to describe to him the use of *money*, the materials it was made of, and the value of the metals; that when a Yahoo had got a great store of this precious substance, he was able to purchase whatever he had a mind to, the finest clothing, the noblest houses, great tracts of land, the most costly meats and drinks, and have his choice of the most beautiful females. Therefore since *money* alone was able to perform all these feats, our Yahoos thought they could never have enough of it to spend or to save, as they found themselves inclined from their natural bent either to profusion or avarice. That the rich man enjoyed the fruit of the poor man's labour, and the latter were a thousand to one in proportion to the former. That the bulk of our people was forced to live miserably, by labouring every day for small wages to make a few live plentifully. I enlarged myself much on these and many other particulars to the same purpose: but his Honour was still to seek: for he went upon a supposition that all animals had a title to their share in the productions of the earth, and especially those who presided over the rest. Therefore he desired I would let him know, what these costly meats were, and how any of us happened to want them. Whereupon I enumerated as many sorts as came into my head, with the various methods of dressing them, which could not be done without sending vessels by sea to every part of the world, as well for liquors to drink, as for sauces, and innumerable other conveniences. I assured him, that this whole globe of earth must be at least three times gone round, before one of our better female Yahoos could get her breakfast, or a cup to put it in. He said, That must needs be a miserable country which cannot furnish food for its own inhabitants. But what he chiefly wondered at was how such vast tracts of ground as I described should be wholly without *fresh water*, and the people put to the necessity of sending over the sea for drink. I replied, that England (the dear place of my nativity) was computed to produce three times the quantity of food more than its inhabitants are able to consume, as well as liquors extracted from grain, or pressed out of the fruit of certain trees, which made excellent drink, and the same proportion in every other convenience of life. But in order to feed the luxury and intemperance of the males, and the vanity of the females, we sent away the greatest part of our necessary things to other countries, from whence in return we brought the materials of diseases, folly, and vice, to spend among ourselves. Hence it follows of necessity, that vast numbers of our people are compelled to seek their livelihood by begging, robbing, stealing, cheating, pimping, forswearing, flattering, suborning, forging, gaming, lying, fawning,

hectoring, voting, scribbling, star-gazing, poisoning, whoring, cant-
ing, libelling, free-thinking, and the like occupations. But besides all
this, the bulk of our people supported themselves by furnishing the
necessities or conveniences of life to the rich, and to each other. For
instance, when I am at home and dressed as I ought to be, I carry on
my body the workmanship of an hundred tradesmen; the building
and furniture of my house employs as many more, and five times the
number to adorn my wife.

Sometimes the voice of Swift rose thus in mockery or invective,
and sometimes it subsided into something softer but no less
piercing:

> The Scriptures tells us that *oppression makes a wise man mad*:
> therefore, consequently speaking, the reason why some men are not
> *mad*, is because they are not wise; however, it was to be wished that
> oppression would, in time, teach a little *wisdom to fools*.

No doubt there about his sanity or his astringency; what about
his faith? Most modern scholars insist, and they have substantial
evidence on their side, that Swift's religious convictions cannot
be questioned. They show that he was a most diligent parson.
They show that he served the Anglican church with a fighting
spirit. Nobody can deny that. They show that he was careful not
to reveal the evidence of his scepticism, if indeed he had it. The
case is not argued here, but some of his contemporaries, it may be
noted, were not so certain as some of the modern scholars. There
was the famous rhyme, pinned to the door of St. Patrick's
Cathedral when Swift arrived there:

> *Look down, St. Patrick, look we pray,*
> *On thine own Church and Steeple.*
> *Convert the Dean on this great day*
> *Or else God help the People.*

Despite the strong evidence to the contrary, it is not so easy to
abandon the suspicion that Swift wrote those lines himself. And
he was the author of a sentence which seems to disavow all pretensions to piety. Life is not a farce he explained: 'it is a
ridiculous tragedy, which is the worst form of composition.'

He certainly did write, too, the greatest epitaph a man ever had, as Yeats called it, and in that epitaph there is not a tincture of Christianity, just as there is no trace of madness. He was, for about two centuries, confidently consigned to hell-fire, but now, under the power of modern scholarship, he almost joins the angels. The Church has claimed him, but so did Voltaire. He loved England, but it was Ireland which inspired him. He knew what crawling self-seekers politicians could be, but he knew too that politics was concerned with the great question of rich and poor. He saw how human nature could be rootedly conservative yet he saw too how common decency so often required that it should be convulsively revolutionary. He served human liberty. That was his own secular boast. He did, and still does.

And he was something else besides. He was, after all, a comic genius, like Rabelais or Cervantes or Charles Dickens or Benjamin Disraeli or Charlie Chaplin or Groucho Marx or Spike Milligan; along with all his other attributes, he belonged to that exclusive company. A few (or, if you like, not so few), like Alexander Pope or Henry Fielding or John Gay or Dr. Arbuthnot or Patrick Delany or Thomas Sheridan or Stella or Vanessa were clever or lucky enough to be able to see for themselves from the start. The flow of satire, soft and savage, poured forth in verse and prose in an endless flood. The invectives can still turn the stomach; yet it was he who described how mankind could be furnished with 'the two noblest of things, sweetness and light'. Nothing could hold his humour and his wit in check for long. Let attention be addressed at last to the Voyage of Laputa, the merit of which, by the way, has sometimes been shamefully depreciated, the bad fashion having been set by Dr. Arbuthnot, who, despite his love for Swift, possibly found the attack on the medical profession within it too near the bone. Anyhow, Laputa contains many varied treasures, such as these two sentences:

He had been eight years upon a project for extracting sunbeams out of cucumbers, which were to be put into vials hermetically sealed and let out to warm the air in raw inclement summers. He told me, he did not doubt in eight years more, that he should be able to supply the Governor's gardens with sunshine at a reasonable rate; but he complained that his stock was low, and entreated me to give him something as an encouragement to ingenuity, especially since this had been a very dear season for cucumbers.

According to Dr. Johnson, the man who wrote that was deficient in both wit and humour, and could not conceivably be related to the author of the vastly superior work, *A Tale of a Tub*. Thus the greatest of English critics or, at least, the greatest of English Tories would have banished Jonathan Swift to damnation and oblivion. It was fortunate that the magnanimous English Left, led as usual by the Irish, was able to come to his rescue.

Index